BERTIE AHERN
AND THE DRUMCONDRA MAFIA

Michael Clifford is a journalist with the *Sunday Tribune* where he writes a weekly column. He regularly contributes to a variety of programmes on Irish radio and TV. He is author of *Love You to Death: Ireland's Wife Killers Revealed.*

Shane Coleman is the Political Editor of the *Sunday Tribune* and is a regular analyst of Irish politics on television and radio. He is the best-selling author of *Foot in Mouth: Famous Irish Political Gaffes* and *Up the Poll: Great Irish Election Stories.*

BERTIE AHERN
AND THE DRUMCONDRA MAFIA

Michael Clifford &
Shane Coleman

HACHETTE
BOOKS
IRELAND

First published in 2009 by Hachette Books Ireland

1

A CIP catalogue record for this title is available from the British Library.

The publishers would like to thank Mark Condren/*Sunday Tribune*,
Photocall, Press Association, RTÉ Stills Library and Collins Agency for
permission to reproduce photographs within this book, and the *Irish Times*
for permission to reproduce text on pages 357-8.

ISBN 9 78 0340 91904 0

Typeset in Sabon by Hachette Books Ireland
Printed and bound in Great Britain by CPI Mackays, Chatham ME5 8TD

Hachette Books Ireland policy is to use papers that are natural, renewable and
recyclable products and made from wood grown in sustainable forests. The
logging and manufacturing processes are expected to conform to the
environmental regulations of the country of origin.

Hachette Books Ireland
8 Castlecourt Centre
Castleknock
Dublin 15, Ireland
A division of Hachette UK Ltd
338 Euston Road, London NW1 3BH

www.hbgi.ie

Contents

A wide range of people cooperated with the authors in researching this book through interviews and the provision of documentary information. In nearly every case, the cooperation was on the basis that the individuals concerned would remain anonymous.

The authors would like to acknowledge the contributions of these people and thank them. They know who they are. Without their help the book wouldn't have been possible.

They also wish to acknowledge the staff at the Planning Tribunal. The Tribunal transcript was of great assistance.

PROLOGUE

THE END OF THE LINE

That day, neighbours wouldn't have paid much attention to the ministerial Mercedes. It was 27 March 2008, and the car carrying Brian Cowen pulled into the driveway of 44 Beresford Avenue in Drumcondra, home of Taoiseach Bertie Ahern. Ministerial Mercs were no big deal in Beresford, an estate of comfortable houses off Griffith Avenue, on the northside of the city. Everybody knew Bertie. His car was a familiar sight there. However, closer inspection on the day in question would have revealed that this wasn't Bertie returning home, but a highly unusual house call by his most senior minister.

Cabinet members were routinely summoned on government work to Ahern's constituency office in St Luke's, down in the heart of Drumcondra. This particular visit was to his home, far from any prying eyes that might be staking out St Luke's. And Cowen wasn't responding to a summons to deal with a problem. He had come of his own volition, and the problem at hand was Ahern himself.

The Tánaiste and Minister for Finance had returned the day before from Malaysia and Vietnam, combining ministerial duties for St Patrick's Day with meeting his family for a short holiday in Vietnam. His sojourn in South-East Asia had been punctuated by urgent phone calls from home. Party colleagues had been in touch about the evidence emerging from the Mahon Tribunal in relation to their leader's finances.

Ahern's personal secretary, Grainne Carruth, had endured a torrid time in the witness box. After she had been presented with relevant banking records, she was forced to admit that she must have deposited sterling amounts on behalf of Ahern. This was a direct and irrefutable contradiction of his evidence.

Public perception of Ahern's finances had taken a nosedive. Carruth had been a modestly paid employee, who appeared to have been left swinging in the wind by her former boss. The sterling revelations were causing enormous unease and tension in the Fianna Fáil parliamentary party.

For some time it had been obvious that Ahern's tenure as Taoiseach was coming to an end. He had stated that he wouldn't lead Fianna Fáil into the next general election, which would fall in 2012 if the Dáil ran its full term. Most commentators were of the opinion that he might go after the European elections in 2009, but the previous November the *Sunday Tribune* had run a front-page story citing informed sources who declared that the widespread view among government TDs was that Christmas 2007 would be Ahern's last in office. Now things were moving faster than anybody had anticipated. In the wake of Carruth's evidence, it was clear that unless Ahern could provide a logical explanation for the sterling deposits, his position was immediately untenable.

Brian Cowen was the heir apparent. Ahern had anointed him as his preferred successor after the 2007 election. His popularity within the party was unmatched. However, loyalty is one of Cowen's predominant personality traits. For months he had resisted the strong urgings of some supporters to make a move against Ahern. Given his status as leader in waiting, any such move would have been decisive. That wasn't Cowen's way. He believed strongly in backing the leader through thick and thin.

Carruth's evidence had clearly changed everything. It wasn't just about Ahern any more. It was about Fianna Fáil and, perhaps more importantly in Cowen's mind, the upcoming Lisbon referendum. Party TDs had held the line in support of their leader, but behind the scenes, cracks in this united front were appearing as the tribunal's revelations mounted.

Informed sources have confirmed to the authors of this book that one junior minister was planning to resign on the grounds that they could no longer serve under Ahern, given what had emerged. If this had happened, there would have been a likely domino effect. The result would have been an unseemly and demoralising end to a leadership that had brought three consecutive election victories.

It was against this backdrop that the meeting between Cowen and Ahern took place at Beresford Avenue. The venue was ironically appropriate. One of the issues being examined at the tribunal was Ahern's purchase of his home. He had bought the residence from a friend, Micheál Wall, in unorthodox circumstances that had given rise to a number of questions.

The exact details of what was discussed between Cowen and Ahern is known only to them. We do know the Mahon Tribunal wasn't the only subject they covered. They talked about the not insignificant chaos on the world financial markets. In relation to Mahon, Cowen has said the two men "discussed things generally" and that he was "supportive of my Taoiseach".

That is likely to be accurate. However, nobody at a senior level of Fianna Fáil is in any doubt that the conversation went beyond that. Cowen would have pointed out that if Ahern remained as Taoiseach, his personal finances would be a central feature of the campaign. If that campaign was lost, Ahern would be forced to resign – going out on a distinctly sour note. However, if Ahern opted to go of his own volition, he would no longer be a target. The media circus surrounding the Mahon Tribunal would largely evaporate. It would not be an issue in the Lisbon referendum. Ahern had been invited to address the joint Houses of Congress in Washington. That would be a fitting end to the tenure of the state's second longest-serving Taoiseach.

At the end of their meeting the two men shook hands. Ahern closed the door and Cowen got back into his ministerial car. The tenor, rather than the specific dialogue, of their conversation dictated exactly what would happen next. As Cowen was driven away, he brought with him the balance of power within the party. It would take a few weeks to formalise but Ahern's career at the top of Irish politics had just ended.

PART I

THE RISE

1

WOULD THE REAL BERTIE
PLEASE STAND UP?

Bertie Ahern stepped down as Taoiseach in May 2008 under a cloud of controversy, if not scandal. The examination of his finances in the Mahon Tribunal had left him in an untenable position. He has always maintained that his unusual financial activity in the mid-1990s was connected solely to the legal separation of his marriage. In the space of two years, money to the value of more than three times his annual salary flowed through his own or associated accounts. Most was in cash.

But it wasn't just the amount of money that was significant: there was also the involvement in Ahern's finances of a group who were central to his political career. Men like the former Fianna Fáil fundraiser Des Richardson, who was also involved in raising money for Ahern's constituency organisation as well as for Ahern personally. Men like Tim Collins, described as a party activist, but whose political activity was strictly confined to Ahern's constituency machine, and Ahern's best friend Joe Burke, who had been an integral part of his political organisation for more than thirty years. Others played a role in Ahern's finances: they were less central to his day-to-day political life but were only too willing to give him a "dig-out".

The one characteristic that united all of them was their commitment to the career of the most successful Irish politician of the last fifty years. By their own account, most were not natural political animals. In the main their loyalty was not to Ahern's Fianna Fáil party, or even to his local cumann. They were Bertie men, first, last and always. Their status as such led to them being dubbed the "Drumcondra Mafia" by no less an observer than Charlie Haughey.

The name would stick. The Drumcondra Mafia was not a political party but it succeeded in putting its man in the state's most powerful office. Its base was St Luke's, an innocuous two-storey red-brick former doctor's surgery, in the heart of Drumcondra village. While nominally a Fianna Fáil building, it was acquired in unusual circumstances. The names on the deeds were not those of party stalwarts but of Ahern loyalists. It was, to all intents and purposes, Ahern's power base.

During Ahern's tenure as Taoiseach, St Luke's was as pivotal as Government Buildings to the running of the state. While the cabinet sat in the handsome Edwardian surroundings of Merrion Street, Ahern's unofficial cabinet was based in its more modest location.

Uniquely for a political leader, Ahern didn't draw a kitchen cabinet from senior elected members or party strategists. He confined his inner circle to a small cabal, most of whom he had known since he started in politics. The role played by the Drumcondra Mafia in Ahern's ascent to, and retention of, high office has never been fully explored. His own political nous and that of the people around him ensured that he built up the most formidable and professional political machine seen in

Irish politics. They were pioneers in some of the strategies they employed and, when required, they dealt ruthlessly with opponents. They got their hands dirty, which allowed their leader to remain aloof, pristine and affable.

Through his career, Bertie Ahern achieved much. He has correctly received huge credit for his central role in the Good Friday Agreement in 1998 and the subsequent peace process, which brought peace to Northern Ireland. Two biographies have already been written about him, and his own political memoirs are forthcoming. He was an outstanding politician – arguably the greatest Irish practitioner of the art of pure politics since de Valera. But ironically for a politician whose popularity was based on personal and individual appeal, he would remain hugely dependent on the small cabal around him, a group who were both remarkable and unremarkable. Individually, they came from modest backgrounds, devoid of privilege, and were remarkable in that they helped to create the most powerful Irish political figure of his generation.

This is the story of the members of that cabal, the story of Bertie Ahern and the Drumcondra Mafia. Money is of central importance to it. The electoral machine that was created was the best funded in the state. Ahern and his people introduced unique and often lucrative fundraising techniques, most notably in an annual dinner that has assumed almost mythical proportions.

The money acquired was well spent. Ahern's operation introduced new and expensive election promotional tools and regular constituency literature. As with general political fundraising at a time before ethics legislation was introduced, the source of much of this money is not, and never will be, known.

Money was central to Ahern's downfall. The discovery that large sums had flowed through either his own bank accounts or those of his associates, and the less than convincing explanations he offered, led directly to his departure from office.

St Luke's was to loom large in the investigation into Ahern's finances. Its acquisition, its status as Ahern's residence, and the safe in a downstairs office where Ahern stored large quantities of cash would all be teased out in public in the more official surroundings of Dublin Castle.

We examine Ahern's explanation of the large sums of money he acquired and we ask whether or not an alternative might be more plausible. If the money in question did find its way to him in the manner he outlined, then this most astute politician was naïve, unwise and displayed greed at odds with his well-cultivated public image. If the money was not sourced as he has claimed, then it raises the most serious questions about the life and times of an exceptionally successful politician.

Either way, at every step of his career, through the highs, the lows and the days when money flowed through his accounts in highly unusual circumstances, the members of the Drumcondra Mafia were at his side.

2

THE MAN FROM NOWHERE

As general elections go, 1977 was a humdinger. The ruling Fine Gael-Labour coalition was shown to be more out of touch than anybody imagined. Their four-year administration had been beset by global economic problems and, at home, continued fears of the Troubles spilling over from Northern Ireland. But their biggest problem was communication.

Taoiseach Liam Cosgrave often appeared to be a man out of time, stuck in the past before Ireland had opened up to the world. He was consistently lampooned in the satirical *Hall's Pictorial Weekly* as the Minister for Hardship. Yet, despite a lack of enthusiasm for the government, few believed it would be defeated in the upcoming election.

They hadn't bargained on Seamus Brennan. In 1976, the Fianna Fáil general secretary travelled to the US and observed the presidential election. He returned with his head full of new ideas for electioneering, determined to drag Irish elections into the late twentieth century, kicking and screaming. His boss, party leader Jack Lynch, saw the merits of the new approach, which would, among other things, put him forward in a more presidential style than any party leader heretofore had aspired to.

The election was a runaway success. The campaign to "Back Jack" – allied with the basic and underestimated unpopularity of the outgoing national coalition – resulted in a majority of twenty seats for the new Fianna Fáil administration, the biggest ever Dáil majority. The government backbenches were heaving with young, hungry politicians. Among them was a man from Dublin's northside, an understated individual, a little unkempt but highly personable. He wasn't someone whose potential jumped out. If, for instance, you had suggested that young Bertie Ahern would turn out to be the most successful politician since Éamon de Valera, you would most likely have been asked to pull the other one.

* * *

Ahern wasn't meant to be elected in 1977. The seat he won was effectively earmarked for the Labour Party. At least, that was how Jim Tully, the local government minister in the Fine Gael-Labour government, envisaged it when he controversially redrew the state's constituency boundaries. Tully's attempt to gerrymander the constituencies to ensure his government's re-election was so breathtakingly blatant it quickly became known in political circles as the "Tullymander".

The incumbent Fianna Fáil TD in the newly created Dublin Finglas constituency was Jim Tunney, a party grandee with a stylish dress sense – known locally as the "Yellow Rose of Finglas", for his habit of wearing a flower in his lapel. Tunney's bailiwick was the predominately working-class Finglas area in north Dublin. But the new constituency also spread south into the more middle-class Drumcondra and Glasnevin, which accounted for around 40 per cent of the electorate.

Given the number of voters in those areas, there was certainly an electoral logic in having somebody on the ticket from the southern end of the constituency. Unfortunately for the party, there appeared to be a dearth of potential candidates. Former Fianna Fáil government press secretary Frank Dunlop recalls – in his political memoir *Yes, Taoiseach* – discussing the absence of credible candidates in the constituency with the then number two in the party, George Colley. Colley told Dunlop there was "a young fellow there called Ahern", but in virtually the same breath dismissed his chances: "I don't think he'll amount to much."

Ahern had grown up on Church Avenue in the heart of Drumcondra. The family lived in a red-brick terrace house that came with his father Con's farm manager's job at All Hallows seminary. Con was a veteran of the War of Independence and Civil War. Fianna Fáil was in the blood. "The *Irish Press* was the Bible," is how Bertie's brother Noel describes it. One family tale has it that at the age of twelve, Ahern wrote an essay entitled "Why I Want to be Taoiseach". The family has never been able to locate it, but one of his sisters swears it existed.

By the age of fourteen, Ahern was shimmying up lampposts in the 1965 general election, putting up posters for his teacher Stan O'Brien, who was a Fianna Fáil candidate in Dublin North-East. O'Brien performed creditably but didn't come close to winning a seat. Years later, it emerged that Ahern was known as "king of the poster boys" for his performance in that election. As with much about the Ahern legend, the story may be apocryphal, but it does chime with the reputation he would acquire for dogged hard work.

The 1965 campaign also brought his first meeting with his future mentor, Charlie Haughey, who topped the poll in the constituency. The young Ahern was introduced to Haughey, then agriculture minister, at a polling booth, where the two future taoisigh chatted for a few moments.

A decade later, the boy had become a man with his own Dáil ambitions. Ahern had joined the O'Donovan Rossa cumann in Drumcondra, named after the legendary Fenian Jeremiah O'Donovan Rossa, who is buried in Glasnevin Cemetery. The cumann was then peopled mainly by elderly activists. Some remember it as little more than a social outlet. The young Ahern quickly displayed his energy and had soon become its secretary. Under his stewardship and, later, reign, it would become the most high-profile cumann in political history.

He had been championed by Noel Booth and Tom Houlihan, who ran O'Donovan Rossa. The two were neighbours of the Ahern family. Noel's son, Robin, was friendly with Ahern and worked with him on Stan O'Brien's campaign. Within a short time, Ahern was the organising secretary of the Comhairle Dáil Cheantair – the Fianna Fáil managing body in the constituency. He was still in his early twenties. His brother Noel recalls Bertie "dragging me and a lot of other pals into a cumann in 1973. I can't say whether he was just being the great organiser or if he was being far-seeing. The political system works on the basis of having friends at cumann level. That would have been 1973. In three or four years he would have needed the delegates. I'd say he did plan it," Noel would later tell a journalist. Already the group that would one day be described as the Drumcondra Mafia was forming around Ahern.

His close friend and lieutenant Tony Kett – destined to take over Ahern's seat in Dublin Corporation and become a senator – was at his side. (He died in April 2009 aged just fifty-seven.) Kett and Ahern met when both men worked in the accounts department of the Mater Hospital – where Ahern quickly developed a reputation for getting things done on a limited budget; as young men, they had founded their own football club, All Hampton United. Also in the group were Dáithí O Broin, who is today deputy principal of Ard Scoil Rís in Dublin's Marino, Brian Curran, who married and moved to Galway, and Paul Kiely, currently chief executive of the Central Remedial Clinic.

Kiely has remained out of the limelight but he is spoken of in almost reverent tones by those involved with, and opposed to, Ahern's political machine. He has been described as "very smart" and "the brains" of the Drumcondra Mafia. He and Ahern worked together at An Bord Bainne, the Milk Board. More than three decades later he was present for Ahern's address to the US Congress. Kiely's father was an insurance agent who worked the Finglas beat. His standing and contacts in the area were a huge benefit to Ahern.

As with most of the group around Ahern, Kiely didn't have a Fianna Fáil background – it has even been suggested that some of his family was Fine Gael. Impeccably dressed and smooth, he was a serious operator: "He didn't ever say much – Kett or Ahern did the talking – but he was always there with his hand at the back, directing everything. He was the strategist. He set the direction," recalls one former rival in Dublin Central.

Paddy Duffy was also involved pretty much from the beginning. In terms of the rough and tumble of Drumcondra politics, he was perhaps not a central player. His strength was not the grind of the door-to-door canvass. But throughout Ahern's ascent to the top, he retained an influence. Many in Fianna Fáil credit him with transforming Ahern's appearance, which had earned him the unkind soubriquet "the Rat in the Anorak". Duffy had been a Jesuit seminarian: he was well educated and had a passion for the arts and Celtic mythology, which showed in Ahern's speeches while Duffy worked for him as press officer at the Department of Finance, and as an adviser at the Department of the Taoiseach.

In the 1970s, Duffy was teaching in the De La Salle school in Finglas and was involved with the local Erin's Isle GAA club. He had joined Fianna Fáil in 1975 and one of the first people he met was Ahern. The two had struck up an instant friendship. Duffy was charged by the party with setting up a cumann in south Finglas and later unsuccessfully contested the local election in that area.

Ahern also became active in the Federated Workers Union of Ireland. He had joined up while still a teenager, and begun a relationship with trade unionism that would last for the next forty years and inform much of his industrial-relations policy. He did some part-time work as a scrutineer in union elections and, at the age of just twenty-one, was short-listed for a job as FWUI branch secretary. The story goes that he lost out only because he was deemed too young for the position. In later years, Ahern would recall with fondness the union conferences or heading down to the Labour club and the free steak dinners. "I never got a free dinner out of Fianna Fáil," he said.

As with his working and sporting life, Ahern stayed local when it came to romantic attachments. In the early 1970s he started going out with Miriam Kelly, a bank clerk from Clonliffe Road in Drumcondra. The couple were married on Ahern's twenty-fourth birthday, 12 September 1975, and set up home at the new Pinebrook estate in Artane, around three miles up the Malahide Road from Drumcondra. Kelly was from a family of thirteen, a good starting pool of voters for any fledgling politician.

* * *

Despite his already obvious street savvy and developing union contacts, Ahern lacked political pedigree. He wasn't a city or county councillor. There was no hand-me-down seat in his family, ruling out the route for political aspirants that had been prevalent in post-colonial Ireland. This meant that securing the party nomination for the 1977 general election would be extremely difficult, and so it proved. Despite the obvious advantage that he was based at the opposite end of the constituency from Jim Tunney, Ahern lost by three votes to a much more established candidate, a councillor by the name of Danny Bell.

Bell was a hardworking and suave businessman, well liked in the area. He was a general-election candidate on merit, but by the time the campaign had begun, the Tunney-Bell ticket had had a third name added to it: Bertie Ahern. A member of the Fianna Fáil national executive at the time recalls leaving a meeting of the executive in the early hours of the morning, just weeks before polling day, when there had been no mention of any additions to the ticket in Dublin Finglas. However, some time after his departure, Ahern became a candidate.

It says everything about Ahern's Fianna Fáil upbringing that his elder brother Maurice believes his mother's proudest moment came on the day she saw her son's face on a Fianna Fáil poster on a street corner during that campaign. "I don't think anything that happened after that really matched that moment for her."

But why was Ahern added to the ticket? The official version is that, with two Finglas-based candidates, it lacked balance and the hole at the Drumcondra/Glasnevin end of the constituency had to be filled. The party needed a "sweeper" to bring in Fianna Fáil votes outside Finglas – an entirely plausible explanation.

Geographical considerations weren't the only reason for bringing Ahern forward. Bell had done well in the local elections and was putting out flyers everywhere. Given the expectation that only one Fianna Fáil candidate would win a seat in the constituency, Tunney, typical of sitting deputies, became worried about the threat from Bell. Not the least of his concerns, apparently, was Bell's place at the top of the ballot paper – the positioning is set by alphabetical order – which in those days was reckoned to guarantee at least 700–800 votes straight off for Fianna Fáil candidates. The best way of neutering that threat was to add a name to the ticket, particularly if the new candidate's surname began with 'A', which would place him above Bell on the ballot paper. Even members of his own inner circle admit that Ahern would not have been seen as an immediate threat to Tunney, certainly not in comparison to Danny Bell.

Tunney's key strategist was Ray Walsh: "He organised everything for Tunney. He was superb. Ray could read the numbers and you needed his approval before you got anywhere. Bertie got his approval after much courting by him and his associates and was added to the ticket at the last minute," recalls one veteran of that 1977 campaign. "Ray Walsh got a hold of [Jack] Lynch and persuaded him that they were in dire straits," says another.

Ahern would have the southern part of the constituency to himself, but Drumcondra was far from the Fianna Fáil stronghold it later became. It was "blueshirt territory", says one of Ahern's supporters, dominated by Fine Gael's Alice Glenn.

Ahern later admitted that he had agreed a sideline pact with Tunney whereby the sitting TD would "take a slip in his support to bolster my first preferences and he would stay out of my areas. He came down in votes and I went up." The bell was clearly tolling for Danny's Dáil prospects.

Whatever the motivation behind Ahern's addition to the ticket, it wasn't supposed to matter in terms of seat numbers. With Fianna Fáil widely expected to win only one seat, Ahern was "a nobody", with "no pedigree", who "came from nowhere", his friend Dáithí O Broin later told the RTÉ documentary *Bertie*, aired in 2008. But nobody, not even those closest to him – perhaps not even Ahern himself – realised the quality of the candidate that had been selected. As the new kid on the block, Ahern had to get his own crew in to survive. He had little choice. But what was done out of necessity turned into a virtue. They weren't the well-drilled, almost military-style Drumcondra machine that became the stuff of legend in the 1980s, but they were hungry, enthusiastic, unconcerned about reputations and totally loyal to Ahern.

"They were not bleary-eyed Fianna Fáilers. These were Bertie men," one then senior Fianna Fáil figure recalls. That much remained unchanged over the next three decades.

In the 1977 general-election campaign, local sports clubs were a big source of Ahern supporters. Players from All Hampton United and the GAA club that he had once lined out for, Whitehall Colmcilles Gaels, were happy to help, as were athletes from Clonliffe Harriers running club, with which his brother Maurice was strongly involved, and members of the local tennis club. Ahern's connections from his involvement with the FWUI also came in useful, while friends from Drumcondra and colleagues at the Mater swelled the ranks.

* * *

The Ahern camp has often contended that the tally of his votes in that election showed a significant number of transfers to

Labour and Fine Gael. This, they argue, points to a significant personal vote: he was getting the first preference votes of people who would normally vote elsewhere than Fianna Fáil.

Perhaps. Although a close study of all the counts in Dublin Finglas shows that Ahern didn't do particularly well with transfers from non-Fianna Fáil candidates, so it's difficult to believe his own votes were particularly strongly transferring across party lines.

Whatever his intial appeal, there is little argument that the main reason for his election in 1977 was the national swing to his party. It not only neutralised the Tullymander, but turned it in Fianna Fáil's favour. The tactics behind the Tullymander had been far from complicated: in Dublin, where Fianna Fáil was weakest, the city was divided into a series of three-seater constituencies, which, based on the voting patterns of previous elections, would inevitably deliver a consistent return of one Fianna Fáil, one Fine Gael and one Labour.

In rural areas, Tully went for four- or five-seaters. This would ensure that, despite Fianna Fáil's strength, it would be confined to a share of the spoils with Fine Gael and Labour. The 50:50 split outside Dublin, allied to the 2:1 advantage the coalition would hold in the capital, seemed to guarantee that the coalition government simply couldn't lose.

Certainly, that was how people in Fianna Fáil saw it. Many senior party figures despaired that the general election was unwinnable. Fianna Fáil, the party that had benefited from imaginative redrawing of boundaries in past elections, had been out Fianna Fáil-ed.

Although some in Fine Gael had serious reservations – most notably future Taoiseach Garret FitzGerald – many National Coalition TDs were cock-a-hoop at the prospect of doing to Fianna Fáil what Fianna Fáil had done to them so many times in the past when Fianna Fáil local government ministers had drawn up electoral boundaries that favoured their party.

However, there was a fatal flaw in Tully's plan. It was based on the assumption of little change in the first preference votes of the main parties and would work perfectly if that was the case. For example, if the new constituencies had been in place for the 1973 election, the National Coalition's majority would probably have increased from four to around fourteen. But if that was not the case – if, for example, Fianna Fáil's vote increased – the potential existed for enormous gains by the opposition. This potential weakness was spotted by a few election experts. However, a sizeable increase in Fianna Fáil's national vote seemed highly unlikely.

With opinion polls then in their infancy, most commentators believed that, if anything, Fine Gael and Labour had strengthened their hold on the electorate. How wrong they were. Days after the election was called, key members of the coalition commissioned their own private opinion poll. The result showed Fianna Fáil at a staggering 59 per cent. The election was as good as over, a point illustrated by Garret FitzGerald's joke to his colleagues on receiving the poll figures: "Can we undissolve the Dáil?" Shock set in, which lasted the length of the campaign.

What the political commentators hadn't realised was that the voters had had their fill of the National Coalition. Fianna Fáil's massive give-away election manifesto, including promises to scrap domestic rates and car tax, certainly helped, as did its decision to embrace the glamorous US-style election campaign with plenty of razzmatazz and glitz. In comparison, Fine Gael and Labour appeared staid and boring.

The huge swing to Fianna Fáil turned the Tullymander on its head. Outside Dublin, it meant that Fianna Fáil was taking three out of four or five seats in many constituencies. In Dublin, its huge vote was delivering two out of three seats. The result was a massive and unprecedented twenty-seat majority.

In Dublin Finglas, Fianna Fáil's three candidates secured more than 51.5 per cent of the first preference vote. Ahern attracted 3,729 first preferences – less than half of Tunney's total and more than three thousand votes short of the quota. But, crucially, he was at least 1,100 votes ahead of Danny Bell. Bell did marginally better on transfers for the next few counts but it wasn't sufficient to dent Ahern's advantage.

Ahern was elected on the seventh count, getting an astonishing 3,042 of Bell's 3,363 votes that were transferred – a testimony to Fianna Fáil's ability to persuade its supporters to vote first, second and third for its candidates. It would be the last time Ahern would ever depend on somebody else's transfers to win in a general election.

In that campaign he enjoyed another slice of luck. A split in the Labour camp, which saw Matt Merrigan run as an Independent Labour candidate, did serious damage to that party's prospect of winning a seat. On the Monday following the election, the *Irish Times* analysis of the votes in Dublin Finglas said the in-fighting had handed the second seat to Fianna Fáil, adding that "Bert [*sic*] Ahern, a 25-year-old accountant got the second seat by default for Fianna Fáil."

Given Fianna Fáil had in excess of two quotas in the constituency, that is probably an exaggeration. But not for the last time in his political life, Bertie Ahern had found himself in the right place at the right time. "Bert", as the *Irish Times* called him, was a TD. His life, and the lives of those around him, had changed for ever.

* * *

His early days in Leinster House didn't make a major impact on those around him. Mary Harney has spoken of how, when he started out as a TD, Ahern "went out of his way to conceal his potential" from his colleagues and the media.

Those closer to him knew differently. They were shocked and delighted that Ahern had won the seat, but they quickly noticed a change in him. Paddy Duffy describes it as a Damascus-like conversion: "It was a real awakening for him. Before that his priorities were football, a few pints and a bit of Fianna Fáil. Suddenly he had a future in politics ... Bertie went from being 'one of the lads' to being a leader with ambitions and plans." It became apparent that Ahern had "talents above and beyond the rest of us. Suddenly we realised, 'He's still Bertie but he's gone to the top storey. We're in the day jobs. He's going places [and we're not] unless we tag along with him.'"

Just how planned and orchestrated Ahern's subsequent rise was is a matter of some debate, even among those closest to him.

One version of events is that, roughly four to five months after the election, a meeting took place in Malahide. Among those present were his core team of Tony Kett, Paul Kiely, Paddy Duffy and Joe Burke.

Ahern had first met Burke, a Donegal-born builder, when they became neighbours in Artane. Both became involved in the residents' association, Burke as chair, Ahern as secretary. The two men and their wives became good friends. Burke was then a foreman on building sites, and had spent a few years with Northside Motors and a crash-repairs business in the north inner city. Eventually he set up as a general builder but went on to specialise in pub refitting. Quite a flash individual with a good sense of humour, Burke didn't play a huge role in the constituency workload, although he was always present at social gatherings. Knocking on doors wouldn't have been seen as his strong suit, but he was regarded as a "good man to get things done". He was "a great man to put eight-by-fours and big [election] posters on Amiens Street", says one insider.

Fianna Fáil members recall Burke, in the early days, driving a Mercedes or "some type of limo" at the time. He would transport Ahern to functions, giving the upcoming politician a certain cachet and earning himself a nickname, "The Chauffeur", among some in Dublin Central.

Following that meeting in Malahide, Paddy Duffy says that – in a strange echo of the young Ahern's school essay – a document titled "How to Become Taoiseach in Twenty years" was produced, which he himself typed up. "I'm not saying we ever went back to it" but it showed "the clarity of his ambitions," Duffy says. Others close to Ahern insist that it never existed.

However, the reality is that Ahern indeed became Taoiseach within twenty years. And, with the benefit of hindsight, it was clear he wasn't in politics to be backbench fodder. Jim Tunney, having seen off the threat from Danny Bell, quickly became aware of the challenge on his hands. In responding to good-natured jibes from other Fianna Fáil TDs, he would dismiss potential difficulties with the line: "Jim Tunney is not concerned about anybody." He was right to be untroubled – not because Ahern was no threat but because another redrawing of the boundaries – this time by an independent body – would return Drumcondra and Glasnevin back into a reformed Dublin Central constituency. From that point on, Ahern wasn't Tunney's problem. Instead another, even bigger, Fianna Fáil name had cause for anxiety: the Fianna Fáil deputy leader and Tánaiste, George Colley.

* * *

Colley was seen by the party grandees as the heir apparent to Taoiseach Jack Lynch, but it was becoming clearer that the succession might not be a foregone conclusion. Despite its overwhelming victory in 1977, Lynch's government was quickly facing trouble on several fronts. PAYE workers took to the streets in huge numbers to protest about the unfairness of the tax system, unemployment was rising; there was major industrial relations unrest and there was serious backbench discontent that Lynch's Northern policies were at odds with Fianna Fáil's republican roots. In the summer of 1979 the government put in a feeble performance in the local and European elections, a result that only made backbenchers more jittery. The end of Lynch's tenure as Fianna Fáil leader was in sight. After thirteen years in the job – nine as Taoiseach – he was ready to hand over the reins to his right-hand man, Colley. But the young turks elected in 1977 had other ideas. They wanted Haughey to lead them. And one, Bertie Ahern, planned on taking the fight to the streets and housing estates of Dublin Central.

3

SPREADING TENTACLES

On his election, Bertie Ahern made a promise to himself that people couldn't and wouldn't ever say, "The only time we ever see you is at election time." From that resolve emerged the most powerful local political machine the state has ever seen.

Unfortunately for the people of Finglas, Ahern's resolve wouldn't be felt in the constituency that first elected him. In 1980, an independent constituency commission had unravelled the Tullymander and its hotch-potch of three-seater constituencies across Dublin. At the heart of the redrawn map of the capital lay Dublin Central.

Ahern followed his political base of Glasnevin and Drumcondra to the new five-seater constituency. The boundaries ran from leafy Griffith Avenue and the Tolka river in the north to the Liffey in the south, and from the Malahide Road and the North Wall to the Phoenix Park. It was a big, sprawling urban constituency with around thirty thousand houses. Although areas such as Drumcondra, Glasnevin and Phibsboro were pre-dominantly middle class, the majority of the constituency was working class and included areas of huge deprivation in the inner city. The principal issues in the constituency hardly changed throughout the 1980s: unemployment, housing, crime, vandalism and drugs. In the grim recessionary 1980s, that held for many constituencies, but nowhere in the country were these issues as profound as in Dublin Central.

The constituency was pockmarked with virtually entire streets of derelict sites. In the more deprived inner-city districts, unemployment in the 1980s was estimated at more than 70 per cent among those under twenty-five. Drugs were a huge problem. The constituency was also conservative: of all the constituencies in Dublin, it recorded the highest pro-life vote in the 1983 abortion referendum and the biggest "no" vote in the 1986 divorce referendum.

Ahern was joined in Dublin Central by five other sitting TDs along with Labour's Pat Carroll, who had lost in the 1977 election by a handful of votes. Two other prominent politicians also had bases in the constituency. Tony Gregory and Alice Glenn were recognised as forces with which to be reckoned.

Nine into five simply doesn't go. From the outset Ahern was determined that he wouldn't be one of the four left behind. The six TDs included two other Fianna Fáil members, Tom Leonard – who had pipped Pat Carroll to the post in Dublin Cabra in 1977 – and, more significantly, the Tánaiste and Minister for Finance, George Colley.

Colley was following his political base of Marino and East Wall – two settled, strongly community-based working/lower-middle-class areas – which were now part of Dublin Central.

* * *

Colley was a Fianna Fáil blue-blood – in so much as Fianna Fáil has blue-bloods. His father Harry was a veteran of 1916 and the War of Independence and was a TD for Dublin North-East before losing out to Charlie Haughey in 1957. Four years later, Colley reclaimed the family seat, coming in behind Haughey. By 1965, he was a cabinet minister and being groomed by some of the party elders to succeed Seán Lemass. Although they had been school friends, Colley and Haughey soon became adversaries in a cabinet full of strong personalities, vying to take over from Lemass as party leader and Taoiseach in the 1960s.

Jack Lynch emerged as a compromise candidate, defeating Colley to become Fianna Fáil leader and Taoiseach in 1966. The showdown between Colley and Haughey was postponed.

Lynch lasted far longer than anyone had expected. But, notwithstanding Haughey's period in the wilderness after the sensational arms trial of 1970, it was inevitable that one day Colley and Haughey would go head to head for the leadership.

In December 1979, just over two years after the Fianna Fáil landslide, Lynch was effectively forced out by an increasingly mutinous parliamentary party. Colley was his anointed successor, and Lynch's departure had been timed to maximise his chance of taking over. The plan went awry. Colley was an old-style gentleman politician, with an almost diffident manner. His strength, as Bertie Ahern would happily discover over the next few years, wasn't in soliciting votes. He was out-fought, out-thought and out-plotted in the leadership contest by the ruthless and wily Haughey.

The level of enmity between the two men, allied to the relative tightness of the result, was such that Haughey couldn't command total loyalty from his party after he had become its leader. A sizeable minority of the parliamentary party, led by Colley and Des O'Malley, distrusted him. Over the next four years, a succession of heaves against Haughey's leadership almost tore Fianna Fáil asunder.

At the time of the leadership contest, Ahern's political base was still in Dublin Finglas. The constituency commission didn't report until the following spring. A large number of cumann people in Dublin Finglas, including many in Ahern's O'Donovan Rossa cumann, would have been Colley supporters – Jim Tunney was certainly in the Colley camp. But Ahern surprised some by voting for Haughey in the leadership contest and stayed loyal to him throughout all of the turmoil that followed. Years later, he explained that although he had met Colley he "didn't really know him".

In contrast, Ahern's involvement – via his association with the Mater Hospital – on an internal Fianna Fáil committee that advised Haughey as health spokesman meant he knew Haughey better. While Colley was seen as part of an aloof hierarchy, Haughey actively cultivated the new crop of deputies elected in 1977. Many of the younger TDs were also attracted by Haughey's republican credentials, and it's hard to imagine this wasn't a factor for Ahern, who had grown up in a staunchly republican household. But he must also have seen a better future with Haughey than with the more establishment Colley.

Although the ever-genial Ahern avoided confrontation or acrimony with the Colley-O'Malley faction, his electoral contests with Colley in Dublin Central in 1981/2 came to resemble a quasi-leadership battle. As we will see, those contests were often bitter, and there would be only one winner.

* * *

The approaches of Colley and Ahern to Dublin Central politics couldn't have been more different. Although Ahern had moved out of the constituency with his new wife Miriam, he had been born and bred in Dublin Central. He mightn't have slept in the constituency now, but his every waking hour was devoted to it. Colley was a national figure who had simply followed his vote there.

Method was the essence of Ahern's philosophy. Many people might regard Dublin as a small city, but not Ahern. To him, even his own constituency was a collection of distinct areas, each with their concerns and problems, so he divided it into twenty-five wards – essentially a group of streets with perhaps a thousand homes. He appointed a "boss" in each ward, who would be in charge of up to ten people whose job it was to canvass each of those streets at least three or four times a year.

The ward bosses were Ahern's eyes and ears in that section of the constituency. They would know everything that was going on – births, deaths, football games, sales of work – and would notify him of events he should attend and accompany him. While out canvassing, it was their job to know each house and ascertain how long should be spent at each door. If there were six potential votes for "Bertie" then it was worth giving it some time. However, if the householders were supporters of a rival candidate, they might be looking to delay the Ahern canvass. The ward boss had to know the difference.

The bosses took their responsibilities seriously. One politician recalls talking to one after a redrawing of the constituency had moved the series of streets he was responsible for to an adjoining constituency. The ward boss was genuinely "broken-hearted" by the loss of an area he and his team had assiduously cultivated for Ahern.

Many of Ahern's closest associates served as ward bosses, including Joe Burke and Paul Kiely. Liam Cooper, still a key figure in Dublin Central today, was another, as was Cyprian

Brady, who in later years would run Ahern's office and become his running mate in the 2007 general election. Cyprian's father, Ray Brady, was also involved in helping Ahern build a base in the inner city when he first made the move from Dublin Finglas. Other ward bosses included Dominic Caulfield and Dominic Dillane.

Dillane was a latecomer to the Ahern organisation: a Kerry-born lecturer in tourism management at DIT Bolton Street, he began canvassing for Ahern in the 1990s. He has a degree in actuarial science and a PhD in statistics; insiders describe him as "borderline genius". His talents, particularly his ability with figures, were quickly spotted and he was brought into the inner sanctum of St Luke's, becoming treasurer of the constituency organisation and establishing himself as a key figure in Ahern's organisation.

John Grange was another ward boss. He is a landscape gardener who, insiders say, was responsible for the hanging baskets at St Luke's that Ahern has been credited with nurturing. Brian Bogle, Charlie O'Connor, Maurice Ahern and John Stephens also served their time, as did Paddy "The Plasterer" Reilly, who in later years would become a household name because of his close friendship with Ahern.

During election campaigns, there was competition between the ward bosses to see who could deliver the highest increase in first preference votes with prizes given to the winners. "It had more the feel of a club than a political party. It was fun. Out on a Tuesday night canvassing, then into Kennedy's or Fagan's for a few pints. Many of them weren't members of Fianna Fáil. It was Ahern. He was a project they took on and they ended up running the country," one close observer from a rival party recalls. This was echoed by a participant. "You felt as if you were part of something. A little bit untouchable. Our man was on the rise."

Former Dublin Lord Mayor Royston Brady, a brother of Cyprian who also became a ward boss, has compared it to "something out of *Goodfellas*" – the legendary Oscar-winning film about the Mob – and the process of becoming a made man. But perhaps the best comparison is with legendary Chicago mayor Richard Daley. Dublin Central was Ahern's personal fiefdom in the way that Chicago in the 1960s and 1970s was Daley's.

The ward system later evolved to include parish leaders, based around the churches and local schools. Knowledge was power. Every opportunity was used – collecting kids from school or football, going to mass – to build information, to get to know people in the locality and, crucially, the area's problems.

Everybody connected to the Drumcondra machine was involved in intelligence gathering. If the children of a canvasser saw a light missing on a road, they would go home and tell their parents. A letter would be typed, stating the matter would be addressed, and put through doors on the road in question. When the light was fixed, another letter would be dispatched pointing it out. It was time-consuming and unglamorous work, but it meant Ahern's name was always out there in Dublin Central. As he had at the Mater Hospital, he quickly developed a reputation as a man who got things done.

In tandem with this, Ahern set about perfecting the constituency's political clinic structure. Every part of the constituency had one – eventually there would be fourteen – and six or seven clinics would be held throughout the month. Initially, Ahern tried to attend them all and even years later, as Taoiseach, he would monitor them closely. Paddy Duffy recalls "a huge mountain of work" being created. In the early 1980s,

Ahern also opened one of the first full-time constituency offices in the country, over Fagan's, the pub that became synonymous with the Drumcondra Mafia. Celia Larkin, who was among the extended Ahern network, became the constituency secretary, running the office. She would go on to become central to Ahern's life, both personally and politically.

The attention to detail was phenomenal, as evidenced by a story that emerged about a young Finglas man who, after returning from abroad in 1977, contacted Ahern's clinic, saying he heard some jobs were going in Post and Telegraphs (later An Post and Telecom Éireann). A letter came back saying Ahern was investigating job opportunities in the public sector. Not long afterwards the man was offered work in Post and Telegraphs. He ended up taking another job. Four years later, he received another letter from Ahern, recalling the initial contact and suggesting that, although the man couldn't vote for Ahern in the Finglas area, he might have relatives living in Dublin Central who would. No stone was left unturned in the hunt for precious number one votes.

At the core of everything lay Ahern's enthusiasm and work ethic. He was known to members of his team as "the bossman" but also, because of his appetite for the canvassing grind, as "part machine, part man". It rubbed off on all those around him: "Everyone bought into it. Everyone wanted to impress him. They weren't afraid of him as people were of Haughey," recalls one figure involved in the 1980s. But neither were they necessarily close to him: "Bertie doesn't really have friends and you were under no illusions about that," one insider says.

His workload in the constituency became the stuff of legend. Every year Ahern personally canvassed huge chunks of the constituency – unless an election was in the offing, the canvassing season ran from St Patrick's Day to September –

41

and he continued to canvass regularly in non-election years long after he had become Taoiseach.

Even political rivals, for whom Ahern holds little appeal, concede he was "brilliant" on the doorstep: "He was very, very personable. And women loved him because he was cute," says one.

It was in the early 1980s that the Ahern Christmas and Easter letters became a permanent feature in his strategy. The Ahern team would sit down in November and a month before Easter and decide on the big issues in the constituency. Paddy Duffy would shape their deliberations into a circular, which was delivered to the entire constituency by up to sixty people, divided into teams. In the Drumcondra office a master board would be marked with all the streets in the constituency, which were allotted to the teams, who headed off to do the "drop". It was finished within one day, first to ensure efficiency, and second, to build team spirit. Afterwards, everyone would meet up in Fagan's for a drink.

In the early 1980s, Chris Wall became involved with Ahern. He had known Bertie's older brother Maurice for some years through athletics. (Wall went on to become one of Ireland's leading athletics administrators.) Shortly after he and his wife Myra moved to Drumcondra, Myra was canvassing for Ahern. When Wall was dropping her to the constituency headquarters, then based at the Ahern family home on Church Avenue, he figured out the connection with Maurice, and presently joined his wife on the canvass. He was soon the most important figure in Ahern's local organisation. "Bertie's ambassador", "Bertie's plenipotentiary" and "Bertie's enforcer" are just a few of the descriptions applied to Wall by those who have witnessed the Drumcondra Mafia at close hand. "There are a lot of people who thought they were players, but it was Bertie and Wall," remembers one constituency figure. "He was Bertie's general. If you wanted something done, you went to Chris," says another.

Wall is affable and pleasant, with a sense of mischief, but those who know him describe an operator who is "tough as nails" and politically ruthless. Wall first made a name for himself at a meeting of the Dublin Central Comhairle Dáil Cheantair – the body in the constituency that oversees all the Fianna Fáil cumainn – when he bluntly reminded George Colley that Haughey had polled more votes than he had in the leadership contest. "Chris didn't suffer fools. What you see is what you get," says one Fianna Fáil figure from Dublin Central.

Unlike other members of the Drumcondra Mafia, Wall's involvement with Ahern was purely political. He had no involvement whatsoever in Ahern's complex financial dealings that would be investigated by the Mahon Tribunal. He was also the only member of the Mafia to play politically at a high level. When Ahern became Fianna Fáil leader, Wall would sit on the party's election committee, and was the Dublin Central Comhairle Dáil Cheantair's constituency delegate to the Fianna Fáil national executive. Although he enjoyed a successful career in business and knows politics inside out, sources say his input at those meetings was generally limited. It was not for nothing that he was regarded as "Bertie's eyes and ears".

Those who have worked with him at close quarters say Wall has great qualities. He is straight and, unlike many involved at constituency level, able to see the big picture. Back in the 1980s, he brought Ahern's machine to a new level. He typed up a hugely detailed strategy document based on classic marketing philosophy. It included a marketing operation, a selling operation and a buying operation. The marketing was about providing the service to the public on an ongoing basis, the selling underlay the election campaign, and the buying took place on election day, when the "purchase" was a vote for Ahern. The marketing side was crucial: it kept Ahern's name in front of people all the time.

By the general election of June 1981, Ahern had been a TD for four years. He had also been a member of Dublin Corporation since February 1978: Jim Tunney, his constituency colleague in Dublin Finglas, had ceded his seat to him on the corporation after he himself had been appointed a junior minister. The local elections of 1979 showed, perhaps for the first time, that Ahern was developing a formidable electoral machine. On what was not a good day for the party, he still headed the poll in his electoral area. He garnered 2,710 first preferences, which was just a couple of hundred votes shy of the quota and well ahead of the next candidate, Fine Gael's Alice Glenn. Ahern hoovered up the Fianna Fáil vote: the next Fianna Fáil candidate was Ahern ally Paddy Duffy, in tenth place, with 462 votes. The following year, the new Taoiseach, Charlie Haughey, made Ahern his assistant government whip. This followed an Ahern-inspired move to propose involving backbenchers in back-up policy committees. The leadership saw this as a good way to head off potential dissent.

Ahern's new position was a largely meaningless one, particularly when the government of the day had a majority of twenty. However, the actual chief whip, Sean Moore, was ill throughout 1980 and Ahern filled in for him, which provided the young TD – he was still only in his twenties – with invaluable experience and access. Despite this, though, his national profile was still pretty low. A constituency analysis carried out just a couple of weeks before the 1981 general election in the *Irish Times* predicted that Colley would "probably" top the poll, adding that Ahern "probably has the edge on Tom Leonard but it will be close". Once more, the man from Drumcondra must have revelled in being underestimated. Although the signs had been clear in the local elections of two years earlier, national commentators hadn't realised that the Drumcondra machine was already giving Ahern a cutting edge in the constituency.

Colley was no pushover. He had a strong team of supporters. The main thrust of his vote came from the East Wall and Marino, along with an element from traditionalists in areas such as Phibsboro, who supported him because of his father. Such voters were called "plumpers" – the most prized of all because they would vote only number one.

Some within Colley's camp had serious reservations about how in touch he was with the constituency, certainly compared to Ahern. Both men lived outside the constituency, Colley in the ultra-exclusive Palmerston Gardens, situated between the upmarket areas of Dartry and Ranelagh on the southside of the city. By 1981 Ahern had moved to Muldowney Court in affluent Malahide, the picturesque coastal village in north County Dublin. But there was no disputing where his roots were firmly planted. He had an innate understanding of the constituency. When he spoke about summary justice for the heroin dealers that blighted the lives of so many in the flat complexes of the inner city and suggested that the gardaí be allowed to box a few ears now and again, he knew that while liberal commentators mightn't approve, he was echoing what many of his constituents believed.

Colley started out as a TD for Dublin North-East, moved to North Central – which for the 1977 election became Dublin Clontarf – and now he had to rebuild his base in another new constituency. It didn't help that he didn't really do constituency stuff and, according to his critics, had a rural style of canvassing. "He didn't knock on doors of non-Fianna Fáil people," recalls one Ahern canvasser. "In contrast, we called everywhere. We took it as a challenge." Colley had spent two decades as a cabinet minister, so it is understandable that bread-and-butter constituency business no longer appealed to him in the way it clearly did to Ahern.

It was quickly obvious to Colley's shrewder supporters that they had a serious challenge on their hands. Ahern could call on huge numbers of young people to work for him. "They covered more ground. Got in before us. He had the numbers," one Colley backer recalls. "It was obvious [he was a threat]. We knew he had lots of foot soldiers. They were not party people. It was totally different. Maybe we were in the comfort zone. Colley was Tánaiste. He had been around for years. Also he had big demands on him to go visiting other constituencies.

"And while we had to go canvassing without Colley, Bertie was a great man for giving the impression that he was in five different places at the one time. I remember Michael Keating [the then Fine Gael TD for Dublin Central] asking me: 'Do you know Bertie? Has he a twin? Because he can't be everywhere. How can he do it?'"

There was also a different emphasis in the two campaigns. "It was totally an Ahern campaign. It wasn't a Fianna Fáil campaign. Colley was canvassing for Fianna Fáil," a member of the Colley team says.

The Colley camp weren't the only ones unhappy with the tactics used by the Drumcondra Mafia. Tony Gregory ran for the first time in that general election. One of the dominant national issues was the H-block hunger strikes. H-block candidates took votes from Fianna Fáil in a number of constituencies and won two seats.

Gregory was not directly involved in the H-block campaign, backing the hunger strikers, but he was sympathetic to their cause. He had put down a motion in a Dublin Corporation meeting supporting the five demands of the prisoners; when it was defeated he had walked out of the chamber, generating a fair amount of publicity in the process.

A few months later, on the morning of the general election, Gregory rose at five a.m., ready for his tour of the constituency's thirty-plus polling stations to check his posters. He found he wasn't the first to be up and about: an earlier bird had caught the worm.

The constituency was filled with new posters: "Support the Five Demands, Vote Tony Gregory. Support the H-block Hunger Strikers." Disastrously for Gregory, they had been tactically placed in areas where there would be little sympathy for the hunger strikers. They were also pasted on shop windows and postboxes – which would irritate many voters – and even delivered to some homes on middle-class streets where there was little support for the H-block cause. Gregory tore around the constituency that morning pulling them down, but many were seen by people on their way to work. He was eliminated in the ninth count and, although the result was not as tight as was suggested later, he blamed the posters for his defeat.

Rightly or wrongly, Gregory felt that the Ahern organisation was the only one that could have carried out the rogue postering. In recounting the story years later to journalist Katie Hannon for her book *The Naked Politician*, Gregory said: "I've a terrible temper. I went up to the HQ of the H-block committee like a lunatic. They thought I'd gone bananas. They said they hadn't put up any such posters." Then he had heard that one of his campaign vans had been driving up Church Avenue – around the corner from Ahern's base – that morning and had come upon a gang pasting up the posters. After the election, he said within earshot of Ahern that he thought he would have taken a seat were it not for the smear tactics. "Bertie just said: 'Now, Tony, you don't think I'd do anything like that.' I said that anybody putting up any shite about me in future will get a hatchet in the back of the head. I said, 'I'll be driving around the area all night. I'll have a hatchet in the car with me. Spread the word.'"

It was clear from that interview, given two decades later, that Gregory remained angry about the incident and, as Hannon wrote, "never fully accepted Ahern's assurances".

He received consolation in the following general election just nine months later when he became a TD, holding the balance of power in the Dáil. A few weeks after that poll, Ahern had to suffer the ignominy of driving Haughey to Gregory's office in Summerhill to negotiate the "Gregory deal", a major investment package in the north inner city to be delivered in return for Gregory's vote. "He had to wait in the car for three and a half hours while I did the deal. What a suck-in!" Gregory remembered.

But there was plenty to admire in the military-style precision of the Ahern camp. Activists recall the walls of the living room in Ahern's mother's house in Church Avenue being filled with boards containing lists of every street in the constituency. They were colour coded: streets canvassed once were blue; those done twice were red; and those visited three times were green. On the night the Dáil was dissolved, a letter was dropped to every home and a second – pushed through letterboxes by "an army of people" starting at one a.m. – on the morning of polling day.

It had the desired effect. When the votes were counted, it

was Ahern, not Colley, who headed the poll with an impressive 8,738 votes, a thousand over the quota. Colley also reached the quota on the first count, polling 8,011 votes to take the third seat.

Ahern topping the poll in Dublin Central wasn't by any means the biggest story on the night of the count. The election of hunger-strike candidates in Louth and Cavan-Monaghan and the overturning of what should have been an impregnable twenty-seat Fianna Fáil Dáil majority were much bigger.

However, political pundits everywhere would have noticed the eclipsing in his own constituency of the man who was still seen as a potential leader of Fianna Fáil. In Dublin Central, at least, a new order was emerging. Bertie Ahern had arrived, big time. Now he had to consolidate that new order.

4

WHEN ONE TRIBE GOES TO WAR

Familiarity breeds contempt and the Ahern and Colley camps
certainly became familiar with each other between June 1981
and November 1982 when the country went to the polls three
times. Ahern had laid down a marker by coming in ahead of
Colley in the June 1981 general election, but the gap between
the two men was tight. However, by the conclusion of the third
election, there would be no doubt over who was top dog in
Dublin Central.

The second of the three elections came the following
February. The minority Fine Gael and Labour government, led
by Garret FitzGerald, fell over a budget proposal to impose VAT
on children's shoes. The Ahern machine kicked into action. The
Colley camp, under pressure, was becoming increasingly
irritated by the tactics of the Drumcondra Mafia. There were
five seats to fight for and other parties to compete against, but
Ahern's people saw Colley as the number one threat.

Tony Gregory has told of how he called to the house of an
elderly lady whom he knew to be a Fianna Fáil supporter. He
was mildly surprised at the warm welcome he received, then

discovered that Ahern had been there not long before, asking her to vote Ahern, number one, another Fianna Fáil candidate, Tom Leonard, number two, and Gregory himself number three, ahead of Colley. The story is put into further perspective by the fact that there has never been any love lost between Ahern and Gregory.

The Colley camp felt Ahern's people were putting the word around in their canvassing that "George is OK", implying that he would easily be elected. They also had serious reservations about some of the Ahern team's tactics. Etiquette demanded that if you wanted to canvass a road and others were there already, you waited for them to finish. But in the heat of election battle, such niceties went out the window.

A senior Colley ally recalls how one Saturday afternoon, during one of the three elections, a woman in her forties was doing a drop in Drumcondra on behalf of the Colley camp. A big group of Ahern canvassers came along, said they were Fianna Fáil and effectively took over.

The "Bertie first, Fianna Fáil second" approach included individual leaflets for Ahern that did not mention the names of other party candidates. The party logo was also displayed in a less than prominent position. At the time such individual-isation was unique. Breaches of agreement over territories were commonplace. When Ahern's team got wind that a particular area was being canvassed by a rival, they would immediately go there, even if it had been covered a few days beforehand.

The February general election saw Charlie Haughey fall agonisingly short of the overall majority, but the party's eighty-one seats would be enough, with the votes of others, to propel Fianna Fáil back to government. In Dublin Central, the general election confirmed the result of the previous June. Ahern's vote was down a fraction, but he was again elected on the first count with 8,570 votes. Colley's vote dropped by more than five hundred, leaving him eighty-two votes short of the quota. It was a virtually inconsequential amount and merely delayed his election until the second count.

The symbolic significance of falling short of the quota was that, for the first time since the 1960s, Colley had to depend on somebody else's transfers to be elected. Now firmly on the hind tit in Dublin Central, Colley was dealt another blow when Haughey refused to make him Tánaiste in the new government. Colley reacted by declining a role in cabinet. In contrast, Haughey made Ahern chief whip, putting him at the cabinet table, although not as a voting member.

Between the election and the Dáil reconvening, the O'Malley-Colley camp made a move against Haughey. Their plan was to propose O'Malley as the Fianna Fáil nomination for Taoiseach when the new Dáil opened. The challenge collapsed ignominiously after Haughey brought forward the parliamentary party meeting to confirm his nomination as candidate for Taoiseach. At that meeting, O'Malley announced he was not allowing his name to be put forward as nominee for Taoiseach. Despite the débâcle, it was a clear sign that the leadership of the anti-Haughey faction had passed from Colley to Des O'Malley.

Ahern's appointment as chief whip was short-lived. Unlike when he had filled the role in an acting capacity a couple of years earlier and Fianna Fáil had a massive majority, the government was always going to struggle to win key votes with just eighty-one seats – two shy of an effective majority. The new administration also proved disastrously scandal and error prone and came to be known as the "GUBU" government. The term, coined by Conor Cruise O'Brien, was an acronym of the words "grotesque, unbelievable, bizarre and unprecedented", which Haughey used when it emerged that Malcolm Macarthur, wanted in connection with two high-profile killings, had been found in the home of Attorney General Patrick Connolly (the entirely innocent Connolly was unaware that Macarthur was a wanted man).

The government was in turmoil for most of its eight months in power, and there was another leadership challenge to Haughey – instigated by Charlie McCreevy – in October. Haughey survived the no-confidence motion in his own party (by fifty-eight votes to twenty-two), but a month later, on 4 November 1982, his government lost a confidence vote, plunging the country into its third general election in eighteen months.

Just prior to the Dáil defeat Ahern, in his role as chief whip, was involved in approaches to the Labour Party to ascertain if it would be interested in voting with Fianna Fáil on the confidence motion. Labour didn't bite.

But, as ever with Ahern, he wasn't just working on a plan B for his party, he also had his personal plans C and D in train. Within hours of the fall of the government, early on 5 November, voters in Dublin Central received a professionally printed circular from Ahern. It informed constituents of how hard he had worked for them since February, getting more gardaí for the area, saving a factory that had been in danger of closure and generally doing his bit for each and every constituent.

By this point, the Ahern machine was unstoppable. Its canvass was so efficient that the team could make a fair assessment as to how many Ahern votes were coming from each house – priceless information in terms of focusing on the waverers and undecided. The level of organisation was such that the Ahern team had a dedicated director of transport, whose job it was to organise cars for those voters needing transport on election day. They also had a director of postering.

With Fianna Fáil struggling nationally and Ahern utterly dominant in Dublin Central, Colley knew he was up against it. Ahern, as part of his blitz of the constituency's letterboxes during the three-week campaign, sent a letter to voters asking for number ones, but making no mention of Colley or the other Fianna Fáil candidate, Tom Leonard.

"This was clearly an attempt by the Ahern camp to screw George Colley," one of Colley's supporters said at the time. Colley's response was the clearest sign yet of how the balance of power had shifted in the constituency. The man who had served as a cabinet minister for the best part of two decades – and who just three years earlier had been Taoiseach-in-waiting – wrote to voters saying: "Because I have been in the Dáil for the past 21 years, some people believe that I will automatically 'sail in' in a general election. This was certainly not the case in the last election and let me tell you that on November 24th, George Colley needs every vote he can get." Unlike Ahern, however, he went on to urge voters to support him and his colleagues in the party. Colley's supporters said at the time that the decision to issue their letter had been taken "very reluctantly" and only in response to "massive intimidation" from the Ahern camp.

The general election marked the first time that the tensions between Ahern and Colley were aired prominently in the national media. On the day of the general election, there was open hostility between the two sides. Both were represented at most polling stations in the constituency. The *Irish Times* reported the next day that one group handed out "leaflets on behalf of the official Fianna Fáil slate, while the other stood some distance away, openly canvassing only for Mr Colley".

There were fist fights between the rival groups outside the polling station in Marlborough Street, at the back of O'Connell Street. The brawl happened after a Fianna Fáil official stepped in: eyewitnesses recounted that the Colley man was "dragged to the ground while an attempt was made to strip him of the offending leaflets". Less serious confrontations between the factions were witnessed at other polling stations. From conversations with those involved at the time, it is clear that heated exchanges between the competing teams of canvassers were common.

One senior figure from the Colley camp recalls an incident outside a polling station in Drumcondra on one of the election days during that period. Teams of canvassers from Fine Gael, Labour and the Colley camp were making their pitch to voters on their way in. At around eight p.m., a van pulled up. "We were on one side, Labour and FG on the other," the Colley supporter said. "Six or seven of these 'black suits' got out with Ahern posters. They blocked us up and wouldn't go away. Pat Colley [George's son] was seriously put out. Their language was appalling. We were told to fuck off. We couldn't move in front of them. Michael Keating [the Fine Gael candidate] said to one of ours, 'It's not FG or Labour you have to worry about, it's them [Ahern's people].'"

Such friction was by no means confined to Dublin Central. In the heat of a general election, incidents occur all the time between rival supporters. But there was no disguising the animosity of some exchanges. Nevertheless, some of the tricks Ahern's team got up to were a lot more innocent: during one of the election campaigns, two members rang Colley's headquarters and left the phone off the hook all day, making it impossible for any calls to be made or received.

Such pranks notwithstanding, there is no question that the

Ahern team generally played by big-boy rules. Tony Kett, Ahern's close friend, gave a clear insight into their thinking in an interview with journalists Ken Whelan and Eugene Masterson for their book *Bertie Ahern: Taoiseach and Peacemaker*: "When the election machine went into action it was purely for Ahern. We have some leeway now, but in the early days we were ruthless. Other Fianna Fáil candidates would complain about the way we ran things. We just ignored them. We were determined to run Dublin Central and we were determined that nobody, not even our own people in our own party, would get in our way. Even in our first election we ignored warnings not to go into Jim Tunney's area and we made forays there all the time. We succeeded, and we still run the constituency in the same way today. Anyone who says otherwise doesn't know what they are talking about."

This is borne out by other Fianna Fáil figures from Dublin Central. "They wouldn't stop at anything, particularly in the heat of the action. They'd stand on your head ... It's not vindictive. They believe what they're doing is right," was how one close observer put it.

* * *

The tensions between the Ahern and Colley camps didn't go away between elections. "There was no harmony, no camaraderie. It came to a situation where there were very few who could sit on the fence," recalls a Colley supporter.

During this era, the meetings of the Dublin Central Comhairle Dáil Cheantair were held in the Belvedere Court on Great Denmark Street in the north inner city. They were often bitter, rancorous affairs – even at times descending into fisticuffs – as the rivalry between Haughey and Colley, and the latter's refusal to accept Haughey's leadership, was played out at a local level.

Colley's people believed Ahern's supporters were being totally disrespectful. "I'd never experienced such venom as was directed at Colley," one Colley supporter recalled. "The stuff said at him, to him and about him at those meetings was heartbreaking. I started to dread Comhairle Dáil Ceantair meetings. You wouldn't treat a dog the way Colley was being treated."

Ahern rarely spent much time at those meetings. He would come in and leave, and Colley supporters say that nothing untoward ever happened when he was in the room.

The level of paranoia was such that Colley people felt Haughey was funding part of the Ahern campaign – which seems unlikely. But as far as the Colley camp was concerned, Ahern was running his own highly sophisticated and hugely expensive personalised campaign and they were surprised that the young TD could afford such an operation.

There is no question that money was a significant factor. A source close to the Drumcondra Mafia says they "realised very quickly that you need a lot of money to be bigger than your competitors", adding that the higher up the ladder Ahern went, the easier it was to access political funding. In the beginning the machine depended on race nights and draws to raise funds, but by the mid-1980s, it had become more sophisticated, with the annual dinner in December for the O'Donovan Rossa cumann attracting guests from business and political circles.

However, the more realistic of Colley's supporters know that it didn't simply come down to money. "Politics was Bertie's life and Bertie's life was politics. Colley couldn't compete with that. He hadn't the energy or the enthusiasm at that stage to start getting into fist fighting or dog fighting." For a hugely experienced politician, Colley could be quite timid. He "didn't have the steel at that point. He didn't have the stomach for it. He was deeply hurt by it," recalls one of his team. He also acknowledges that Colley wasn't entirely blameless in all of this. Making statements about reserving his position in relation to the leader of the party was hardly conducive to harmonious meetings.

At its most benign level, it was over-enthusiasm by some in support of their man. Others from that era, not connected to either faction, play down the whole thing: "It wasn't that nasty. George Colley didn't know how to play nasty . . . He was living on the southside. This was a tough area. He wasn't in that league. He didn't know how to be tough. What was tough to Colley was bread and butter to us," said one Fianna Fáil figure. And others who know Ahern well question the idea of him crushing all would-be opponents. "Ruthless? He wasn't that ruthless. He didn't like confrontation."

Whatever did or didn't happen in 1981 and 1982, there could be no disputing the result of the November 1982 general election. Ahern garnered an astonishing 10,542 first preference votes, almost double Colley's tally and nearly one and a half quotas. His surplus elected Colley on the second count. In the Dublin Central quasi-leadership battle, there could be no disguising the thrashing Colley had received.

Despite the swing to Fine Gael nationally, Ahern was also well ahead of Michael Keating, who took the second seat. And despite predictions in some quarters that, after his deal with Haughey, Gregory could challenge Ahern for the number one spot in Dublin Central, Ahern was more than four thousand first preference votes ahead of the Independent deputy.

Nationally, Fine Gael and Labour won the election with

seats to spare. Fine Gael's seat tally was just five short of Fianna Fáil's, new territory for the traditional party of opposition. With Labour's seats added to the mix, the coalition had a comfortable majority. For Charlie Haughey contemplating, at best, a long period as leader of the opposition, the one piece of good news from that election count was the subjugation of his nemesis in Dublin Central.

Although Ahern was still only thirty-one, the result left nobody in any doubt about his status as an emerging figure in Fianna Fáil. The party struggled badly in Dublin in that general election, and Haughey – who bestowed the "Drumcondra Mafia" title on the group around his young apprentice – would have seen the Ahern machine as the blueprint for replication across the capital at the next general election.

5

LAYING DOWN THE LAW

Dull moments in politics were few and far between in the early 1980s. Following the November 1982 election contest in Dublin Central, Ahern found himself thrust into the cauldron of another heave against his mentor, Charlie Haughey.

In early 1983, with the Fine Gael-Labour coalition in government, files were released detailing the tapping of two journalists' phones under Haughey's last administration. For his enemies within the party, this was the latest stick they could use to beat him out of the leadership. A committee of inquiry was set up within the party to determine who knew what and whether culpability accrued to Haughey or others. Ahern was appointed to it, and it was chaired by his former constituency colleague Jim Tunney. The report exonerated Haughey, finding that he had no knowledge that Minister for Justice Sean Doherty had authorised the tapping. Doherty took the hit, but he would return, bearing a cold dish of revenge, a decade later to claim that his boss had known exactly what was afoot. Years later another committee member, David Andrews, would describe the inquiry as a farce.

To be fair, its powers were very restricted. Evidence was not given under oath and was not covered by privilege. Journalist Raymond Smith, in his book *Charles J. Haughey, the Survivor*, wrote that because of the absence of privilege the committee had to seek legal guidance from a prominent senior counsel to ensure it didn't walk itself into a court action. The senior counsel was one Hugh O'Flaherty, who would later – as a Supreme Court judge – become embroiled in a scandal that almost brought down Ahern's first government. The exoneration was crucial to Haughey. Despite a widespread belief in political circles that he was finished, he managed to survive, by just seven votes, a parliamentary party motion calling for his resignation.

Throughout his career, Ahern would pointedly avoid making enemies, and despite the turmoil and bitterness of the leadership heaves, he was one of the few senior figures in Fianna Fáil who managed to come through it all largely unscathed. He had backed his mentor in the crucial votes, and had managed to stay on good terms with the dissident wing of the party. He did this by keeping his head down during the three heaves, as demonstrated in a telling television clip of then RTÉ journalist Pat Cox quizzing Ahern about what had gone on at a particular Fianna Fáil parliamentary party meeting during one of the challenges. Ahern repeatedly stonewalls questions about who said what behind the closed doors. Finally, he declares: "I take the minutes of the meeting, my head was down."

His ability to keep his head (down) while all those around him were losing theirs – a trait noticeable throughout his career – has been remarked upon by some of those at the forefront of the heaves. Charlie McCreevy, a key Haughey opponent at the time and later finance minister in two Ahern governments, says he can never remember Ahern making a comment that would antagonise anybody at those ferocious meetings. "In fact, now that I think about it, during all those heaves, when nearly everybody spoke at the parliamentary party, I don't think Bertie ever spoke." Another former cabinet minister concurs: "He didn't seem to be getting to the middle of the turmoil like some of the rest of us," was Michael Smith's wry assessment twenty-five years on. He added: "He'll obviously live a lot longer."

Politically, Ahern's life was only beginning. There was no point in burning bridges that could stymie his future progress, particularly when during the third heave it appeared inevitable, until the last minute, that Haughey was finished. After he had come through that final parliamentary party vote, Haughey's position as leader became impregnable. A number of the dissidents had lost their seats the previous November. And, after three years in which their lives were turned upside down, it was understandable that many in the anti-Haughey faction yearned for a return to something resembling normality. A couple of years later a number would follow Des O'Malley into the Progressive Democrats. The rest swallowed hard and accepted that Haughey would be leader for the foreseeable future.

In the new Fianna Fáil front bench, Bertie Ahern was made chief whip, a continuation of the role he had fulfilled in government the previous year. Over the next four years of opposition, he would make the transition from coming man to one of the country's highest-profile politicians.

As Ahern's star rose, that of his rival, George Colley, was in serious decline. Although in political terms he was a veteran, Colley was still a relatively young man. However, politicians never like to show anything that can be construed as weakness, and his supporters say that in retrospect it was obvious that his health was not great. Not long before the end, there was a cumann meeting at which Colley was the principal speaker. There was a good degree of aggravation at the meeting, with Colley being criticised from the floor. There is, of course, no way of knowing if this was the cause, but later that evening he had an angina attack.

He had been suffering with angina pains for the previous year. In the autumn of 1983, he told friends he was going into hospital for minor surgery. The treatment, at Guy's Hospital in London, was intended to avoid a heart bypass operation – a much less routine procedure then than it is nowadays. Guy's had pioneered a method of clearing blood clots. However, after the treatment started, serious complications set in and doctors had to perform an emergency bypass. Although initially Colley appeared to be making steady progress, his condition deteriorated and he passed away on 17 September, twelve days after he had entered the hospital. The suddenness of his death was an enormous shock to everybody.

His remains were brought back to Dublin Airport, where Haughey and his entourage were in the VIP area to pay their respects. Despite their bitter political rivalry, Haughey and Colley went back a long way together, and many of Haughey's team were genuinely upset. But some close to the Colley family circle have never forgotten that just one man with Haughey was actually crying that evening: the demise of his great rival was too much for Bertie Ahern. He was unable to keep his emotion in check.

Once the shock had passed, attention turned to the ensuing by-election to fill Colley's seat. What happened has passed into the annals of great election stories. Haughey wanted John Stafford to be the party candidate. The Stafford family, who ran a successful undertaking business, were close personal friends of the Haugheys. John's father, Tom, had been Lord

Mayor of Dublin. The family had a record in politics, and plenty of resources behind them.

There were two other potential candidates. As is routine in Irish politics, the family of the deceased man put one forward: Colley's widow Mary. The other was Tom Leonard, who had been a TD between 1977 and 1981 and had unsuccessfully contested the previous three general elections in Dublin Central.

Mary was a reluctant candidate and, for obvious reasons, neither Haughey nor Ahern was keen on her getting the nomination. But the Ahern camp were not enthusiastic about Stafford either. They wanted Leonard. The fifty-nine-year-old ran a family business, started by his grandmother at the end of the nineteenth century, in Dublin's fruit markets. A prominent footballer in his younger days, he was well known and liked in the constituency. In the markets area, it was estimated that he could pull in a guaranteed 1,600 votes. Remembered to this day as a gentleman who was, to quote one Fianna Fáil Dublin Central politician, "too good for politics", Leonard – who died in 2004 – would not have been regarded as "the most energetic politically". His catchphrase was "I'll come back to you on that" and he was known as "Lazarus" because he had been politically dead and revived so many times. The Ahern camp saw Leonard as less of a threat than Stafford, even if this put them on a potential collision course with the ultimate boss, Haughey.

Matters came to a head in a meeting between Haughey and the Drumcondra Mafia, in Ahern's constituency office over Fagan's, to decide who would be the chosen candidate in advance of the convention. Along with Ahern and Haughey, those present included Chris Wall, Paddy Duffy, Tony Kett, Joe Burke and Paul Kiely. Ahern had prepared his team thoroughly as to what arguments they should put to the boss in suggesting that the candidate had to be Leonard. For the party's sake, of course.

"We had to explain that Leonard was the only candidate we could ensure would get elected. Otherwise you're not going to get the seat," Duffy recalled. It showed how far Ahern had come in just six years as a TD. He was politely but firmly laying down the law in his constituency to the party leader. Ever the pragmatist, Haughey wasn't impressed, yet had little option but to go along with his wishes – success in any by-election requires the local organisation to support the candidate. At the end of the meeting, he turned to the Ahern team and said: "I don't care who you run, including the widow, but win that fucking seat."

They adjourned to nearby Kennedy's – one of the Drumcondra Mafia's favourite watering holes – where Haughey pulled a typical stunt. With a flourish, he ordered a drink for everybody in the group, then felt, very deliberately, for his wallet. It wasn't in his pocket. He turned to Ahern and said: "I'll take a loan from you, Bertie." Needless to say, Ahern never saw the money again. It was a "kick in the arse" from Haughey: "You got your way on this one but I'm still the boss and don't forget it." Later Ahern, reputedly himself never the quickest to buy a round, would use the same trick.

* * *

A meeting was scheduled between Ahern's team and Mary Colley for her to set out her stall with the sitting TD in the hope of attracting crucial support. But before the meeting took place, she made a statement expressing less than full loyalty to Haughey. After that, she was contacted and told there was no point in a meeting going ahead. Media reports at the time noted that her candidature had been "coolly received" by leading members of the organisation in Dublin Central.

The convention to select the Fianna Fáil candidate was held at the Royal Dublin Hotel. According to some recollections, there was a free bar for the delegates on the night, and by the time the vote came, several were well oiled. Along with the three main contestants, one of Ahern's closest allies, Paul Kiely, had also been put forward as a candidate. This was a standard ruse by Ahern at conventions to allow him to reserve his position as to which of the real contenders he would support. Kiely withdrew his name at the last minute. "There was always a stalking horse at every convention so he wouldn't have to commit his support to anyone," one insider recalls.

When the votes of the 124 delegates from forty cumainn were counted, Stafford was ahead on forty-eight, followed by Leonard on forty-three and Colley on thirty-three. Colley, the odds-on favourite when she first announced she was putting her name forward, was therefore eliminated. But in the second count, Leonard came out ahead of Stafford by sixty-seven votes to fifty-five. When news of the result reached Fianna Fáil supporters outside the room, it was greeted with "frank and open disbelief", the *Irish Times* reported. One person present recalls Haughey's cold fury after the vote was announced.

There are extremely knowledgeable and well-informed Fianna Fáil people in Dublin Central who, to this day, swear that Ahern wanted Stafford to win. They contend that, having failed to deliver the votes for him, Ahern and his people were happy to let the impression go out that they had orchestrated the result. However, the majority view is that Ahern's camp really did manage the whole thing from start to finish. It was, as one Colley supporter later ruefully reflected, an exercise in "organised democracy".

When the result was declared, Ahern addressed the meeting as director of elections, and gave what can only be described as an unkind speech that was a less than ringing endorsement of the new candidate. "Tom has had more than his fair share of failures. He has been described as a three-time loser. But, as director of elections, I will ensure he will be a first-time winner," Ahern told delegates. He went on to warn that anybody who ran away from the coming fight would be a traitor to their party. It is not known who or what he was referring to, but perhaps it was simply night-of-convention fighting talk.

In the political world, all the talk was of the result and Leonard's shock victory. It wasn't long before the joke was doing the rounds at constituency meetings that the convention had "screwed the widow, buried the undertaker and elected the corpse". The joke was unpleasant and unfair to Leonard, a decent man who had already served as a TD. When asked by the *Irish Times* later what he thought of Ahern's introduction, he replied: "I didn't like it very much." He added that maybe Bertie hadn't been thinking about what he was saying.

A week after the convention, the Fianna Fáil organisation was jolted by the resignations of three local officers – including Phil Colley, sister of George – from the Harry Colley cumann because, they said, the party in the constituency lacked democracy. "I feel that if democracy is to continue in the party that a different attitude will have to be taken at comhairle level," Colley said. She added that people felt they had no say in the running of the constituency and that it was being manipulated by those at the top. In a thinly veiled swipe, she said the leadership should be more aware of what was happening in Dublin Central and in Dublin South Central to make sure certain members "do not have all the say in the running of the party".

Although the resignations came as a shock, the reality was that the result of the by-election was never in doubt. With the Fine Gael-Labour government already struggling with low opinion-poll ratings, there was little question that Leonard would win the by-election: he had the formidable Drumcondra machine working for him. A week away from polling, Ahern "confided" – he rarely confided anything that he didn't want in the public domain – to journalists that they had already covered the twenty-nine thousand houses in the constituency twice and hoped to intensify the campaign in the final weekend.

On election day more than a hundred cars were on hand to ferry Fianna Fáil supporters to the polling stations. Leonard won the by-election at a canter, getting 47 per cent of the vote, more than twice the number of votes of the Fine Gael candidate, Mary Banotti.

Leonard's second term in Leinster House was to prove his last. The Ahern camp felt he wasn't doing the business and he was frozen out. In January 1987, he failed to secure the nomination at the constituency convention. In all likelihood Ahern knew that, to ensure his place at cabinet after the next general election, he would have to deliver three seats out of five in Dublin Central. Leonard, although he was a sitting TD, had failed to win a seat in the 1985 local elections, which might well have sealed his fate.

* * *

Following the devastation of George's death, there was no sense of tragedy for the Colley family in failing to win the nomination. While the media wrote and spoke in the aftermath of the convention about a distraught Colley family being consoled by supporters, those close to them say it simply wasn't like that. Mary Colley wasn't a member of the party and hadn't attended cumann meetings since the early 1970s. They do recall the atmosphere on the evening being "terribly tribal".

Tribal or not, Ahern had demonstrated with the by-election that he was his own man. It wasn't the first example of this. At the very beginning of the general election campaign of February 1982, Paddy Duffy received a call from Haughey asking him to come to Kinsealy. He drove through ice and snow to Haughey's fabulous residence. After his wife Maureen had brought in tea, Haughey told Duffy he wanted him to work at Fianna Fáil Headquarters in Mount Street during the election. Duffy left Kinsealy and, on arriving home, rang Ahern to tell him. Haughey was not just leader of Fianna Fáil but, given how the Fine Gael-Labour government had fallen, very likely Taoiseach-in-waiting. Ahern's response was both unequivocal and uncompromising: "You will in your fuck. Leave that with me." The matter was sorted – presumably with Ahern persuading Haughey that Dublin Central's need was greater. Duffy never went to Mount Street.

At this point Ahern's public image may have been as a not overly impressive Haughey acolyte. As ever, his ability and the extent of his ambition were underestimated. He might have kept his head down when the party storms were raging but he knew exactly where he wanted to be when those storms had abated. Ahern was loyal to Haughey, but it was not a blind loyalty, particularly when it conflicted with his own interests. According to Duffy, "Bertie was his own man, doing things his own way."

In some accounts, Ahern fell out of favour with Haughey for a time after the Dublin Central by-election, such was the leader's displeasure at what had happened. However, Haughey clearly saw something in Ahern that he liked: he had plucked him from the massed ranks of backbenchers and given him responsibility while he was still very young, and it would take more than a squabble over a by-election candidate to do long-term damage to their relationship.

The way Duffy puts it is that while Ahern was loyal to Haughey, within that loyalty he was "exercising his own independence on issues that were important to him and to his future". That marked him out from many other Haughey supporters. "Bertie was very proactive in determining his future." According to Duffy, there was a great *esprit de corps* among the group: "In front of our eyes, he was growing. Exercising his skills. Growing in stature. It was a big personal growth period."

There could be no doubting the advances he had already made in just a few years after coming into the Dáil as a political novice. Nationally, the next level beckoned, but locally the Drumcondra Mafia still had unfinished business to take care of.

6

A LITTLE LOCAL DIFFICULTY

By the time the local elections of 1985 came around, life in politics was looking good for Ahern. The internal turmoil within the Fianna Fáil parliamentary party was effectively over. Des O'Malley had been turfed out of the party in February of that year for "conduct unbecoming" and was about to set up the Progressive Democrats. A number of dissidents would follow him. Those who opted to stay were exhausted and demoralised by the turmoil of the previous years and were ready to toe the line. Ahern's mentor, Charlie Haughey, finally had control of his party.

Fianna Fáil was still in opposition and a general election was still some way off, but the Fine Gael-Labour coalition elected at the end of 1982 appeared bereft of strategy to cope with the worst recession in a generation. The two governing parties could not agree on the cutbacks that were so clearly required to bring order to the near out-of-control public finances. They did manage to stop the massive national debt increasing any further, but it was done by levying punitive rates of taxation that served only to depress the economy further.

Unemployment rocketed, with the rate reaching the high teens. Tens of thousands of people were forced to emigrate each year to find work. Ireland was described internationally as the "sick man of Europe". It was like the bleak 1950s all over again. Ireland, as a viable state, seemed to have little future. The signing of the Anglo-Irish Agreement in 1985 gave the coalition a brief fillip in the polls, but realistically a change in government was only a matter of "when", not "if".

Ahern badly wanted to be in the next cabinet. Although he had moved steadily up the ranks in the eight years since he had been elected to the Dáil, he was still well behind more experienced figures such as Albert Reynolds, Gerry Collins and Brian Lenihan in the pecking order. That would soon change.

In his final years as Taoiseach, Ahern appeared to develop a serious distaste for the media. During his rise to the top, his affable and genial manner meant he was popular with journalists. He played the media game more than any politician before or since. Whether he liked the media or not, he understood brilliantly how it worked and used it to build his profile. He attracted positive headlines in the summer of 1984, during the traditional silly season, for his idea of holding the Oireachtas committees in the Dáil chamber and opening them up to the public. In October, Haughey reshuffled his front bench, promoting Ahern to spokesman for labour and the public service.

By this time, Celia Larkin – who would later become Ahern's "life partner" – was running his constituency office with determined efficiency. She had become involved with Fianna Fáil in Dublin Finglas in 1976, and stayed in the Finglas area after Ahern moved to Dublin Central. A career civil servant, she worked for him when he was chief whip. When Fianna Fáil returned to the opposition benches, she initially helped Ahern set up his constituency office before returning to the civil service. Later, she took leave of absence from the civil service to become Ahern's full-time constituency secretary. "She ran the office with an iron fist and very effectively," according to one of Ahern's Drumcondra team. Larkin had plenty of political savvy but she also did what Ahern respected above all else: she knocked on doors and canvassed.

Larkin brought order to the administration of the huge constituency workload. During Ahern's time as government chief whip in 1982, she established a filing system with index cards. When the operation moved to the apartment above Fagan's, she computerised the files, establishing the database that is still used today by Ahern's team in Dublin Central. Every contact between Ahern and a constituent was noted on the system, resulting in an immediate follow-up letter and, if necessary, further correspondence.

She was tough when required: "She didn't rule by fear but she certainly didn't suffer fools," is the verdict of one close observer. This was perhaps one of the reasons why she wasn't popular with the boys in the Drumcondra Mafia. She and Chris Wall – the central figure in Ahern's constituency machine – never got on. In *Bertie*, the television documentary on Ahern in 2008, it was put to Wall that Larkin was very important to the operation. Wall paused – the silence spoke volumes – before finally answering, "No." It was public affirmation of what people in politics had known for years: the Drumcondra lads and Larkin barely tolerated each other. "Celia has no problem with Chris. In fact she has a certain admiration for him. But Chris has a problem with her," says a friend of Larkin's.

According to one insider, it was the wives of the Drumcondra set who tended to have the most problems with

Larkin. Others say there was jealousy and resentment among the Mafia towards her because of her unparalleled access to, and influence over, Ahern. And there is no disputing her influence over Ahern: "When Celia shouted, Bertie jumped," is how one close observer puts it. "She ruled the roost," is the verdict of another.

According to another Fianna Fáil figure in the constituency, "Bertie Ahern wouldn't be Taoiseach only for Celia Larkin. He changed completely. He got much more focused – she gave him a sense of focus. [As a woman], she thought differently. Bertie had grown up with the lads. She brought a bit more finesse to him."

While Larkin brought "finesse" and additional profession-alism to the already impressive Ahern machine, Ahern didn't have control of the Fianna Fáil organisation in his con-stituency, despite the power of the Drumcondra Mafia. There were forty active cumainn in Dublin Central at the time – each had three votes at any constituency convention – but Ahern controlled just six. This meant he had only eighteen guaran-teed votes out of the 120-plus delegates in the Dublin Central Comhairle Dáil Cheantair.

In 1985 the level of resistance to Ahern in the constituency manifested itself in the selection process for local elections. Nobody saw it coming. Although he was a senior figure in Fianna Fáil and one of the country's biggest vote-getters, Ahern had to endure the embarrassment of failing to secure a nomination for the Inner City Ward.

At the vote, which took place in Barry's Hotel in the city centre, he came in behind Ernie Beggs and John Stafford – the man who had lost at the by-election convention less than two years earlier. In practical terms, it was only a brief setback. After the meeting, the Fianna Fáil national executive local election committee unanimously added his name to the list – some of those at the executive meeting recall a "spluttering" and highly indignant Ray Burke immediately putting Ahern's name on the ticket, even though technically he lacked the power to do so. Although the Stafford family insist that it had had nothing to do with the *coup d'état*, many Fianna Fáil people in the constituency saw it as revenge for what happened in the by-election convention. "Stafford's gang did it," is the verdict of one member of Ahern's Drumcondra set. Ahern was "in total shock": "He couldn't believe it." Perhaps he had become complacent. "He couldn't entertain the thought that he wouldn't get through," recalls a then delegate.

There are those, once close to Ahern, who say that to this day he has never forgotten or forgiven those involved in embarrassing him that night. They claim it is not coincidental that a person supposedly involved in plotting against him in 1985 was sidelined for the 2009 local elections, twenty-four years on. But others dispute this, claiming that Ahern, while certainly chastened, quickly moved on.

He had plenty to move on to. The Drumcondra Mafia were planning a *coup d'état* of their own in Dublin Corporation. Up against a hugely unpopular coalition government, Fianna Fáil would make big gains in the local elections, taking nearly half the seats available and control of councils nationwide. Across the northside of Dublin, Ahern's troops were marshalled with a plan to elect as many as five councillors to the Corporation, in the process putting Ahern at the front of the queue to become the first Fianna Fáil Lord Mayor of Dublin in twenty years.

Ahern and his long-time friend Tony Kett ran in the North Inner City, with the aforementioned Beggs and Stafford. In Drumcondra, where Ahern might have been expected to run, his brother Noel was the candidate. In Ahern's old stamping ground of Finglas, Celia Larkin was on the ticket. And over in Clontarf, his old friend Joe Burke was the candidate. In Cabra, Tom Leonard – whom Ahern had helped put into the Dáil less than two years earlier – was running as a sitting councillor.

Although there were reports of serious tension between the Ahern and Stafford camps during that election, Ahern's main rival in North Inner City was Tony Gregory. The inner city was Gregory's political base, whereas Ahern was leaving his core area, Drumcondra, to his brother. Did he run in the inner city to make a point? It was no secret that he had found the 1982 Gregory deal – whereby in return for his vote in the Dáil Gregory had secured a massive investment package for housing and facilities in the inner city – particularly hard to stomach. Dublin Central was "his" patch. He, Ahern, was supposed to be the one who delivered for his constituents. It clearly irritated him that Gregory was being presented as a saviour for the inner city. Whatever his reason for running in that ward, Ahern regarded the 1985 local election as a plebiscite for who ran the inner city.

Years later, he gave a pretty brutal assessment of Gregory's performance in that election to Ken Whelan and Eugene Masterson: "Tony Gregory was small fry. When I went head to head with him in the 1985 local elections, people soon stopped talking about how great he was. I got 5,000 votes and he got 1,800. The argument was about who ran the inner city. I did. It was as simple as that," Ahern said.

It wasn't, though, quite "as simple as that". The facts beg to differ. Ahern did top the poll with an impressive vote haul, but he actually got 4,316 votes – 1.6 quotas – and Gregory was less than 600 votes adrift with 3,766. Hardly small fry and certainly not as comprehensive a victory as Ahern presented it.

The mutal enmity between the two men appeared to soften in the final years of Gregory's life. While Ahern dismissed out of hand suggestions that one of his lieutenants had offered Gregory a junior minister's job to support his minority government in 1997 – "in his dreams" – he did indirectly offer the job of leas-Cheann Comhairle of the Dáil to Gregory in 2007, but it came to nothing.

Despite his impressive haul, Ahern failed to bring in Tony Kett alongside him. Kett got just 174 votes and Stafford took the second Fianna Fáil seat. But there was better news in the neighbouring ward, with Noel Ahern's 2,282 votes enough to get him elected. In Clontarf, Joe Burke polled half a quota and, although he was behind both the sitting Fianna Fáil councillors after the first count, managed to pick up enough transfers to unseat one.

In Finglas, Celia Larkin fell short in a hugely competitive ward that included four candidates who were either current or future TDs, three of whom would eventually reach ministerial office. In Cabra, Tom Leonard failed to win a seat. But, more alarmingly for Ahern, there was a big Fianna Fáil success story in the ward: Paddy Farry topped the poll. According to estimates at the time, he had spent between £12,000 and £14,000 on a campaign that included the use of a pipe band on an open-top bus and big teams of canvassers. That was a huge amount of money in those days and Farry seemed to be a coming man. A brilliant criminal solicitor with a high-profile practice in Phibsboro, he was handsome and suave and, not unlike Ahern, combined ambition with amazing drive. Once elected to City Hall, he set up an office staffed by two secretaries. Alarm bells rang in Ahern's head. If this was what he did in a local election, what might he do in a general election?

That question would never be answered. Farry was squeezed out. He narrowly failed to get the nomination in the 1987 general election. As ever with Ahern and Dublin Central, there are many different versions of the events. Some say Farry's failure to win the nomination was nothing to do with Ahern. Others insist that Ahern saw him as a threat that had to be snuffed out. Without referring to anybody in particular, Chris Wall would later tell the *Bertie* documentary that "There were lots and lots of people whose ambitions were cut short in those days." Farry, as many involved then in the constituency believe, was one of those people.

On balance, the local elections were a success for the Ahern machine with three out of the five targets secured and Gregory outpolled. But, as ever, not everybody was enamoured by the Drumcondra Mafia's tactics and this time they trod on the toes of a senior party member.

Fianna Fáil front-bencher Vincent Brady secured a massive vote and topped the poll in Clontarf, but was reportedly unamused that Ahern had canvassed there on behalf of Joe Burke. The same went for another TD, Michael Barrett, who was apparently not impressed by Ahern circulating literature on behalf of his brother Noel in Drumcondra.

The word in political circles was that Ahern remained out of favour with Haughey, who was still smarting over what had happened to John Stafford in the by-election convention. For all these reasons, there was a particular reluctance among all the aforementioned parties to see a northside Ahern dynasty emerge.

As a result, even though Fianna Fáil had twenty-six of the fifty-two seats in the Corporation, Ahern would have to wait a little longer to become Lord Mayor. A few weeks after the local elections, his old constituency colleague Jim Tunney was voted into the mayoral chain. Ever the diplomat, it was Ahern who had proposed him at the first meeting of the new Corporation.

As Fianna Fáil leader on the Corporation, he had a key role in divvying up membership of the committees. First-time member Joe Burke secured an attractive posting as vice-chair of the planning committee.

One other vignette from that local election campaign gives an insight into the tricks of the trade used by the Ahern machine. A householder in the North Inner City reported hearing somebody at his door and immediately went to answer it, only to find nobody there. However, a leaflet had been popped through the letterbox containing printed script closely resembling Bertie Ahern's handwriting, saying: "Sorry I missed you. Called today seeking your support for the forthcoming local elections. Bertie Ahern." It emerged that similar "Sorry I missed you" messages were being left by Joe Burke, Celia Larkin, Tony Kett and Noel Ahern. In the case of Joe Burke, not only was the message virtually identical to Ahern's, but the handwriting looked suspiciously similar!

There is divided opinion even today in Dublin Central as to whether or not the loss of face Ahern endured in having to be added to the ticket for the local elections was a factor in "Operation Dublin". This was the name given to the drive to restructure and reform the cumann system in the capital, rebuild the organisation and close down moribund cumainn.

The initiative certainly came from Fianna Fáil Headquarters and Haughey in particular. In recent general elections Fianna Fáil had struggled in Dublin, dropping to 38 per cent in the November 1982 contest, well below its support in the rest of the country. Just two out of the seventeen front-bench spokesmen in 1983 were from Dublin. The receipts from the national collection had fallen in the capital. There was an obvious need for new structures and new talent. However, many of Ahern's opponents believe it was a plot by the Ahern camp to take control of Dublin Central and ensure there would be no repeat of the local election convention.

The truth probably lies somewhere in between. The system did need to be reorganised. Certain cumainn had no delegates to the Comhairle Dáil Cheantair. Others, in the words of one Fianna Fáil constituency figure, "could have held their meetings in a telephone kiosk". But while the initiative did come from Headquarters – and involved Liam Lawlor and Brian Lenihan senior – there is little question that Ahern's people played a key role in the reorganisation.

Ahern's close friend Joe Burke's comment that "some people refer to it as the slaughter of the innocents" is telling. Despite this remark, the Ahern camp insist that Operation Dublin was nothing to do with settling old scores. The idea was to divide up the constituency on more practical lines, based on the same area, same population and so forth. "It was nothing to do with politics. It was about applying business criteria to how the constituency was run," says one person involved.

The reforms might have been necessary but they weren't always well received. "It was dog rough," admits one Ahern supporter. A constituency delegate remembers: "The old traditional Fianna Fáil people were getting on. They were outflanked and there was often little or no resistance." Another observer says: "The elderly stalwarts were not relevant. They were pushed to one side."

The stories surrounding Operation Dublin, which may or may not be true, have become the stuff of legend. A meeting of a cumann that had passed its sell-by date would be set to start at eight p.m. However, the chair, secretary, treasurer and a member would arrive early, one constituency figure recalls.

"They would change their watches or arrive with carloads of people never seen before and just take over a cumann." So even though their watches said it was eight p.m., the meeting would actually begin at seven thirty or seven forty-five. They would quickly put forward a motion that, as the cumann had not been active, not returned collections and so on, it should be dissolved for six months or until further notice. This would be done and dusted by eight o'clock by which time the rest of the members would have begun to file in and normal business could be dealt with. It was only at the end of the meeting when the minutes were being read back that the rank-and-file would realise what had happened.

Ahern's rivals contend that Drumcondra loyalists would move from cumann to cumann to maximise Ahern's influence. They also say that Ahern had his own so-called paper cumainn. "Bertie would put his own people into cumainn to put manners on them," recalls one senior constituency activist.

By the end of Operation Dublin, the number of cumainn in Dublin Central had been reduced to around twenty-five. Six were closed in Tom Leonard's stronghold of the markets area. Ahern's opponents in the area say this didn't happen in any other constituency.

Was it necessary? Most Fianna Fáil people in Dublin Central believe that, while it was ruthless, on balance the cull was required. Others says it was done purely for the Ahern machine's benefit. They acknowledge that there may have been only three or four meetings a year at certain cumainn, but argue that the members knew everything that was happening in their area and, come election time, they produced the vote. Joe Tierney, a former member of the Fianna Fáil national executive, who was a key figure in Dublin Central for decades, has said the Ahern machine "wiped out the Fianna Fáil operation and built a parallel organisation".

But the counter argument to that from the Ahern camp is that Ahern never really succeeded in taking total control of the constituency because other politicians – such as Dermot Fitzpatrick, a doctor with a large practice on the Navan Road at the opposite end of the constituency from Ahern, and the Staffords – had their own bases. "There were always elements that prevented a total takeover. There were always thorns in the side," is how one of the Drumcondra Mafia puts it. Other, more neutral, observers say there is truth in this and that Ahern only succeeded in achieving dominance of the organisation in Dublin Central after the 1992 general election when Dermot Fitzpatrick lost his seat. By then, a redrawing of the boundaries had resulted in John Stafford moving to Dublin North Central.

But it seems beyond doubt that the "thorns in the side" were less numerous after Operation Dublin. Whatever the motive behind it, it sent a clear message: don't mess with the Ahern machine. As if anybody should have needed reminding. Secure in his immediate bailiwick, Ahern and his team could now concentrate on bigger prizes.

7

FROM DRUMCONDRA TO
DAWSON STREET AND BEYOND

In July 1986, Bertie Ahern spread his wings beyond Dublin Central: he crossed the river to take up residence in one of the city's most prestigious addresses, the Mansion House on Dawson Street, official residence of the Lord Mayor of Dublin.

Ahern was elevated to first citizen of Dublin after he defeated Carmencita Hederman, twenty-seven to twenty-four, in a vote by the city's councillors. Fittingly, it was his former running mate in Dublin Finglas, Jim Tunney, who, as outgoing Lord Mayor, placed the chain of office over his head.

The next twelve months would change Ahern's life, both politically and personally. By the time his stint as Lord Mayor ended, he would be one of the best-known politicians in the country and a cabinet minister, with a burgeoning reputation as a man who got things done.

Although his wife Miriam accompanied him in the mayoral coach, their marriage was apparently in serious difficulty. Perhaps for reasons more connected with the difficulties of raising a young family in the official and public surroundings of the Mansion House, Miriam ultimately chose to stay at the family home in Malahide where their two girls were attending school. Years later Ahern's close friend Tony Kett would tell Ken Whelan and Eugene Masterson that the "plain reality was that Bertie was never home and when he got home Miriam's family were *in situ*, keeping her company. It was no way to keep a marriage going. Like many marriages in politics and other walks of life, one partner got careless and that led to the collapse of the relationship. At that stage Celia was not involved." Later Ahern admitted that his marriage was in many ways a victim of the long hours he spent attending to the offices of Lord Mayor and then as Minister for Labour. He would also claim that the fall-out from the marriage breakdown was the source of all the problems that arose in his finances.

While his personal life was in difficulty, though, things couldn't have been better politically. Ahern saw the public relations opportunity the position of Lord Mayor offered and grabbed it like no politician before or since has, building an enormous profile in the process.

Although the role is largely ceremonial, with few real powers, he immediately declared that unemployment, tackling dereliction and restoring vitality to the Quays and the docks were his priorities. He called for Dublin Corporation to cease building houses in areas such as Tallaght, Clondalkin and Blanchardstown and concentrate on the inner city, where there was plenty of disused land to be developed. In terms of good planning, his logic was indisputable. Politically, the area he wanted developed was in his own constituency.

He also demonstrated his common touch by indicating that he would get in touch with the protocol section of Dublin Corporation to ask them if the prefix "Lord" was necessary in his title. He would prefer to be "Mayor of Dublin". It didn't lead to anything, but it added to his credentials as a man of the people, uninterested in fancy titles with roots in a colonial past.

As well as attending every opening of an envelope in the city – a practice he would perfect while Taoiseach – and a high-profile chairing of the Dublin Millennium Committee, he kept his name in the headlines by generating controversy from time to time. Towards the end of his tenure as Lord Mayor, he urged Dubliners to stop "moaning, bitching and growling" about their city. In a speech that bore the fingerprints of his erudite adviser Paddy Duffy, he said: "When the Norsemen settled in the Dublin area in the ninth and tenth centuries, they did so for a good reason. It was perfectly located in their trading network, it was the key access point between the north and south of the country and it was a sheltered harbour for their long ships." And, yet, he challenged, "When was the last time you said to someone, 'Great city this, I'm glad I live in Dublin'? … Do we not need to occasionally tell ourselves that we live in a great city?"

It wouldn't be last time in his political career that Ahern let fly at what he saw as whingers and moaners, particularly those whose whingeing and moaning didn't suit his own agenda.

Perhaps out of frustration at the limitations of the role, he also called for the introduction of a directly elected mayor – similar to what happens in the US or on the Continent – who would hold power for five years. But his real goal lay elsewhere. In early 1987, the Fine Gael-Labour coalition finally fell apart and a general election was called for 17 February. The economic climate was still dire, with the twin evils of unemployment and emigration as bad as ever. The electorate had had enough of the sitting government. Change was inevitable.

Charlie Haughey was chasing that elusive overall majority

and Ahern, who badly wanted to be in cabinet, was under pressure to deliver in Dublin Central. Despite his hugely impressive vote-garnering abilities, Fianna Fáil had taken only two out of the five seats in the previous three elections. To nail down a place in cabinet, Ahern would have to deliver three.

Tom Leonard, winner of the by-election in 1983, had lost his council seat two years later. He was unceremoniously jettisoned. Although he was TD for the area, he was refused automatic selection on the grounds he had been returned in a by-election and was therefore not a "sitting deputy". Reports at the time said his defeat was "inevitable when he lost the support of the cumann controlled by the Lord Mayor, Mr Bertie Ahern". Ahern himself was selected unanimously because he was a sitting TD.

The result of the election convention suggested that, less than two years on from Ahern's embarrassment at the selection contest for the local elections, he was finally establishing control in Dublin Central. On the first count, Stafford got sixty-two votes, Paddy Farry, the high-profile solicitor who had polled so well in the local elections, scored ten, Leonard six and Dermot Fitzpatrick just one.

Stafford was thus selected. On the second count, Fitzpatrick came from last place in the first to get forty votes, beating both Farry and Leonard, who got thirty-five and four votes respectively. Farry had come close, but not close enough, and Ahern had the ticket he wanted.

Leonard had every reason to feel hard done by, though the result wouldn't have come as much of a surprise to him – he had been told by the Ahern camp that this would be the outcome some time before the convention: he and Farry had both been deemed *persona non grata*. Of the two victors that night, Stafford had known a similar fate less than four years earlier at the by-election convention. Twenty years on, Fitzpatrick's daughter Mary would also be shafted at general-election time by the Drumcondra Mafia. Nothing personal. Just business.

* * *

The 1987 general election was a partial triumph for Charlie Haughey. Fine Gael's vote collapsed, but a strong performance by the new Progressive Democrats meant that while Haughey would be Taoiseach, he fell two seats short of an overall majority. Not that any blame could be attached to Bertie Ahern. He delivered for the party, big time. Not only was the Haughey family's good friend John Stafford safely delivered to the Dáil, but Ahern also brought in his other running mate, Dermot Fitzpatrick.

And he managed to do so with pretty much the same first preference vote as in the previous three general elections. With Ahern the undisputed top dog in the wake of Colley's passing, a strategy was drawn up whereby he was given free rein across the constituency. Some would say this was simply a formal recognition of what had gone on in previous elections. Ahern got 13,635 first preference ticks, almost twice the quota, and a higher total than Haughey in the adjoining constituency. And, as with the previous elections, the percentage of Ahern's transfers staying in the Fianna Fáil fold was hugely impressive. Almost 80 per cent of his surplus went to Stafford and Fitzpatrick, who were both elected without reaching the quota.

The votes of Stafford and Fitzpatrick were spread more evenly than had been the case with Colley and Leonard in previous elections, allowing both men to stay in the contest and eventually be elected.

Not that the election was without its tensions. George

Colley might not have been around but, in Stafford, Ahern had a new foe within the party ranks. There was ill feeling on both sides over what had happened at the conventions for the by-election in 1983 and the locals two years later.

The Stafford supporters were not shrinking violets. "There was a lot of physical stuff in that election," one Fianna Fáil figure recalls. Area divisions for canvassing, in so far as they existed, were ignored. Some of those on the ground recall how the Drumcondra crew were "past masters" at getting the other Fianna Fáil candidates drawn into long meetings, taking up their time. Ahern, of course, was never at these meetings: "You never saw Bertie. He was at somebody's hall door."

But by the end of the campaign, with three Fianna Fáil seats secured, everybody was happy.

Ahern's reward was a place at the cabinet table, ten years on from his entry into Dáil Éireann, and at the age of just thirty-five. The Department of Labour wouldn't have been seen as a particularly plum posting but, once again, he had been in the right place at the right time.

Haughey was keen to involve employers and the unions in his strategy to get the economy moving again and a national wage agreement was seen as a key plank in it. It fell to Ahern – building on the work he had done as opposition labour spokesman when he had developed close ties with ICTU – to negotiate the programme for national recovery.

With Ray MacSharry as finance minister, the Haughey government – with the Dáil backing of the main opposition party Fine Gael – finally moved to tackle the crisis in the public finances. Despite swingeing cuts in public spending, the economy showed signs of growth. Confidence started to return and there were huge approval ratings for the minority Fianna Fáil administration.

Aside from a growing reputation as the Red Adair of industrial relations disputes, Ahern utilised his spell in the Department of Labour to build up his profile in other ways. PR man Frank Dunlop, later a central player in the planning tribunal, was commissioned by the new state training agency, Fás, to do PR work. It involved publicising the opening of new training centres throughout the country and ensuring they received plenty of coverage in the local papers. As the line minister, Ahern was in a position to use the openings as a major PR opportunity. Conscious of the need to cultivate Fianna Fáil grass roots, he availed himself of these opportunities to meet up with the local party organisation. Fifteen years on, it was his own state-sponsored version of Charlie Haughey's 1970s chicken-and-chips circuit, which Haughey had used to build up support within Fianna Fáil during his post-Arms Trial wilderness years.

There were also some important benefits for Ahern's local constituency. Ahern was the minister responsible for CERT, the state training agency for the hotel and catering industry. In 1989 he persuaded it to move from its rented office in Dublin 4 to a new £3 million headquarters to be built on a derelict site on Amiens Street in the north inner city. It was exactly the type of stimulus the run-down inner city needed. At a cost of just £500,000 for a 1.8 acre site right beside the IFSC, the state got a bargain. Within a few years, the site would be worth many multiples of that. But what was also interesting about the deal was the involvement of several people who were very close to Ahern. The chairman of CERT at the time was Jim Nugent, an old friend of Ahern, dating back to their involvement together in the FWUI. He would later emerge as one of the contributors to Ahern's first alleged dig-out at Christmas 1993 and an attendee of Ahern's annual Dublin Central fundraising dinner.

Two sets of architects were appointed to the construction of the new office block, one of which was Pilgrim Group. Two of its main figures were Des Richardson and Tim Collins. The two men were close friends of Ahern and key members of the Drumcondra Mafia, although their role on the ground in the constituency was virtually non-existent. The CERT headquarters became a regular haunt of some of the Drumcondra crew. One night in the early 1990s when a group of them were leaving in the early hours, a member of the party fell out through a plate-glass window but was unharmed.

While Ahern was becoming a more established figure in national politics, he was also keeping a close eye on his constituency. In an interview with the *Irish Times* in 1988, he spoke about his typical weekend. Friday evening involved a jar with councillors and staff before he attended three or four local functions – a parish social, a football club, the prison officers' club, a residents' association meeting. Between seven and midnight, "I might hit anything between six and ten locations, though I'd never stay at any one of them."

Saturday was for clinics, always starting with the Tolka House pub close to the Botanic Gardens in Glasnevin at ten thirty a.m. Then he went on to the Fianna Fáil constituency headquarters on Amiens Street, where he would stay until four o'clock. He would normally see around fifty people in that time.

Weather permitting, Ahern and his team would do "walkarounds" for a couple of hours, selecting an area and knocking on doors, meeting and greeting. Ahern found this "especially important when you can get so bloody isolated in this bloody place [the Dáil]".

Saturday night was his only chance to spend time with his family and friends. They generally stayed in because Ahern didn't like pubs on a Saturday night as they were "too bloody packed". A meal out left him vulnerable to somebody approaching, looking for a problem to be sorted, pulling up a chair at the table. If they did go out it was to a club – but not on Leeson Street. The kind of club Ahern had in mind was of the local GAA variety, such as Na Fianna or Whitehall.

Sunday was based around where "the Dubs" were playing. Ahern, the man of the people, wouldn't get a seat in the stand: "Always to the terrace and to the same place so people nearly always know you and you don't get hassle," he said. If there wasn't a cabinet meeting in the morning, he would meet up after mass, at around eleven a.m., with some of his constituency team to plan tactics or do more "walkarounds", stopping for "a jar" at twelve thirty and then home for lunch.

During the summer, he brought his daughters along to community events. (In later years, when he was separated, he set aside Sunday afternoon for them. They would have lunch in the Berkeley Court, then head to Croke Park. That was sacrosant. Staff and officials knew not to ring him during those hours unless there was literally a national emergency.)

On Sunday night he would meet up "with a few of my own guys" for a drink and hit a few different places in the constituency. Other than Kennedy's or Fagan's, favourite pubs included the Beaumont House, the Brian Boru in Phibsboro, the Tolka House in Glasnevin or the Goose Tavern in Marino. Even after he became Taoiseach, Ahern liked to chill out with a few pints in one of these hostelries. The clientele was accustomed to seeing him on the news in some far-flung location earlier in the day and then arriving in shortly before closing time for a late pint. "A lot of friends say I work hard on a Sunday because I might have been in Cabra at mass, back to a cumann meeting in Fairview, one or two community things or garden fêtes, indoor or outdoor things for the CRC [Central Remedial

Clinic] or other charities in the area. But I don't regard that Sunday thing as work, really," he told the *Irish Times*.

While some of the legend surrounding Ahern's eighteen-hour days may be exaggerated – some of those who know him say he is never great in the morning and wouldn't be a particularly early riser – there is no question that he worked harder and longer than anybody else in politics during his time in the Dáil. And despite his rise up the ladder in national politics, many of those long hours were put in at the coal face in Dublin Central. It was the larger-than-life US Democrat politician Tip O'Neill who famously commented that all politics was local, but no senior politician would subscribe to this dictum more than Bertie Ahern. He was destined to be a major player on the national stage but Drumcondra would remain his hub.

The Ahern machine was by now becoming the envy of TDs across the country, but to its key players something was lacking: the most professional political operation in the state had no home to call its own. That was about to change.

8

THE GOSPEL OF ST LUKE'S

Since the 1940s, the Fianna Fáil organisation in Dublin Central had operated from premises at 72 Amiens Street, near Connolly Station. The building housed the constituency's party TDs and a whole slew of councillors. By the 1980s, it was past its sell-by date, particularly for an operation like Ahern's. The place was run-down, Amiens Street itself was suffering from an increase in antisocial behaviour and, with the range of different public representatives in the constituency, it actually became difficult to book a room for meetings.

A decision was made to sell the building, and Ahern set about looking for a place closer to the heart of his operation in Drumcondra. Since 1983, he had hired two rooms above Fagan's pub, which facilitated clinics, but now a more permanent base was required.

Ahern would explain later that after the sale of 72 Amiens Street the party was effectively homeless. "Fianna Fáil hadn't got a base in the constituency. So Fianna Fáil got a new base in the constituency and the base was St Luke's. It was bought by a trust who were Fianna Fáil supporters, to be held in trust for

Dublin Central and the party nationally." He left out the crucial detail that St Luke's was bought before Amiens Street was sold. And it wasn't entirely accurate to say that Fianna Fáil was behind the purchase of St Luke's.

St Luke's, a residential house owned by a doctor, went on sale in 1987. Ahern's people saw it as ideal. The relatively modest two-storey red-brick detached house was situated at 161 Drumcondra Road, just across the road from Fagan's, between a boutique and a building society on the hugely busy thoroughfare that connects Dublin Airport to the city centre. In November 1987 Des Richardson, Tim Collins and Joe Burke entered a contract of sale to buy it. Burke was the only one of the three who was a member of Fianna Fáil, and even he could hardly be described as an enthusiastic member of the O'Donovan Rossa cumann.

The composition of the named purchasers emphasised that St Luke's was to be an Ahern base, rather than a direct replacement for Amiens Street. It was one of the more obvious examples of "Ahern first, Fianna Fáil as an afterthought" that informed the *modus operandi* of the Drumcondra Mafia.

Over the following decades, St Luke's became a lot more than Bertie Ahern's constituency office or even his place of residence. It is a byword for Ahern and the Drumcondra Mafia: the physical manifestation of Ahern's power base. Virtually every significant move he has made in politics over the past two decades was teased out under its roof. It would also be central to the narrative of Ahern's finances.

Now that Ahern's team had their hands on a property, they had to fund its purchase. Efforts to raise money resulted in an alleged meeting at the Gresham Hotel on 3 December 1987. At least twenty Ahern supporters were reported to have been present. None has ever been identified, or come forward, when questions about St Luke's were raised at the planning tribunal. The group would come to be known as the St Luke's Club. There is no record that this alleged meeting actually took place. Many Fianna Fáil people in the constituency weren't aware that this it was to take place. Liam Cooper, an officer in the O'Donovan Rossa cumann then and, at the time of writing, would tell the planning tribunal more than twenty years later that he hadn't been aware of it.

According to Ahern, a strategy was laid out in which each supporter would pay £1,000 a year for either four or five years to fund the purchase of premises and pay off any loans that might accrue. This scenario echoes other elements of Ahern's finances, which would emerge in later years, in which any money that was accruing to Ahern or his operation was the result of small contributions from a large number of people and, in this case, paid over a long period of time. Over the years the existence of the "St Luke's Club" gained further credence. In 1997, prior to the general election that year, Ahern commissioned senior counsel David Byrne to draw up a document outlining the history of St Luke's because rumours were afoot in the media about the exact status of the premises. Ahead of the general election, rumours had circulated that friends of Ahern had bought the house for him, and that he was the legal owner. Naturally, the man who would be Taoiseach – he was Fianna Fáil party leader in 1997 – wanted to deal a swift blow to them.

He explained the situation at the planning tribunal: "Queries had been put to them [the trustees of St Luke's] a number of times, and they were anxious that we would pull one document together and certainly one or two of them were anxious that this would be done before the general election. And, as I recall it, they asked Gerry Brennan (Ahern's solicitor) if he would pull that together. He subsequently asked Mr David Byrne and myself to work with him in drawing that document together."

In the report, Byrne noted: "To raise the funds necessary to purchase and renovate the premises, the St Luke's Club was informally established at a meeting held in the Gresham Hotel on the 3rd of December 1987. This meeting was attended by over 20 people, most of them from the constituency who resolved, having regard to the funds required, that this sum could be raised over a period of four to five years by 25 people giving a commitment to provide £1,000 each per annum."

Byrne was reporting on the basis of what he was told by Ahern, rather than any official record of the meeting because, of course, none exists. No blame accrues to the lawyer in so doing as he was merely asked to draw up a document based on the information given to him.

The lack of any documentary record of the event taking place, or the loose formation of the St Luke's Club, seems extraordinary in an organisation that was as professional and efficient as Ahern's. His office had records of thousands of constituents and issues that might affect them, yet it failed to maintain records on the accumulation of tens of thousands of pounds to buy St Luke's.

An alternative explanation for the absence of records is that the meeting at the Gresham never took place. If this was so, then the money used to buy St Luke's was sourced elsewhere. No such alternative funding was identified in the investigation at the planning tribunal but, as with much of Ahern's story, there are more questions than answers in relation to the purchase of St Luke's.

In any event, the money was raised. The purchase price was £56,000 and up to another £75,000 was required to renovate the premises to suit the needs of a political party, and to accommodate some structural work. By the standards of the day, this was a phenomenal amount of money to raise for what was ostensibly a small organisation.

The declaration of trust was drawn up in May 1988, and signed by Richardson, Collins, Burke and two other close confidants of Ahern, Jimmy Keane and Paddy Reilly. A local priest, Father Hugh Daly, said mass in St Luke's at its official opening in 1990. It would be the only mass said on the premises during Ahern's tenure, but in terms of financial well-being, all prayers were answered. St Luke's would always maintain good financial health.

* * *

When the renovations were complete, the former doctor's residence had been transformed into a fine headquarters for the ambitious local politican. Downstairs there is a constituency office and a private office with a safe, in which Ahern stored huge sums of cash through his early years in St Luke's. During his time in office, his desk was always messy, strewn with the mementoes and small gifts that political leaders receive virtually every day. The walls were adorned with pictures of Ahern meeting various world leaders. There is also a kitchen, a bar – where Ahern's favourite beer, Bass, is available on tap – and a large meeting room.

Upstairs is effectively a separate entity, consisting of a small apartment. It includes a kitchenette, a bedroom, bathroom and living room that, in time, Ahern would refer to as a meeting room. The second floor was fitted with underfloor heating, relatively unheard of in pre-Celtic Tiger Ireland. In the bathroom, there are gold taps. Those who have been upstairs recall that teddy bears decked out in the Dublin colours were prominent.

Outside, the only hint that this is not a standard business or residential address comes from the presence of two security cameras.

In 1992 Ahern moved into the apartment as his full-time residence. Years later, at the planning tribunal, he would dispute its status, claiming that party workers had effectively free run through the living or meeting room. However, a number of party sources have confirmed that upstairs was off-limits. Ahern was not one of the trustees of the premises, but nobody was in any doubt as to who was in charge. "Everybody treated St Luke's as Bertie's house," was how one former party activist described it.

Once he was ensconced in his new office and home, St Luke's became the focal point of Ahern's career.

The Taoiseach is accorded an office in Government Buildings on Merrion Street, right beside Dáil Eireann. This has been the traditional centre of government since the foundation of the state. It is a stunning Edwardian building, constructed around a courtyard. At the rear of the site there is a domed central block, which is visible from the street through a columned screen and gateway and is connected via a walkway to Leinster House. Although originally a college of science, it is a worthy headquarters for a government of the people.

From 1997 to 2008, while Ahern was Taoiseach, St Luke's was effectively a second centre of power in Irish politics, proving equally pivotal to the running of the country. There has never been an official residence for the Taoiseach, but during Ahern's years at the helm, 161 Drumcondra Road was Ireland's answer to Number 10 Downing Street.

There were few days when Ahern didn't appear at St Luke's when he was running the country. The telltale sign was the ministerial Mercedes parked on the footpath outside. Quite often there were two, indicating that the Taoiseach had summoned one of his ministers for discussion on official matters. During the crucial talks around the peace process in Northern Ireland, for which Ahern received deserved plaudits, many meetings with main players were held in the building. At other times, particularly times of crisis, the cars of his closest associates were also parked outside, including Des Richardson's Jaguar.

Every Friday during Ahern's years as Taoiseach, civil servants in his office at Government Buildings prepared two big briefcases for him to take back to St Luke's, detailing what was happening in every government department. He would spend Friday evening until ten o'clock there rooting through it. Not an early riser, Ahern – who by this point lived up the road in Beresford – would head down to St Luke's and spend all day immersing himself in every detail of the functioning of government.

The Department of the Taoiseach might have been on Merrion Street and the cabinet might have gathered in Government Buildings, but much of Ahern's real work was done in St Luke's and it was where his kitchen cabinet sat. It would be stretching things to say that all the real decisions were made there – but not by much.

* * *

Running a constituency office, staffed by full-time personnel, doesn't come cheap. From the outset, Ahern and his supporters realised that ongoing costs would require an ongoing dedicated method of funding.

Since 1982, the day-to-day running costs had been sourced from a constituency account in AIB Drumcondra in the name of Ahern and Joe Burke. Another of the fabled Mafia came up with a method for keeping the account in the black. Des Richardson organised the first O'Donovan Rossa fundraising dinner in 1987. Over the following two decades it would grow into a major social event, attracting the great and the good from all sectors of the economy and society. The first dinner was held in the Mansion House while Ahern was still Lord Mayor. From there, it was moved to the Royal Hospital Kilmainham, and then to Clontarf Castle. Ironically, the main knees-up for Dublin Central was never held within the constituency boundaries.

In 2001 the *Sunday Tribune* newspaper provided a unique insight into the event. Reporter Shane Coleman visited Clontarf Castle with a photographer on the appointed night of the annual fundraiser, just before Christmas. At the entrance to the dining room, a list was pinned to the wall: the plan for twenty-five tables, including the host at each one. It was snapped by the *Tribune* photographer, and made fascinating reading.

Among the guests was John Finnegan, a controversial auctioneer who was a key witness at the planning tribunal. He was also a long-time associate of former Taoiseach Charlie Haughey. He had been named as one of the holders of the controversial and illegal off-shore Ansbacher deposits. He was also investigated by the tribunal about how £10,000 of his money had ended up in a Ray Burke off-shore account. The tribunal eventually found that it was a corrupt payment.

Also as table hosts were several people who would later come to public prominence as having claimed to give Ahern money in alleged dig-out payments. These included publicans Charlie Chawke and Dermot Carew, businessman Dave McKenna and former CERT chairman and Central Bank director Jim Nugent.

Other prominent names on the list included those of builder Jerry Beades, an associate of Ahern, property developer Sean Dunne, hoteliers Noel O'Callaghan and Jim Mansfield, auctioneer Ken McDonald and top builder Bernard McNamara. Businessman Vincent McDonald, who used to socialise with Ahern in Kennedy's pub in Drumcondra, hosted three tables. Ryanair chief executive Michael O'Leary was there as a guest. Bertie Ahern's school friend Robert White, who was associated with the Sonas Centre – the mooted but then abandoned casino and national stadium project in Dublin's Phoenix Park – also hosted a table. It would emerge at the planning tribunal that White's business partner in the project, Norman Turner, had, seven years previously, given Des Richardson $10,000 in cash when Richardson had been a party fundraiser. The money was not passed on to the party but used by Richardson to meet on-the-job expenses. Naturally, Richardson and Joe Burke were at the dinner. Burke, who was organising the event, expressed displeasure at a photograph being taken of the seating arrangements.

The name of one man in attendance meant little at the time but grew in significance. Mícheál Wall was a Connemara-born, Manchester-based businessman who featured strongly in Ahern's later travails with the planning tribunal.

Arriving after the majority of guests, Ahern entered through a side door – there is little doubt that the media presence prompted this, but such a discreet arrival was unusual for him. Here, after all, the great and the good were paying tribute to his contribution to public life with their pockets, and one might have expected him to take pride in the occasion. Why be shy at the receipt of large sums of money for his political machine?

Each of the twenty-five tables seated eight. The two hundred guests were treated to a four-course dinner that included roast beef, and the wines available for purchase included a 1997 Pouilly Fumé, Châtelain Prestige, J. C. Châtelain, and a 1996 Nuits St Georges Premier, Château Gris.

The ticket price wasn't revealed, but it was speculated at the time that a table of eight was roughly £1,400 (€1,780). If such a figure was accurate, it would also have been convenient: under ethics legislation, declaration would not be required if the average contribution per guest was below the legal limit, which, at the time, was £500 per person. Therefore, with two hundred in attendance, such a night might raise anything up to £100,000 without the necessity to declare it. Conservative speculation at the time set the tickets at roughly £200 a head, which would have brought in £40,000. In terms of Irish politics at this date, this level of funding from a single event was something most politicans could only dream about.

Despite Ahern's avoidance of the *Tribune* photographer, the event still made front-page news that Sunday because Finnegan had been there. A degree of controversy ensued, which resulted in Dáil questions the following Wednesday. In response, Ahern told the House: "I have not taken money from anybody or asked anybody for money, regardless of whether they are involved in a tribunal." He went on: "If a constituency organises a function and I attend as guest of honour, I neither vet nor organise who else attends, nor do I handle the money."

The reply highlighted his position vis-à-vis funding: others did it for him. He merely showed up as a guest of honour. He had a similar position in relation to the controversy over St Luke's. Questions were asked of the trustees. They responded. Nothing to do with him. Richardson contacted the *Sunday Tribune* in the week after the story appeared, complaining about the headline "Ahern takes cash from key Flood witness", which, he claimed, was unfair. But there was no argument with the substance of the article, which outlined who attended.

The fundraising dinner wasn't the only issue with donations raised by the media at the time. The *Sunday Tribune* also reported that Ahern had failed to provide full information about political contributions he had received in 1997 to the Public Offices Commission – the ethics watchdog and forerunner to the Standards in Public Office Commission – in relation to St Luke's. He had failed to declare the benefit accruing to him from the use of St Luke's on the basis that it was owned by Fianna Fáil trustees. In 2001, he amended his declaration under the Ethics in Public Office Act to cover the use of St Luke's since 1995. The total value on use of the office over four years was put at £23,450.

However, it is arguably impossible to set a value on the benefit to Ahern of St Luke's. No other TD in the history of the state has ever had access to such a set-up. The combination of constituency office, meeting rooms, base for clinics, a centre for social activity and residence, all under one roof, was of incalculable benefit to the local politician.

Despite its nominal status as a Fainna Fáil asset, St Luke's epitomised the cult of Ahern the politician, surrounded by his Praetorian Guard, the Drumcondra Mafia. If the walls in the little red-brick building could talk, many believe they would have some terrific tales to tell.

9

THE MOST CUNNING, THE BIGGEST DITHERER

With St Luke's acquired, it wasn't long before the Drumcondra machine was cranked up again for another general election. In the summer of 1989, against all Ahern's better instincts and advice, Charlie Haughey – still craving that overall majority – went to the country. He wanted to capitalise on the high opinion-poll ratings that his government's tough action on the public finances had brought.

Nationally, as Ahern had feared, the move backfired badly. Cutbacks in health services dominated the campaign, and the government struggled to deal with the issue. Fianna Fáil lost four seats and ended up ditching its old core value of single-party government. For the first time in the party's history, they went into coalition – with Haughey's old enemies, the PDs.

As ever, Ahern emerged smiling. His campaign team now had 280 volunteers, 120 active at any time during the election campaign. Every house in the constituency was canvassed three times. When the votes were counted in Dublin Central he had an astonishing two quotas, or 13,589 votes. It was the highest personal vote he would ever command, although he continued to be a remarkable vote-getter in all his subsequent elections.

Again, the transfer pattern to Stafford and Fitzpatrick was in excess of 80 per cent of Ahern's surplus – which gives some credence to those in the Ahern camp who argue that they were good at delivering votes for Fianna Fáil, not just Ahern. With the two running mates separated by just a hundred votes after the first count, the Fianna Fáil vote was sufficiently well spread to ensure the party retained its three seats, without either Stafford or Fitzpatrick reaching the quota.

At this stage Ahern was probably Haughey's only real confidant in the cabinet and he was a regular visitor to Haughey's home in Kinsealy after the general election failed to produce a decisive result. His stature in Fianna Fáil was reinforced by Haughey's decision to nominate him and Albert Reynolds to negotiate a new government with the PDs' Pat Cox and Bobby Molloy. The talks took place in Ahern's one-time residence, the Mansion House, but initially went nowhere: Reynolds was strongly opposed to the notion of coalition with the PDs. But Ahern, always a believer in the old adage of politics being the art of the possible, was working to deliver a deal on the basis that it was the least bad option for his party. It would avoid another election or the prospect of Fine Gael putting together a minority government.

Not everybody was so pragmatic: at a cabinet meeting during the height of the crisis, Reynolds, Pádraig Flynn and others spoke out strongly against coalition, while a number of ministers took the opposite view. Ahern, as ever, kept his cards close to his chest, as did Haughey, still the master to Bertie the apprentice.

Although Ahern was closer to what was going on than any other minister, both he and Reynolds were irritated to discover that Haughey had met with O'Malley and the two PD negotiators without their knowledge. Only Haughey could have brought Fianna Fáil into a coalition, but perhaps only Ahern could have seen it in such clear, uncomplicated terms so quickly. Whatever about Haughey, Ahern was light years ahead, in terms of political strategy, of his fellow ministers.

* * *

Haughey's ground-breaking decision to go into coalition had secured him another term as Taoiseach but, politically speaking, his time was coming to a close. A year later, in 1990, his authority received a massive setback in the presidential election when the senior Fianna Fáil politician Brian Lenihan was defeated by Mary Robinson. Ahern was director of elections but could hardly be blamed for a disastrous campaign that lurched from crisis to crisis. The election seemed to mark a seismic shift in Irish politics and there was a sense that the electorate wanted to move beyond civil-war politics.

That seemed to be borne out in the following year's local elections, which were particularly poor for Fianna Fáil. As a a government minister, Ahern did not contest them. He had previously stood down from Dublin Corporation, with Tony Kett, his friend and running mate in the previous local elections, taking his seat. In the 1991 local elections, Kett retained the seat, polling a highly respectable 1,545 first preference votes. However, he was a long way behind Ahern's old adversary in the North Inner City, Tony Gregory, who attracted more than 4,000.

In Drumcondra, Ahern's brother Noel – who in the run-up to the elections had called on An Post to commemorate the seventy-fifth anniversary of the 1916 Rising by finally removing all pillar boxes with a crown on them – was elected on the first count with more than 2,700 votes. However, in Clontarf, Joe Burke lost. While the perception was that he didn't enjoy the humdrum of constituency clinic work, he was up against it: both his running mates – Ivor Callely and John Stafford, who had moved to the ward from the North Inner City – were TDs, and he narrowly lost to Stafford.

The elections would be the last that Fianna Fáil contested with Charlie Haughey as leader. The "boss" was losing his touch. The time was fast approaching for the apprentice to step out of his shadow. And that was exactly what he was doing. By now Ahern had negotiated a second national pay deal, and sorted numerous high-profile disputes. He was also up for a move to the Department of Environment, a job he clearly coveted. It wasn't to be, but again fortune favoured him because, by staying as labour minister, he was perfectly placed to be cast as virtual national saviour in the 1991 ESB strike. It lasted for four days, plunged the nation into darkness and caused misery in places such as Ballymun where people in the tower blocks had to climb the staircases in total darkness. After a marathon eleven hours of talks, in which Ahern played a key role, the strike was settled. Although his critics have sniped that he only gets involved in resolving a dispute when he knows resolution is in sight, there is little question that his experience and contacts from his days at the FWUI, allied to his interpersonal and negotiating skills, were a huge asset in the Department of Labour.

When the strike was settled, he was portrayed as the hero of the hour – and was a definite contender to succeed Charlie Haughey. His stock was about to increase further.

In the late summer/early autumn of 1991, the programme for government between Fianna Fáil and the PDs was up for renegotiation. The talks hit an impasse and even seemed to threaten the future of the government. Albert Reynolds, by then finance minister and still no fan of the PD coalition, was taking a tough line with the junior party on budgetary matters. Meanwhile, some senior PD figures were of the view that it was time to pull out of government. A series of controversies in the business world, relating to companies such as Greencore, Telecom Éireann and Celtic Helicopters, was causing serious political problems for Haughey. The PDs were afraid of being tainted with guilt by association.

By the middle of October, the talks were going nowhere fast and, with a motion of no confidence in the government about to be debated in the Dáil, nerves were frayed.

The conclusion of that debate on 18 October became the deadline for a renewed deal between the two coalition partners. All of Ahern's negotiating skill – and his cool head – came to the fore. While Reynolds's macho stance with the PDs went down well with Fianna Fáil deputies initially, the mood shifted when a general election looked to be in the offing.

"Bertie Ahern got everybody off the hook," is how Stephen Collins puts it in his book on the PDs, *Breaking the Mould*. Using the old union negotiating ploy of focusing on what had been agreed rather than what hadn't, Ahern brought the deal home: in the early hours of 18 October, he managed to persuade Reynolds to sign it.

Later that day, while Ahern was briefing journalists, Haughey stuck his head in the door, pointed at his protégé and uttered the immortal words that have stuck to Ahern like glue ever since: "He's the man. He's the best, the most skilful, the most devious and the most cunning of them all." Coming from Haughey, that was praise indeed. Ahern was *the* anointed one. Albert Reynolds, however, had different ideas about who would take over.

* * *

Within a few weeks, the "most cunning of them all" had been appointed Minister for Finance at the age of forty. Reynolds, along with Pádraig Flynn, had been fired from government after declaring against Haughey. The Taoiseach comfortably saw off, by fifty-five votes to twenty-two, the fourth heave against him. In keeping with his conduct in the previous three, Ahern backed his leader, resisting approaches from the Reynolds wing. There was no surprise therefore when he was appointed to fill the vacancy Reynolds had left.

By the time he came to present his first budget he would be in the centre of what turned out to be a phony leadership race – a leadership race that would see his judgement, his "bottle" and his close ties with his Drumcondra friends called into question. But before that there was a piece of personal business to take care of.

On 11 January 1992, he went on the *Kenny Live* television chat show and came clean about the break-up of his marriage. The interview was aired just two and a half weeks before he delivered his first budget. The tradition on budget day is for the Minister for Finance to appear beforehand with his wife on one arm and a briefcase on the other. This would not be possible for Ahern and he clearly felt he needed to address the issue. He told Kenny that he 'had my own domestic difficulties for a couple of years and shall continue to have them'. He also expressed support for a change in the law on marital breakdown and divorce.

The issue of his marriage should have been overtaken by the sensational events that followed over the next couple of weeks. Instead, his private life became a central feature in the race to succeed Haughey. Just five nights after the *Kenny Live* interview, Sean Doherty, justice minister during the phone-tapping of journalists a decade earlier, dropped a bombshell: he stated that Haughey had been aware of what was going on. When the PDs said that Haughey would have to go, his position became untenable. It was just a question of when he would announce his departure.

Reynolds was clearly going to be a candidate for the leadership. It quickly became apparent that Ahern was the only person with a chance of beating him.

The day before Haughey formally announced he was standing down, Ahern presented his first budget, which was generally well received. But what everybody watching him in the government benches wanted to know was whether or not he would contest the leadership. At that point he was the hot 5–2 on favourite to succeed Haughey, and there was huge pressure on him from the Haughey wing of the party to stand and prevent Reynolds winning.

Ahern held a series of meetings with supporters but, even though he was effectively canvassing, he still hadn't announced that he was running. A few days later, he declared he would not contest the leadership and would support Reynolds. He gave a plethora of reasons for his decision – including that in the late autumn he had pledged his personal support to Reynolds on the understanding that Haughey be allowed to go in his own time, and he could not renege on that. However, it was more likely that Ahern and his advisers in Drumcondra didn't feel he had the numbers among Fianna Fáil TDs.

His supporters in the parliamentary party were furious with him. They felt they had been left hanging out to dry while Ahern dithered in Drumcondra over entering the race. Their view was that he had the vast majority of the cabinet with him and that he had a 50:50 chance. They felt he had left it too late to call TDs to solicit support, and when he did this, he refused to make a definite commitment to run.

"How can I give a firm guarantee to a man who has not given me a firm guarantee that he is running?" one TD was reported as saying. Some in the Reynolds camp were even more scathing, suggesting that Ahern had led a "charmed life" under Haughey's protection but had bombed in his first real test on his own.

Neither was his old mentor impressed. Haughey was reported to have said to a political colleague: "What the hell is going on with this man from Drumcondra? I'm not very impressed to know he is going back to Drumcondra to consult with his gang. It's not what you'd expect from a future Taoiseach."

Emily O'Reilly, then a senior political journalist, branded him a "ditherer", writing: "His behaviour at the time smacked of indecisiveness, political immaturity and an inability to extract himself from the poorman Machiavellian clutches of his constituency mates."

But Ahern was not like any future or past Taoiseach. Unlike de Valera, Lemass, Lynch, Haughey or Reynolds, his kitchen cabinet was not made up of a few senior cabinet colleagues or backbenchers in Fianna Fáil. "Consulting his gang" was what Bertie Ahern had done since 1977 and would continue to do until 2007 and beyond. That weekend in Drumcondra, he sounded out Chris Wall and Paul Kiely for their political nous, with Joe Burke and Tony Kett as friends more than political strategists.

His choice to bide his time might have been Machiavellian, but it was hardly politically immature. On the contrary, it showed patience and the ability to think beyond the next few weeks and months. Reynolds was not a young man and

111

wouldn't be leader for a long period. Apparently he had made that clear to Ahern at a meeting the two men had had at the Berkeley Court Hotel on the day before Ahern announced he would not be running.

Ahern was just forty and had been appointed finance minister – only his second cabinet post – just a few months previously. Time was on his side. His older brother Maurice has since said that Chris Wall had crunched the numbers: "We had a victory by one vote but we decided he wouldn't dare go for it." However, others close to the group say that at best the margin was tight but it was more likely that he didn't have the numbers, which would have been clear to Ahern. He might have had the support of the majority of the cabinet, but so did George Colley in the 1979 leadership contest and that wasn't sufficient for him to defeat Haughey.

Hindsight has proven Ahern's choice to have been the right one. When the leadership came around the next time, less than three years later, Ahern was the only choice and was elected leader without a contest.

He insisted afterwards that his decision not to challenge Reynolds in 1992 was unconnected to his marital situation. However, the evidence given more than fifteen years later by his friends to the Mahon Tribunal suggests this wasn't the unanimous view of the Drumcondra Mafia. Ahern's sleeping arrangements, and the perception that his rivals in Fianna Fáil had used them to their advantage, were cited as one of the key motivating factors behind the second "dig-out".

Before he ruled himself out of the contest, Ahern actually criticised what he said were outrageous rumours circulating about his private life, but he said there was a "grain of truth" in stories linking him to Celia Larkin. "We have been out, we have been to functions together. We've been seen and photographed together," he said.

A couple of days later Michael Smith, a senior figure supporting Reynolds, said in an interview with the *Tipperary Star* that Reynolds was the "envy of politicians in terms of his family life". He insisted that he was quoted out of context. Ahern didn't accept that.

Speaking to a reporter from the *Irish Independent*, Reynolds himself had commented to the effect that "people want to know where the Taoiseach is living". He had made the remark as an afterthought to an initial comment that Ahern's marital status was not something he should discuss. Ahern said Reynolds apologised to him for it, claiming it was taken out of context.

Ahern was the only one of four Fianna Fáil ministers to survive Reynolds's unprecedented cull of the outgoing cabinet, and was reappointed Minister for Finance. But although he held the number two posting in politics, he certainly wasn't part of Reynolds's inner circle and would watch in horror as the new Taoiseach oversaw two collapsed governments. In terms of his ultimate ambition, it was now a matter of time. But while he waited, and concentrated on the not insignificant job to be done in finance, he became involved in personal financial dealings that would ultimately prove his undoing.

PART II

THE MONEY

10

THE MINISTER WHO CAME IN
FROM THE COLD

In late 1993 the Minister for Finance felt it was time he opened a bank account. For the previous seven years, Bertie Ahern had been dealing in cash. Every month he received two cheques, one for his salary as a TD and another for his salary as a minister. Every month, he cashed them, more often than not in public houses, like Fagan's in Drumcondra. Cashing cheques in bars was common practice for people in many different lines of work, from the retail sector to construction. For a well-paid senior politician, particularly a Minister for Finance, it was a highly unusual way to manage money.

However, life was complicated for Ahern. His marriage had fallen victim to the fate that dared not speak its name in the Catholic Ireland of the times: it had failed. As was common, he and his wife had had a joint bank account, held in AIB Finglas. When they separated, Ahern no longer used it.

Interest rates were quite high, rising well above 10 per cent. At one stage in this period, the overnight deposit rate was 19.5 per cent. But Ahern kept his savings in two safes, one in the department and the other in his office at St Luke's. He didn't keep a written record of them: "I don't keep records, I don't keep receipts and stuff like that," he said. He just put money into the safe when he could afford to, and he took money out when he required it. He didn't distinguish in accounting terms between the two safes although, generally speaking, he kept his ministerial money in the safe in his departmental office. He was an accountant by training, but in terms of his own finance, he appears to have acted like a mountain man who keeps his stash under the bed because he harbours strong suspicions about banks.

By the end of 1993, according to his version of events, Ahern had the guts of £34,000 in cash in the St Luke's safe, and another £20,000 in the department. Some of the notes had been in the respective safes for seven years. He has no recollection of taking bundles of notes out to have them swapped for new ones. Most of the money was in relatively small denominations, which he had received when cashing the cheques. It was a set-up that might appeal to anybody running a sizeable cash business – but Ahern was a full-time politician, who had never been involved in business.

Apart from the two large bundles of Irish punts, there was a third element to his stash. It would only emerge some fifteen years later, after he had resigned as Taoiseach, that he had another bundle in St Luke's. This one amounted to more than £15,000 and was held in British sterling.

* * *

Most of the sterling in St Luke's was the proceeds of Ahern's salary cheques. A small amount, he claimed to have won on horses at race meetings in the UK. Ahern has never given specific details of where he won the money. He has intimated that the wins occurred during his frequent trips to Manchester, which he had visited regularly since the 1970s.

Typically, he travelled there for a Manchester United game. He had followed the Red Devils since childhood, and was a passionate supporter. His love of the game, and his devotion to United, were well known. His facility for backing winning horses was not something he had ever been noted for, and would remain largely hidden from the public until many years later.

He is unsure as to how much of the sterling he had acquired from betting on horses. He thinks it was a relatively small amount. He did, however, give the bookies in some British racecourse a serious headache in 1996, when he walked away with around £5,500 from two different bets. He has never given details of these wins, either the race meeting or whether he made a big killing with a long shot on the nose, or whether he won the cash after a topsy-turvy day.

Ahern would say later that the bulk of the sterling in his safe originated from his salary. The money had found its way to St Luke's from the Department of Finance via Manchester. On at least six occasions he travelled to the city with a few thousand Irish punts in his pocket, and made the return journey with bundles of sterling.

This unusual behaviour was connected to a plan to make an investment in Manchester. Ahern wanted to build up a sterling deposit to purchase an apartment. As with his arrangements back home, he steered clear of banks in this endeavour. Instead, a friend of his helped him to build up a stash of sterling.

Tim Kilroe was a highly successful businessman. In 1993, the fifty-three-year-old native of County Roscommon was a leading light in the Manchester Irish community. He had emigrated to the city in the mid-1950s. After working initially for the local Dunlop factory, he followed the traditional route of the Irish emigrant into construction. At twenty-eight, he struck out on his own, setting up a sub-contracting firm with his wife, Loretta. Major success followed, and by 1993 his various construction businesses were turning over in excess of £100 million a year.

Among Kilroe's investments was the Manchester Four Seasons Hotel, a venue that would feature later in Ahern's financial narrative. He also invested in the West of Ireland airline Aer Arran, which he subsequently sold. He was a keen racing fan, something he apparently had in common with the prolific punter Ahern. In 1985, Kilroe's horse Forgive 'n' Forget won the Cheltenham Gold Cup, prompting a huge display of Irish tricolours in the winners' enclosure. It is unclear whether Bertie's nose for the nags had prompted him to throw a few bob on the winner. Kilroe died in 2004, two years before Ahern's financial irregularities came into the public domain.

In the early 1990s, the two men were close. Ahern regularly stayed at the Four Seasons and, on occasion, Kilroe entertained him in a corporate box at Old Trafford. At one of these social gatherings, Ahern told Kilroe that he was thinking of making an investment in the city – Kilroe was always talking up the opportunities in Manchester, and at that time something of a building boom was afoot.

One Sunday morning, most likely after the previous day's match, the two men took a stroll in the Salford area. A new development of apartments was going up, built by an outfit called Urban Waterside on a site known as Merchant Arch. Kilroe pointed out the possibilities to Ahern, who appreciated the advice. The price for the unit that took his fancy was

£85,000. He resolved to save up and put a deposit on it.

In one respect, Ahern's planned purchase was unusual: at that time he didn't own a house – St Luke's was his home. And here he was, splashing out on a foreign property. As was already clear from his dealings at home, he avoided banks at all costs. He asked Kilroe how he would be fixed to facilitate an informal arrangement of foreign exchange. Ahern would bring him over some punts, and Kilroe would exchange them for sterling, which Ahern in turn would bring back to Dublin and lock away in his safe in St Luke's.

"I would normally ring him," Ahern said of their currency-exchange mechanism, "and I would say in these phone calls, I would say, listen, I want to change X, which would mostly be £2,000 or £2,500, which, quite frankly, to him was peanuts. Peanuts. I'm not into changing massive money."

The sums might have been peanuts to Kilroe, but they represented a considerable sum to the Irish Minister for Finance. In 1990, £3,000 was one-tenth of his net annual salary. "It was no big deal," Ahern said.

The foreign-exchange transactions took place in a variety of locations. Sometimes, the money was passed over in a car. Sometimes the deal went down in a bar. There is no indication whether it happened late at night, when critical faculties wouldn't have been at a premium, or before the first pint of the evening was sunk. But Ahern believes both cars and bars figured in the exchanges.

On other occasions, they swapped their notes on the day after a match – "Maybe the following morning at breakfast," Ahern explained.

Both men were astute and in tune with currency fluctuations. Back home, Ahern's day job kept him up to speed and Kilroe knew his way around money. Yet there was no specific arrangement between them to ensure that neither was short-changed in the handover: "We would have taken account to make sure nobody was being done either way," Ahern said.

The note-swapping wasn't confined to British soil. On at least one occasion, during a visit by Kilroe to Dublin, the pair set up their makeshift foreign-exchange desk and Ahern added a few more bundles to his sterling stash. At a remove of fourteen or fifteen years, he wasn't sure where this had occurred.

Despite all the work Kilroe undertook to build up Ahern's sterling stash, the plan came a cropper in November 1993 when Ahern changed his mind about the great leap forward into foreign property. It was not for him. Instead he would concentrate on trying to purchase a home in Dublin. By then, he had amassed a considerable amount of sterling, adding up to something north of fifteen grand and south of eighteen. It would be some months before he decided to lodge the money in a bank. In the meantime it sat in the safe at St Luke's, next to his thirty grand plus in savings.

That is Ahern's explanation of why he had a large amount of sterling. As Kilroe was dead when all this came to light, there is nobody to corroborate his story of a proposed investment. As the foreign exchange took place in cars and bars rather than a bank, there is no surviving record that it ever happened.

* * *

The scrapping of the proposed investment wasn't the only change to Ahern's finances in late 1993. The legal separation of his marriage was completed in November, following a hearing in the High Court. Now came the painful business of footing the bill. Since they had separated, he had been paying maintenance to Miriam. Initially, this amounted to £1,300 a month and increased over the years. Now that the separation had a legal imprimatur, he had to make supplementary payments.

The details of how much he was to pay under the legal arrangement are unknown. Family-law matters decided in court are not for public consumption. In 2006, the Mahon Tribunal went to the High Court to apply for access to the Aherns' agreement in pursuit of the money trail. The proceedings were held in camera. The High Court refused the application.

Back in November 1993, Ahern was faced with a considerable bill. His situation wasn't unique: marriage break-ups always carry a financial penalty, sometimes a considerable one. The burden facing him – he was employed in a well-paid job with prospects whether or not he stayed in politics – was much lighter than the average man in a similar situation could expect. His own outgoings were not large. He paid maintenance to his ex-wife and their two daughters. He lived at St Luke's, paying a nominal sum in rent. He was not a man of extravagant tastes.

The bill at the conclusion of the case in the High Court was £19,115.97. This included Miriam's legal expenses, plus £5,000 for her barrister and payment of the balance of a car loan she owed. In dealing with the debt, Ahern took a well-worn route: he decided to apply for a loan. What was highly unusual was that he did so even though he had around £70,000 in safes at St Luke's and the Department of Finance.

Years later, he would offer an explanation as to why he had acted as he did. One consideration was that he had committed to pay £20,000 for his daughters' education. "So I hadn't got £50,000. I had £30,000. If I had have taken that thirty. And that was a commitment that I had made and I had honoured it. The £30,000 I had available, which was my savings from the time I was Lord Mayor [in 1987] right up to that period, which was the twenty-third of December [1993], I had £30,000. If I had have paid that £19,000, almost £20,000, I then only had £10,000. So all my savings having been saved for seven years, I had only £10,000. So I decided not to do that. I decided to take out a bank loan and pay it."

The explanation, while retaining some logic, ignores a few key points. He was prepared to pay interest on a loan in order to maintain large cash savings in his safe. This, while being unusual, is not unique. More to the point, his explanation made no mention of the £15–£18,000 sitting in his safe: he could have used that to pay his legal bills and retained the stash of £50,000.

While Ahern was an able politician, considered to possess a keen intellect, sums don't appear to have been his strong point.

* * *

Philip Murphy was assistant manager of the AIB branch at 37–8 O'Connell Street. In late December 1993, he was beavering away in the office when a colleague called out to him. The Minister for Finance was on the phone. Murphy reacted with a wry smile. Pull the other leg. No, the colleague insisted, Bertie Ahern himself was on the blower.

Still sceptical, Murphy took the receiver. He recalled that he had met Ahern many years previously at a function in the Mansion House. They had also found themselves in each other's company through sporting connections. Otherwise he didn't know the man personally but, like the rest of the country, he knew Bertie.

The familiar voice offered a warm greeting. Ahern recalled their previous meeting. He told Murphy he wanted to take out a loan and that he would be interested in opening a savings account as well. The Minister for Finance was coming in from the cold.

Murphy was chuffed. This was an early Christmas present. It was difficult to imagine a more prestigious client. He prepared for the minister's visit.

On 23 December, when most of the place was hot with festive fever, Bertie Ahern walked into the bank. Murphy met him and brought him to the branch manager, Michael Burns. The three men sipped tea and chatted awhile. They recalled mutual acquaintances from the Finglas branch where Ahern had banked when he was married. Then Ahern and Murphy repaired to another office to do the business.

Ahern filled in the banker on his requirements. The legal separation of his marriage had left him with a bill consisting of three elements. He owed £12,813 in legal costs. He had agreed to contribute £5,000 to his wife's barrister's fee. And he was to pay off a car loan for her, amounting to £1,302. The total came to £19,115.97, for which a loan was quickly agreed. The bank didn't request any security. The only written record of the transaction still surviving was drawn up eighteen months later when Ahern began to make repayments.

On that day the minister also signed and dated a declaration opening a special savings account. Later he would say that he didn't open the savings account until after Christmas when he unexpectedly received a big wad of cash. The bank retained the declaration form, which was signed on 23 December.

"I had told Mr Murphy I was saving money," he said. "I recall he told me I was insane. I shouldn't be saving money that way. I should put it into a bank."

Ahern left and went about his business in the pre-Christmas rush. The meeting had been a success. He was now putting the legal and financial aspects of his court case behind him. Things were looking up. And they were about to get a whole lot better. He was not to know that Santa Claus would be bringing him more than just a bank loan and a pair of socks that year: before the decorations were taken down, more money would be on the way to him. And the New Year would bring a new departure in his life.

For the previous seven years he had had no relationship with banks. Over the coming year, he would find it difficult to stay away from them, lodging and withdrawing money at a fevered rate. And not one of these transactions directly corresponds to the salary cheques he received as a TD and government minister.

11

DIGGING FOR CASH

The way Des Richardson tells it, the first dig-out was conceived over a pint. In the autumn of 1993, Richardson was chief fundraiser for Fianna Fáil. An integral member of the Drumcondra Mafia, he was also a fundraiser for Ahern's constituency organisation. Now he was going to don a third fundraising hat. He was about to ensure that Ahern's personal finances were sorted out.

The matter came up for discussion when he was having a pint with Gerry Brennan, another of Ahern's inner circle. Richardson and Brennan had grown up in the same area of the south inner city. Both had vital, if understated, roles in Ahern's political organisation. While Richardson was the money man, Brennan was the legal brains.

Brennan had trained as a solicitor at night classes, having left school early. He was regarded as highly competent and had a substantial practice in the city. He was also a central cog at St Luke's, acting as a trustee and handling all legal queries. He was also Ahern's personal solicitor, at Ahern's side through the High Court family-law case. He, more than anybody, would have known exactly what Ahern's financial standing was. Naturally, he was also aware of the details of the settlement agreed in court, which left Ahern with a £19,115.97 bill to pay.

Brennan would have been aware of Ahern's cash stash, or should have been, as Ahern had been obliged to declare all his assets to the High Court. Brennan would also have been aware that Ahern intended to take out a loan to cover what he owed Miriam, in addition to his own legal costs, owed to Brennan himself and any barristers that were employed. Brennan died in 1997, nearly a decade before Ahern's financial affairs became public. The extent of his involvement in the alleged dig-out was told by others, principally Richardson and Ahern.

According to Richardson, Brennan came up with an idea. Why don't we have a fundraising dinner to wipe out Bertie's bills? It could be done along the lines of the annual dinner for the constituency, except this one would be personal rather than political. It should be no bother to round up twenty or twenty-five people who would be prepared to fork out for poor Bertie.

The pair approached their friend with the proposition. "Gerry Brennan mentioned to me that they were thinking of having a function at Christmas time, which they would ask the usual suspects along, as he put that to me," Ahern said. He wouldn't play ball. He couldn't have that kind of arrangement for something that was for himself rather than the constituency organisation or the party.

It was back to the drawing board for the two concerned friends. The next plan of attack involved approaching a number of individuals privately, selected friends of Ahern's, and letting them know that the man was in some bother. This would be done without informing him – if he was told he would reject the idea. The money would have to be collected in cash because if Ahern was presented with a cheque he wouldn't cash it.

This was a matter that required sensitivity and confidentiality. The cash aspect shows just how determined the pair were to force Ahern to accept the money. They didn't see their task as merely collecting it: they wanted to ensure that he would have no option but to accept it. They were determined to help him, even if he tried to run away from it at every opportunity.

The criteria for the selection of donors for the dig-out are unclear. "I sat down with Gerry Brennan one evening, and had a chat about the situation, and picked out friends who could probably afford it," Richardson said. Oddly, he didn't approach other key members of the Drumcondra Mafia, such as Joe Burke, Ahern's best friend, or Tim Collins, who was certainly very close to the minister. Richardson maintained that he thought perhaps Collins couldn't have afforded it, but he never asked.

In the end, the names they settled on had a few common denominators. "They are friends of mine," Richardson said. "They are friends of Gerry Brennan. They are friends of Bertie Ahern and they are all from the southside." The last is the most unusual. Richardson has never explained why they had to be from the southside. Ahern had been based in Drumcondra all his life, at the heart of the northside of the city. Why now, at the time of his greatest need, were his two confederates venturing across the river in search of a few bob?

In any event, if they were hoping to exclude northsiders from the dig-out, they didn't know their friends that well. One donor, Paddy Reilly, was a butcher based in Stoneybatter, in Ahern's Dublin Central constituency. Whether his origins were ever an issue is not known because he was the only donor whom Brennan met alone. Both men died before the dig-out came into the public domain.

In the end, Richardson and Brennan came up with a list they thought appropriate for the job at hand. They also devised a strategy of attack. In most cases, they would approach prospective donors together. "When we met these people the conversation took place by and large on the aspects of the separation," Richardson said. "It didn't come from me, it came from Mr Brennan. He explained the situation to the individuals that we met, why we were raising the money. I felt far more comfortable with him doing that than I, because he was the man who was in the position, I suppose, of the knowledge or information at the time."

On the face of it, this strategy would involve Brennan divulging information that was confidential to his client, which is highly unprofessional for a solicitor, but as Brennan was dead when the information came into the public domain, he couldn't explain why he had acted thus, or whether, in fact, he had done so.

Both Ahern and Richardson stressed that they didn't see anything wrong in how Brennan acted. "He wasn't telling anyone any great secrets, to be frank with you," Ahern said. "I'm not going to condemn a person who isn't here. I mean these [the donors] were all friends of mine."

Nevertheless, a different reading of the situation might conclude that the dead man's reputation suffered a blow in the narrative of the dig-out. His friends might protest, but they were also the ones who delivered that blow, by accident or design, through their version of events.

* * *

The alleged eight donors were:

Paddy "The Butcher" O'Reilly: Brennan approached O'Reilly on his own, according to Richardson. As both the solicitor and the butcher are dead, it is impossible to speculate on what allegedly transpired between them.

O'Reilly had been a long-time friend and associate of Ahern's, mainly through his work for Fianna Fáil in the constituency. He was a businessman who made a good living from his shop in the working-class area of Stoneybatter. However, he wasn't a millionaire, or even very wealthy. By all accounts a decent man, he responded positively to the approach from Brennan. So, a dead butcher of modest means was named as one of those who gave a dig-out to the well-paid Minister for Finance.

Charlie Chawke: Chawke is a well-known publican, whose principal premises was the Goat in Goatstown, south County Dublin. One day that autumn, Richardson and Brennan found themselves at the bar in the Goat, and Chawke came over to join them. There is no suggestion that they were there by appointment.

The usual chit-chat ensued. Then the conversation turned to Ahern's finances. Brennan laid out the situation. "He just said that he [Ahern] wasn't a wealthy man and he had legal expenses he would find difficult to meet," Chawke said. He didn't have to be asked twice. He knew Ahern well as a friend. They had met at sporting occasions and funerals. Chawke had never been out to St Luke's and he had never actually gone to any match or race meeting with Ahern. "Our paths would have crossed a lot," he said. He hadn't known that Ahern was going through the courts at the time, but he was willing to do what he could to help out a friend in need.

The boys named the figure they had in mind. "It was agreed

that it would be £2,500 in cash," Chawke said. "I had £2,500 in cash at the time anyway." He was running a cash business: he had no problem in coming up with the sum. He told the boys to call back in a few days' time and he'd have it ready for them. They left that evening with gladness in their hearts. They were one donation closer to saving Ahern. They returned on an appointed day and Chawke handed over his donation. There is no record of the transaction.

Jim Nugent got a phone call from Gerry Brennan, asking him to come into the Berkeley Court Hotel where Richardson had a suite in connection with his fundraising activities for Fianna Fáil. Nugent and Ahern went back all the way to 1970, when both had been active in the FWUI. "We became friends through the branch committee, the operation of that, and we kept up that friendship over the years," Nugent said. "I would have had an involvement in the Fianna Fáil scene in Dublin before he came into it." In 1993, Nugent was a consultant businessman, and chairman of the state training agency, CERT.

Nugent met Brennan in the foyer of the Berkeley Court. "He explained to me that a number of people were putting some funds together," Nugent said. "The figure being proposed was £2,500. I clearly understood that for reasons of confidentiality we would do it in cash."

At one point in the conversation, the two men were joined by Richardson. Nugent agreed to put his shoulder to the wheel. He went away and acquired the cash. He didn't withdraw it from a bank account. "I would have had an amount of cash at any one time," he said. "I'd rather not get into why I would have had that. I certainly know there would have been a lot of cash in funds there from my savings."

The plan to save Ahern was going swimmingly. Another two

and a half big ones had been secured. There is no record of Nugent's donation.

David McKenna and Ahern also went back a long way, although the minister was more than a decade older than McKenna. Their shared history was in Fianna Fáil, in which McKenna had got involved at a young age, joining the Orga section of the party. He was also friendly with Richardson, whom he'd met through business some years previously.

By 1993, McKenna was flying high. A plumber by trade, he had joined the legions who had emigrated to the building sites of Britain in the 1980s. He got involved in recruiting for the construction industry and brought his skills home in 1988. His company, Marlborough Recruitment, was expanding at a rate of knots and would eventually be listed publicly. (In 2001 Des Richardson would join Marlborough as a director, eventually serving as chairman.)

Richardson made the call to McKenna. Drop into the Berkeley for a cup of tea. When McKenna arrived, they were joined by Brennan, who put the arm on the latest targeted donor. "Gerry said that there is an ongoing issue with our friend Bertie, he's got a number of bills to pay, legal bills. And we are looking for a number of people to come together to help him," McKenna said. He didn't even have to consider it. A friend was in trouble.

McKenna didn't know the details of Ahern's travails in the family-law court, but he had an idea that all was not well. "He was sleeping above Drumcondra, he was sleeping in friends' houses. So you can only assume that things are not great." By late 1993, Ahern was indeed sleeping at St Luke's, in an apartment that had been tastefully furnished by his long-term partner, Celia Larkin. Why he might have been sleeping at friends' houses has never been established.

A figure of £2,500 was mentioned, as was the cash clause. McKenna wasn't dealing in a cash business but he said he'd be able to get it. He didn't have to withdraw the money from a bank, or anywhere that would leave a record of the withdrawal. As he got up to leave, Richardson collared him: "I was walking out the door when he said to me, 'Look, if you could give five it would speed things along,' and I said, 'No problem, not an issue, but I'll make it over two payments.'"

There is no explanation as to why the wealthy businessman, who jumped at the chance to donate £2,500 to the down-at-heel minister, wanted to make the donation over two payments.

Within days, McKenna was back on to Richardson. He had the first payment. When would Gerry be there to pick up the few bob?

The three men met in the Berkeley Court Hotel bar. McKenna handed over the cash in an envelope to Brennan, who pocketed it. McKenna told them he would have the second instalment some time after Christmas, but in the end, his enhanced generosity was not called on. "Some time after Christmas I was having a pint with Des," McKenna said. "I said, 'How are we fixed on that other two and a half?' in that type of language, and he said, 'No, it's OK, it's all done,' and I said, 'Grand.'"

Richardson remembers the extra two and a half in slightly different terms. In asking for it from McKenna, he was opting for a change in the strategy agreed with Brennan. "Me and Gerry Brennan decided that we would get ten thousand each and I decided that mine would be two five thousands," Richardson said. "I went back to Dave McKenna and asked for another £2,500 but he didn't have it."

By now, the project was flying. There is no record, in a bank or otherwise, of McKenna accessing £2,500 at the time to contribute to the Poor Bertie Fund.

Michael Collins is another friend of Ahern, and was also on the donor list. The exact circumstances of Collins's donation are unclear because he lives in Australia and didn't give evidence at the planning tribunal. We do know he is no relation to Tim Collins. There is no record of Michael Collins contributing to a dig-out. No bank records were available to the planning tribunal that might suggest he withdrew £2,500 around that time for the purpose of a dig-out.

Fintan Gunne was a well-known estate agent. He died in October 1997 but, by all accounts, he was another of Bertie Ahern's many friends. The exact circumstances of his donation are unknown, but his wife Maureen wasn't surprised that he would have lent a hand to the strapped Minister for Finance. "Fintan was very generous with people who were in need," she said. As with the others, Gunne's donation was in cash. Maureen Gunne told the tribunal that he would have had no problem in accessing the cash from a business the family owned in Carrickmacross. There is no record of Fintan Gunne contributing to a dig-out.

* * *

So far, all the dig-out friends had one thing in common: they donated without a trace. While they were not close personal friends of Ahern in the way that most people understand that description, they were all willing to stump up for him in his supposed hour of need. Not one scrap of paper exists that could confirm that any one of them accessed £2,500 in cash in the autumn of 1993 to help out. Of the six cash donors, two are dead, and another, Collins, didn't give evidence about his donation. Brennan, one of the organisers, is also dead. The only proof that the dig-out was organised and executed is the sworn testimony of Richardson, Chawke, Nugent and McKenna. There was also the sworn testimony of Ahern himself, who related how he received the money and was told about the collection.

The final two donors left a paper trail, and not a few questions about the whole venture.

Des Richardson, the chief organiser, decided he would donate to the collection himself. This was a generous gesture on his part, considering all the work he was already doing for Ahern. His day job as a national fundraiser for Fianna Fáil left him with plenty of headaches. "At that stage, we were firefighting every single day on the funding account of Fianna Fáil," he said. "Every Monday morning when I woke up we had an £8,000 interest bill on top of the Fianna Fáil debt."

On 22 December 1993, Richardson received a cheque from Fianna Fáil, signed by its treasurer, Ahern. The cheque was routine and proper. It was to the value of £18,744, made out to a Richardson company, Willdover, and written to cover fees owing to Richardson and his secretary, Deborah Burke.

Earlier that year Richardson had agreed with the party a fee of £5,000 a month for his services as a fundraiser. The cheque in question covered three months' fees, with the other £3,744 going to Burke. Richardson deposited the cheque in his Bank of Ireland account in Montrose. The lodgement brought the account into credit. On the same day, he made out a cheque from the account, payable to Ahern, to the value of £2,500. He also purchased a draft to the value of £5,000, which was also made out to Ahern.

The transactions at the bank that day involved Richardson delving into his overlapping functions. His account was brought into credit by the cheque he received from Fianna Fáil, signed by Ahern, and due for his work for the party. Then he effected two withdrawals from the account, which included his own contribution to the personal dig-out for Ahern. Richardson would in time tell the tribunal that the account was his own money, and he was entitled to do with it as he pleased.

The draft for £5,000 was allegedly connected with the final donor, a man who says he wasn't a donor at all.

Padraic O'Connor was an unusual person to approach about digging out Ahern. He was an economist by training, who had worked in the Central Bank. In 1993, he was managing director of NCB Stockbrokers. The previous year he had met with Ahern a number of times when the latter was Minister for Finance. A currency crisis was afoot, and O'Connor offered advice to the minister on how to tackle it. Their meetings were strictly business, although O'Connor would say that he became friendly with Ahern as a result. However, he denies that they were friends as such. "I never had a pint with Mr Ahern, I never went to a football match with Mr Ahern. These are things I would do with my friends," O'Connor said.

The only other connection between the two men was tenuous. O'Connor's wife, Helen Hedigan, is from the family who owns the Brian Boru pub in Phibsboro, at the heart of Ahern's constituency. The local TD occasionally drank there, although O'Connor says their paths never crossed when he was in. In any event, O'Connor was not on the inside track round St Luke's way. For instance, he said he knew a few of the other donors, but only by reputation. "I know some of them. I've never associated with any of them. I don't believe that I've met any of them," he said.

In the autumn of 1993, Richardson arranged for a meeting with O'Connor in NCB's head office in Mount Street. O'Connor knew Richardson, but not well. "There was a vague family connection. I knew him on nodding terms, bumped into him in the barber shop in the Berkeley Court."

Richardson, for his part, claims he knew O'Connor very well. "He has never been a friend of mine. He is a very good acquaintance of mine. I would meet him occasionally. He is a gentleman, a person I would have no problem in calling a friend."

Richardson attended at O'Connor's office alone. Brennan was otherwise occupied. According to Richardson, he didn't want to go into too much detail on Ahern's marital circumstances without Brennan. That was the solicitor's responsibility. He said that Ahern's problem was a personal legal expense and he needed a dig-out. O'Connor was eager to help. The figure of five grand was mentioned. The stakes were being raised. This was the first time Richardson pitched for the five big ones straight out.

The stockbroker said, no problem, he'd arrange to do it.

For some reason, there was no mention of cash at this meeting. Not only was Richardson going for the extra money, he was neglecting to tell O'Connor that cash was a prerequisite. Either way, the deal was sealed. Richardson left with another donor in his pocket, another step closer to salvation.

O'Connor tells an entirely different tale. He says Richardson's pitch was for Ahern's constituency operation, a political donation rather than anything to do with his personal life.

Richardson told him that since Ahern had been appointed treasurer of the party nationally, he was having difficulty raising money to run St Luke's. Any chance NCB might stump up five grand?

O'Connor considered the request unusual, but he was willing to go along with it. He says there might have been a suggestion that other stockbroking firms would be tapped. It wouldn't do to be the only one not coughing up. In any case, a request for a political donation from the Minister for Finance was not something that a stockbroking firm would feel comfortable rejecting.

Both men agreed that it would be best to make the donation confidentially, but O'Connor is adamant about its nature. "As far as I'm concerned this was an approach for a political donation and we made the decision to make a political donation," he said.

The two men shook on it and Richardson departed. If, as Richardson and Ahern maintain, O'Connor was giving a personal dig-out, then he behaved in a very unusual manner thereafter. On the other hand if, as he maintains, he was facilitating a company donation to the Minister for Finance, his actions make perfect sense. O'Connor consulted with two of his senior executives, Chris McHugh and Graham O'Brien. Both men confirm that he told them Richardson had approached him for a company donation. Richardson asked for it to be arranged, and authorised a bogus invoice to cover it in order to maintain confidentiality. None of them were particularly happy with that, but it wasn't a big deal.

Richardson issued the invoice through a company called EuroWorkforce for a health and safety audit on an NCB building that had never taken place. A cheque was issued to the value of £5,000, plus £1,050 VAT.

O'Connor thought no more of it until early the following year, when Richardson contacted him to say that there was a problem with the cheque. It had been mutilated in transit. Another was issued, and finally drawn in early March.

Meanwhile, back in Richardson's version, he was on a promise from O'Connor that five grand would be forthcoming to dig out Ahern. On that basis, Richardson himself threw five grand into the kitty, along with the bank draft he had

withdrawn on 22 December. He couldn't even wait for
O'Connor to come up with his few bob – the money had to be
handed over pronto. There is no explanation as to why
Richardson couldn't wait to hand over the money until the
NCB cheque had cleared.

O'Connor denies that he took part in any dig-out, and his
former colleagues at NCB back him up: his donation was from
the company, not himself, and the money he authorised was
issued two months after Ahern received the dig-out. If
O'Connor is correct, the building blocks used to construct the
dig-out scenario begin to crumble.

This begs the question: if O'Connor didn't contribute a vital
component of this dig-out, did it happen at all?

* * *

Meanwhile, back in Dig-out Land, the handover went down on
27 December. For many years it had been a tradition of Ahern
and his friends to attend the Leopardstown Christmas festival
of racing on that day. Afterwards the group repaired to St
Luke's for some festive drinks. There, Brennan told Ahern he'd
like a word with him and the two men left the party
atmosphere for the quiet of the office. Brennan told him what
had gone down.

"We were in St Luke's after coming back from Leopardstown," Ahern remembered, "and he just gave me the £22,500.
He told me that was to assist with my legal fees, collected by
my friends. I told him that I'd taken out the loan if he didn't
know. He probably already knew.

"But I told him that I didn't want it. He said it had been
collected. He said he'd rather I take it. I did take it. I said I'd
take it on the basis I'd give it back another day."

According to Richardson, the two men were gone for fifteen or twenty minutes. He remembered things slightly differently. According to him, when Ahern and Brennan emerged, Ahern approached Richardson. "I'm not quite sure what to do about this but I'll talk with you later," he told his fundraiser.

This scenario doesn't make much sense. When Ahern had taken out the loan four days earlier, he had sent the drafts to pay off Miriam to his solicitor, Brennan. His solicitor therefore knew that Ahern had taken care of his legal bills. Four days later, Brennan was wearing his fundraising hat and handing him a wad of cash and drafts to pay off bills that he, Brennan, knew were already taken care of. Still, that's the way Ahern and Richardson tell it. Brennan, as we know, can no longer answer for himself.

About a week later, Richardson and Brennan were in St Luke's with Ahern when the minister thanked them for the money and insisted he would treat it as a loan and would in time repay those who had contributed. The pair were just relieved that he was going to take the money.

The dig-out had now become a loan. Over the years that followed, Ahern would make what he eventually described as "efforts" to repay the loan. They would consist of him occasionally telling one of his lenders, "I must sort you out for that," and the lender replying, "No problem, Bertie."

Nobody got repaid until the matter exploded into the public domain thirteen years after the dig-out had occurred.

It's a strange tale, but that's the way they tell it. Apart, of course, from Padraic O'Connor, who relates something entirely different.

Strange and all that the story of the dig-out was, the events that followed would lurch further into the surreal.

12

CASHING IN ON THE SAFE

The new year of 1994 dawned bright for the Minister for Finance. New challenges lay ahead, both for the country and for him personally – such as how to re-enter the banking system smoothly. He had the guts of £70,000 in cash, built up during his years in exile. The most obvious route to take – which your average accountant might advise – would have been to deposit the money in one fell swoop, perhaps into a number of different accounts. He could have put some of his notes into a current account, and the remainder to a savings account earning high interest. He could have gone out and bought a house. The £70,000 combined with the £22,500 loan he deposited would have purchased a spanking residence in his constituency.

As with his political career, though, Ahern moved cautiously. He relieved his safe of the cash in a series of moves. He has never explained why he decided to act in this manner. Perhaps, as Minister for Finance, he knew more about the banks than the average man or woman, and reckoned caution was the best approach in dealing with them. So, over the following year, he handed the money over gradually to financial institutions.

While he remained cautious about the banks, he was still determined to dip his toes. Having taken out a loan, and opened a savings account in late December 1993, he made another foray into the world of banking the following month. On 31 January 1994, Ahern opened a savings account in the Irish Permanent Building Society in Drumcondra, just across the road from St Luke's. "I opened a building society account because I knew I was going to look for a mortgage in the next few years," he said. The move made perfect sense. Like thousands of others, Ahern wanted to save for a deposit in an institution that he would ultimately approach for a loan.

Surprisingly, in light of all that already had transpired, he didn't deposit any of his cash stash in the account when he opened it. Instead, the first lodgement was a cheque from a commercial company to the value of £5,000. There is no record of that unidentified company giving him the money, but he is convinced that it was his benefactor.

The money wasn't a personal cheque. Neither was it a political donation, because such monies would have been lodged in one of the constituency accounts. It was a totally new concept, in Ahern's own words, "a political donation for personal use". His explanation of this new departure in democracy was less than lucid. "There are two distinct positions, when a company or individual gives you money, which is for your constituency, or gives you a donation for a constituency use," he said. "My practice is that I give it to my constituency and it's always been my practice. But at times, but not many times, an individual would give you money and say it is for your personal use but you tend to use that anyway in, as any politician will do, expending money on issues in your constituency.

"So, I mean, when I would be asked to buy, to participate in draws or raffles or give donations to humanitarian issues, I would give it out of my own money. I can't take it out of my constituency money." So it goes with a political donation for personal use. The money was not declared for tax purposes. Ahern didn't seek any advice as to whether he should declare it.

The next significant transaction on the account occurred five weeks later, on 9 March. Ahern opened his safe and took out £6,000 in sterling. This was the first tranche of the stash he had built up in Manchester. He called in his secretary, Grainne Carruth, and asked her to bring the cash across the road to the Irish Permanent. "From time to time I would ask my security guard to either make lodgements or to accompany Miss Carruth in making lodgements," he said.

The secretary and the policeman set out with Ahern's winnings and savings. The Drumcondra Road is the main route between the city centre and Dublin Airport. On an average day, traffic can build up at the junction just outside St Luke's. On the far side of the street sits Ahern's fabled watering-hole, Fagan's. The Irish Permanent is a few doors down.

In the bank, Carruth exchanged the sterling for punts and lodged £4,000 to Ahern's own account and £1,000 to each of two accounts he had set up for his daughters. The armed garda hovered nearby, in case anybody got any ideas about stealing the minister's money.

Despite the lengths to which Ahern had gone in acquiring those sterling notes, years later he would have trouble recalling exactly how he came by them. His initial recollection was that the lodgements made by Carruth on that and subsequent days were of Irish currency, the proceeds of his salary. Only later, when faced with the record of sterling transactions from the building society, was he in a position to recall Kilroe, the hand-overs in cars and bars, and the horses.

The following month, on 25 April 1994, Ahern decided he wanted to make another large deposit. This time, he chose his stash of Irish punts to hand over to a bank. He rang the assistant manager at AIB in O'Connell Street, Philip Murphy, and asked him to come out to St Luke's.

Murphy had no problem complying with the request. After all, he was dealing with the Minister for Finance. He attended at St Luke's, where Ahern sat him down, poured out a cup of tea and handed him thirty grand in cash. He wanted the money deposited in the special savings account he had opened the previous December.

The request was unusual, and how it was handled was curious, considering that an accountant and a banker were involved in the transaction. Both men would have known that the limit allowed for the savings account was £50,000 – Ahern had brought in the legislation, and the accounts were popular with savers. Already, the balance in Ahern's account was heading towards £23,000. Therefore, it could only accommodate another £27,000 or so. If the matter came up for discussion between the two men – and it is difficult, under the circumstances, to see how it could not – the obvious conclusion would be to lodge the exact amount to top up the account.

After all, it wasn't as if Ahern had just received a round thirty grand he wanted to lodge. He could have taken the exact amount out of his safe and left the rest there until his next foray into banking. Instead, he gave the round figure to the banker. Murphy got back into his car with the bag of cash and headed for the bank. There is no record of him being accompanied by Ahern's armed guard for safety. A total of £27,164.44 was lodged to his savings account to bring it up to the maximum amount. The rest of the cash, £2,835.56, was lodged to a current account.

By the following month, events suggest that Ahern was not as uptight about banks as he had been because he decided to dive in again with more of his cash. Carruth was instructed to make another deposit in the Irish Permanent, this time for £5,450 sterling. She may or may not have had her armed guard. As before, £2,000 of the money was lodged in Ahern's daughters' accounts.

The first two weeks in August had been downtime for Ahern since he had established himself in politics. For many years, the holidays followed a practised routine. In the first week he would attend the Galway races, always a great social occasion for the country's political and business élites. The highlight for many Fianna Fáil politicians was the fabled party tent, where big noises from the world of business, and particularly construction, would pay tribute to the party with large sums of money. It was a staple of the party coffers throughout Ahern's tenure at the top.

Following a day or two at the races, Ahern would strike out for the Kenmare area in south Kerry. He would book into one of the hotels in the town – or, quite frequently, in the state-owned Parknasilla nearby – and take time out from his hectic lifestyle. Occasionally during the holiday, he would return to Dublin briefly, perhaps to attend to an event that was either unavoidable or unmissable. Often he came back up for a big match, particularly if Dublin were involved in the latter stages of the championship.

In 1994 he returned to Dublin briefly. On 8 August, Philip Murphy from AIB O'Connell Street arrived at St Luke's by appointment. He was shown into Ahern's office. The two men shot the breeze. The Dublin team was doing well in that year's championship. The famine might be drawing to a close. At some stage, Ahern handed over the cash: £20,000. He wanted the money to go to his daughters' accounts, which would be used for their education. By now, Murphy must have been used to the salaried politician approaching him with large quantities of cash. He took the bag, returned to his office in O'Connell Street and lodged the money as instructed.

What with all these forays into the world of banking, Ahern's safe was looking bare. In the course of nine months it had practically been cleaned out. But he need not have worried. Another dig-out was in the offing in Dublin, but before that, he had to get through a whip-around – in Manchester, scene of so much sporting joy, and furtive foreign-exchange ventures.

13

MANCHESTER UNITED IN GRATITUDE

In 1994 Manchester United was riding the crest of a wave following decades cast adrift in the doldrums. They had won the Premiership in 1993, the first time they had won the English league in twenty-six years.

The following year, they retained the title and won the FA Cup to boot. It was to be the start of a golden era for the club and its fans. No longer would they have to endure the brickbats of their illustrious neighbours in Liverpool, or other lesser lights of the league. No longer would the Irish contingent cross the Irish Sea in vain, hoping that this might be the year when they could return home cushioned by victory.

Bertie Ahern was one of the travelling United army. As we now know, he used to return from some of those matches cushioned by pocketfuls of sterling, through his foreign-exchange operation with his friend Tim Kilroe. But on one occasion in 1994 the return flight was even sweeter as he was weighed down with an envelope containing a serious packet of sterling for which he hadn't had to exchange anything. He had hit the jackpot with a whip-around. The only problem is, he can't remember now when exactly during that year this money fell into his lap. All he knows is that it was tied up with the football season.

"The end of the season is late April or May and the season starts in August," he said. "I have never been able to pin whether it was the end. Some of my colleagues were with me because the same people attend with me regularly at these matches and they would dispute with each other whether it was the end of the season or the start of the season."

The only colleague who actually accompanied him on the occasion in question was Senator Tony Kett, and Kett usually only travelled to Manchester towards the end of the season, so he reckons it must have been April or May. Originally Ahern claimed that the whip-around took place in September, but on consideration, he thought it better not to specify an exact time-frame. In any event, it went down on one of his regular trips to see the Red Devils.

Ahern was staying at the Four Seasons, owned by his friend Kilroe. On the eve of the Saturday match, he was invited to attend a private dinner with a number of Manchester-Irish businessmen in the hotel. Naturally, Kilroe was there, as was another old friend of Ahern's, Mícheál Wall. He was another West of Ireland man who had been forced to take the boat to escape idleness and poverty. He had done well for himself in Manchester, and owned a coach-hire business. While he was a man of considerable means, he wasn't in the league of the others at the gathering.

"I would consider Mícheál Wall wealthy, I would consider the others extremely wealthy," Ahern said. "You are talking about serious people. Every one of these people [apart from Wall] was worth fifty million plus at the time."

Wall didn't eat the dinner that night. Maybe he declined or

was excluded for hierarchical reasons: he wasn't worth fifty million. He said later that he drove the bus that transported some of the diners to the hotel. That might have been sufficient reason to refrain from dining if he thought the presence of wine might prompt him to imbibe and therefore render him ineligible to drive them back – the multimillionaires would have had to walk home. Or maybe he just wasn't hungry that night. Whatever the reason, Wall appears later in Ahern's financial narrative in a role that more than made up for missing out on contributing to the whip-around.

Everybody else agreed to sit down in the Four Seasons restaurant and get stuck into the nosh. Twenty to twenty-five individuals were present. By Ahern's calculation, this implies the net worth of the table was in excess of £1 billion, which is as prosperous a gathering of Irishmen as you are ever likely to find.

Despite the status of those in attendance, and that Kilroe was proprietor of the establishment, the dinner took place in the main hotel dining room. If it had been held in a private room, there is at least a slight possibility that a written record would have been kept. Sadly, none was.

Ahern knew many of those present. He had been to a number of such informal functions during his regular jaunts to Manchester. "I would have known a number of them very well," he said. However, when asked twelve years later to identify those present, he was at a loss. "I have tried to track back everybody who was in that room that night, but it is difficult," he said. We do know that Tony Kett was present. He gave sworn evidence to that effect – as did one of the multimillionaires, John Kennedy. "I recall personally donating a sum of £1,000 to Bertie Ahern for his efforts in changing the face of Irish politics," Kennedy said, years later. He had thrown his cash into the metaphorical hat that was passed around.

Apart from Kennedy and Kett, Tim Kilroe was the pivotal figure in the gathering, but he died before the whip-around came to public attention. That leaves seventeen or eighteen Irish multimillionaires living in Manchester who can't be identified for love or money.

Ahern remembers some detail of the dinner: "It was a meal with a group, a hot group, all Irish people, most of them in Manchester for a considerable time, who I have met many times before and since, and it was a meal that, where [it was] informal but still [had] a question-and-answer session, talking about the Irish economy, talking about the country.

"I would have attended an enormous amount of events in Manchester, officially and unofficially, over the years."

The talk of the economy and the Q-and-A session to which he refers occurred once the eating was done. Ahern stood up in the dining room and gave the businessmen his perspective on the economy back home. He was not speaking in his official capacity as Minister for Finance but as a private citizen, whose insights these boys were eager to digest. The status of the address is unclear. Tony Kett recalls it like this: "I would consider it a talk more than a speech. He didn't read from notes. He spoke for twenty minutes to half an hour and thereafter had a question-and-answer session."

When it ended, the gathering repaired to the hotel bar where they remained for some time. Naturally, many of the multimillionaires engaged personally with Ahern, thanking him for his time. Tony Kett also orbited the group, as a sort of appendage to the main attraction. "He was the man of the moment, so to speak," Kett said. "He was the one they wanted to listen to and hear. He asked me to tag along."

At some stage, Kilroe slipped up beside Ahern.

"I remember Tim Kilroe approached me with, I think, one or two of the others and said they appreciated me coming over, appreciated me being there," Ahern said. "I had done questions and answers and talking to them, just general talk, and he said he wanted to make a contribution. He made a contribution and I recall that."

The businessman passed an envelope to the Minister for Finance. Ahern was surprised. He hadn't expected this: "Before, they gave me books and glass and things like that," he said. "On that occasion, that's why I remember it, it was the only time they gave me a financial contribution." Ahern hesitated. He wanted to be sure that the money he was receiving was for performing a function with his Joe Citizen hat on, rather than any ministerial garb. "The only question I did ask him: I asked was it a political contribution as I would have to give it to the party. He said it was a personal contribution for me coming over. It was nothing to do with the party."

Relieved that he could tell himself he was breaking no codes or laws, Ahern thanked his host and slipped the envelope into his pocket. Understandably, he didn't count the money there and then. To do so would have been rude to his host and the other multimillionaires.

The following day, he was at Old Trafford. He hadn't counted the money in the envelope before he went to the match. He didn't count it after the match. It is unclear whether he left the stuffed envelope in his hotel room or whether he was happy to walk around with it for the day. As he can't remember whether it was in May or September, there is no knowing who the opposition was and whether United won the match.

Either that Saturday evening, or the following day, he flew back to Dublin. It must have been a satisfying flight.

Notwithstanding the result – and we can hazard a guess that United won on the basis of their outstanding form that year – the trip had been a success.

While Ahern was accustomed to flying home with large amounts of sterling following encounters with Kilroe, this was different. It was free, the proceeds of a whip-around rather than an exchange of currency. Yet, despite his good fortune, he hadn't yet counted the money.

During the flight, he told Kett what had happened. Until then, Kett had been blissfully unaware of his friend's good fortune at the Four Seasons bar. "He sounded surprised," Kett remembered.

Some time on the Monday, in his office in St Luke's or upstairs, Ahern pulled out the envelope and finally counted out the fifty-pound notes. The total amounted to around £8,000 in cash. The men who had been present had coughed up an average of £400 each for their evening's entertainment. They must all have been accustomed to carrying large wads of cash, as the whip-around had been spontaneous.

* * *

Even though he had rejoined the world of banking at the start of that year, Ahern reverted to type and put the cash into his safe. If he had lodged the money in a bank, a foreign-exchange slip would have recorded the transaction. However, he seemed to retain a sliver of suspicion about banks. He didn't think much about it one way or the other. "It was £8,000," he said. "Let's be frank about it. It was no big deal. It was no big deal."

And so it wasn't, for at that time he had money coming out of his ears. Between cash and his savings account, he had around £70,000, and his building-society account was in credit to the tune of £19,000. He certainly had no money worries. Except, perhaps, that people wouldn't stop handing him cash out of the blue.

Yet, despite his prosperity, others around him remained under the impression that he was short a few bob, that he couldn't even afford the price of a deposit on a house. After all, wasn't he living upstairs in St Luke's, which, for all its strengths as a base, was hardly suitable for the man who would be Taoiseach? It was time for another batch of friends to step up to the plate.

14

HELPING OUT THE HOMELESS

"Where's Bert staying tonight?" With this innocuous question, the second dig-out was conceived. It was posed by Dermot Carew, proprietor of the Beaumont House, a suburban pub in the heart of Dublin's northside.

Carew had come out from behind the bar to sup with his friends, including Bertie Ahern. The gang usually got together on a Saturday night to sort out the affairs of the world from their vantage at one end of the bar. It was a Saturday in September 1994, a time etched in the memory of some of those present: the All-Ireland Football Final was looming. Dublin were playing Down, chasing a crown that had eluded the county for eleven years.

Five of the usual crowd were standing at the bar. Apart from Carew and Ahern, there was Bertie's best pal, Joe Burke. Paddy Reilly, "The Plasterer", was there too, and so was an unusual recruit: Barry English.

At closing time, Ahern bade them adieu and left. He hadn't gone out the door more than two minutes before Carew made an enquiry. The way they tell it, Ahern was a man without a home. "In this period, Bertie lived with his friends, his mother or over a flat at St Luke's," Reilly would remember thirteen years later. "His not having a home was a subject of sympathy among his friends."

In reality, by 1994 Ahern had made his home in the apartment on the first floor of St Luke's. He had moved in two years previously. Celia Larkin had applied her considerable taste to refurbishing and decorating it. If he did stay over with his mother or other friends, it certainly wasn't for want of a home to go to. Yet in 1994 this was not the impression of his closest friends.

"Where's Bert staying tonight?" Carew asked. "It's about time he got a house."

Carew's question forced a particular reality onto the group consciousness. A dig-out would have to be organised. Carew, who accepts he was probably the instigator, made a proposal. Ahern had previously mentioned to him that he was interested in buying a house some time. Now his friends were going to take the initiative. Somebody had to look after him because he was too busy looking after the country.

"It was agreed on the night that I'd collect the money ... The lads said they'd drop it into me in the pub," Carew said.

No figures were discussed. Nobody knew how short Ahern might be. There was no discussion on the price of property in the area. The gathering included the publican, who was well versed in business; Burke, who had years of experience in the construction industry; Paddy the Plasterer, who knew his bricks and mortar; and English, who was a whizz-kid engineer, already earning serious money. Yet there was no discussion on how best to take care of Ahern. They saw their function entirely as coughing up dough for the homeless man.

There would be no pressure applied to donate a minimum

amount. "I left it up to each individual to give what they wanted," Carew said. The only stipulation was that the money must be in cash. "I felt that if I was to try to give Mr Ahern a cheque I would not have been able to prevail upon him to cash it," he added.

By coincidence, this was the reason why the first dig-out – undertaken nine months previously – was also collected largely in cash. The four at the Beaumont House had no idea that there had already been a dig-out for Ahern. Burke had a vague notion that something had happened, but the rest knew nothing at all. Yet they showed the same determination that the money must be in cash because Ahern simply wouldn't accept a cheque.

With that single instruction ringing in their ears, the four dispersed.

There appears to have been a code of *omertà* about the dig-out. For instance, the Saturday-night regulars included two other close friends of Ahern: Tim Collins and Senator Tony Kett. That night, both men were unusually absent. Yet none of those present thought it might be an idea to contact them and let them know what was going on. Two more contributions would have brought Ahern that bit closer to putting a roof over his head. Coincidentally, both men had roles in other areas of Ahern's financial narrative.

* * *

Over the following weeks, the four Beaumont pals dug deep and coughed up. Carew came up with a figure of £4,500 off the top of his head. He duly deposited the cash in an envelope and lodged it in his safe. The Plasterer threw in £3,500, a figure he arrived at without consulting any of the others. Plastering was a cash business and he kept plenty of cash around. Joe Burke threw in £3,500, a figure he, too, arrived at independently. He had cash from his business, which at the time involved large purchases of materials for refurbishing pubs. He had intended to give £5,000 but before he could hand it over, he spotted something he felt compelled to buy his wife for her birthday, which was imminent. The unspecified gift cost £1,500.

The largest donation came from the most unlikely contributor. Barry English was an unusual addition to the dig-out crew. Most of Ahern's wide circle in Drumcondra didn't know him at the time. He had been introduced to the group through Joe Burke some three or four months previously and had met Ahern between four and six times. All of those meetings had been casual, and in the company of Burke and others who drank at the Beaumont House and Fagan's of Drumcondra.

English was a lot younger than the other men. At twenty-eight, he was just six years out of college, where he had studied engineering. Since graduating he had worked abroad for an Irish engineering firm, M.F. Kent, in London, Barcelona and Singapore. In October 1993, he had returned to Ireland, taking up a position with the firm in Dublin. Through his work, he had met Burke and was thus thrown into the Drumcondra milieu. In September 1994, he was still regarded as a fringe member.

English was under the same misapprehension as the other dig-out pals. "He [Ahern] was living with his friends or his mother or over the constituency office. It was suggested that we give him a bit of a help-out," he said. Unlike the others, he didn't work in a cash business. He was a salaried employee. He didn't own a house or a car, both of which were supplied by his company.

He came up with a round figure to donate to what he

characterised as charity. "When you're asked to give to charity, you always try to gauge the correct amount to give," he said. The sum he arrived at was £5,000. There is no record of him withdrawing it from a financial institution because he happened to have the cash on him. "The money I gave was part of cash I returned to Ireland with after working seven years abroad," he said. By then this cash had been back in the country for eleven months.

Once again, the gathering of cash presented problems that were unforeseen at the time. With no paper trail, the only evidence that a dig-out had occurred at all is the sworn testimony of those involved. Any records – such as bank withdrawals – would have strengthened the proposition that a dig-out had occurred.

* * *

Over the next few weeks the donors arrived at the Beaumont House with their offering. Carew took each batch, put it into an envelope and initialled it beside the amount donated. The cash was then stored in the establishment's safe. It totalled £16,500.

Then, one day, the opportunity arose to present their humble offerings to Ahern. It was a mid-week evening when he arrived in Beaumont alone for a pint. By then, the All-Ireland was over, and Dublin had lost. But Ahern wasn't to know that the dark cloud of another Dubs defeat at the hands of culchies had a personal silver lining.

Carew came out from behind the bar and joined his friend. Presently, the publican excused himself and returned to his office. He took a bulging envelope from the safe and rejoined the Minister for Finance. He presented it to him. Years later the exchange of words that followed was related by Carew to the planning tribunal.

"Bert, the boys and myself want you to have that," Carew said.

"What is it?" the minister asked.

"It's a few pounds towards the deposit on a house."

"No, no," the minister said.

His protestations could be attributed to a number of different things. By September 1994 he must have been accustomed to friends or strangers presenting him with the proceeds of a dig-out or whip-around. Maybe he gave a here-we-go-again shrug. Perhaps he was exasperated that, once more, he was being handed cash, which he couldn't refuse. If the donation was in cheque form, he could have declined to cash it.

It is also possible that his protestations were associated with a more lucid judgement that informed him it wouldn't be advisable for a Minister for Finance to take the money. So he mulled over his predicament.

Carew, seeing the minister's hesitation, turned up the heat. "The boys won't take it back," he extolled Ahern. "No fecking way."

This was the clincher. "I'll take it as a loan," Ahern said.

"Fine, Bert," his friend replied.

The minister took the envelope and placed it under his coat, which was on the couch beside him. The two men returned to the real world, perhaps raking over the defeat the Dubs had suffered at the hands of County Down.

Ahern didn't need the money. At that time, he was in rude financial health, having access to around £90,000. At the time, it could have bought virtually outright a house on Iona Road, the most prestigious address in his constituency. His building society account, ostensibly opened to save up for a house, had a balance of £19,000, well above the requirements of any deposit on a property.

Some time later that evening, Ahern and Carew were joined by another regular, Senator Tony Kett. Although he was one of the inner circle at Beaumont House, Kett had no idea of what had just gone down. He positioned himself at the table, just a few feet away from the coat with the stuffed envelope. Years later, when informed of the goings-on of his close friends under his nose, Kett would profess himself totally ignorant of everything associated with the Beaumont House dig-out.

* * *

As was his custom, Ahern didn't lodge the money directly into a bank account. He brought it home to St Luke's and placed it in the safe, next to the other bundles of cash. A few weeks later he decided to lodge the money.

On Tuesday, 11 October 1994, somebody made a large deposit to Ahern's account at AIB O'Connell Street. Ahern says he assumes he made it, although he has no specific recollection of the event. That very day in the Dáil, he had found himself defending a recently awarded pay hike to ministers: "Virtually every prime minister in the European Union, with the exception of Ireland, has one or more official residences with staff provided," he told the House. "The British Prime Minister has a country house as well as 10 Downing Street . . . Practically all the European prime ministers are in the £80,000 to £100,000 pay range, with the crucial difference that the other prime ministers have an official residence provided, which is a valuable form of benefit in kind."

Coincidentally, within hours of making that speech, he was fattening his bank balance with proceeds he received while serving as a minister, although the money had nothing to do with his official function.

Ahern's failure to remember making a cash lodgement of more than £25,000 is troubling. "It wasn't some huge day in my life that I was walking in and going to remember for ever more," he said. "My belief is that I made it. I just don't recall the event."

The monies he was depositing consisted of two elements. There was the £8,000 in sterling he had received in Manchester, and the £16,500 loan he was given by his friends in Dublin. The total amount deposited was recorded at £24,838.49.

There is a snag that may be just another coincidence. If the exchange rate for the day is applied, and a five-pound standard charge subtracted, the figure deposited equates to exactly £25,000 sterling. The exchange rate applicable in this instance would be the one used for sums of up to £2,500 and would therefore have been technically the wrong rate. However, records show that elsewhere in Ahern's narrative, a bank has applied the wrong rate to the bank's advantage.

A banking expert may well say that doing this would be a breach of procedure, but countless examples through the last decade testify that this procedure is routinely broken, whether by accident or design.

There is another coincidence. Records show that, on the day in question, the bank took in £27,491.45 worth of sterling. Over a six-month period, the average intake of sterling at the branch amounts to between £2,000 and £2,500.

If Ahern's version is accurate, another customer also came into the branch on the same day and made an unusually large sterling transaction, amounting to more than £15,000. No big sterling transactions for months on end, and then two show up on the same day.

Ahern and seven others gave sworn evidence to the Mahon Tribunal that the second dig-out and the Manchester whip-around took place. Ahern is adamant that the proceeds of these two events constituted the deposit of £24,838.49.

The alternative version is provided by written record and circumstance and disputes the evidence of Ahern and his friends. If he, or somebody on his behalf, did make a deposit of £25,000 sterling to his account, as the records indicate to be the case, then glaring questions arise: did the second dig-out or Manchester whip-around ever occur, as laid out by Ahern and his friends? If they did, what became of that money? The lodgement on 11 October does not necessarily correspond to the money allegedly gathered.

The question of whether or not the two events ever took place would not arise if there was any written record to support them. For instance, even if one element of the money given in the Beaumont House dig-out had been accessed through a bank, a record of the withdrawal would survive. If the Manchester event had been recorded in the most cursory manner – by booking a private room, even – there would be supporting evidence.

Equally, if enough of the missing Manchester multi-millionaires could have been found to verify the whip-around, the event would have been more credible.

As it is, there is only the word of those who say they were present. The written record, or what survives of it, begs to differ. That may just be one more coincidence.

Whether it was £8,000 or £25,000 sterling he lodged on that day, Ahern wasn't finished with sterling. Just over a fortnight later, his secretary Grainne Carruth walked across the road from St Luke's and handed over £4,000 in cash to the Irish Permanent Building Society for deposit in Ahern's savings account. This was the last of the money he had converted to sterling in Tim Kilroe's cars and bars or won on the horses.

Another large tranche of sterling would pass through Ahern's hands before the year was out. At least, that's how he tells it. The written record would again beg to differ: it throws up the possibility that on the next occasion a large deposit would be made to his accounts, it would consist of another currency entirely.

15

THE HOUSE THAT MICK BOUGHT

Mícheál Wall arrived in town on Friday, 2 December 1994. He drove off the boat at Dublin Port and struck out for the city. Earlier that day, at his home in Manchester, he had placed a briefcase in the boot of his car. Inside it there was around £30,000 in sterling. He was in Dublin for Ahern's big shindig, the annual fundraiser for his constituency operation, which was then held at the Royal Hospital Kilmainham.

But Wall had even bigger fish to fry. He would also be using the trip to take care of some personal business between himself and Ahern. They were about to enter into an agreement on the purchase and renting of a property. Having spent more than a year obsessing about a house, Ahern now seemed to be moving in the direction of acquiring one.

This was Wall's second appearance in the narrative of Ahern's finances. When last we met him, he was on the periphery of the Manchester whip-around, driving the bus and declining to eat the dinner. Now he was about to move centre stage. This time he would be fed in fine style.

* * *

Wall is a member of the Manchester-Irish set. From the Galway village of Lenane, he emigrated to the northern England city in 1959 at the age of seventeen. He began work as a joiner. He was endowed with the entrepreneurial spirit and established a coach-hire business while still in his early twenties. The business grew. Wall diversified into property in the Manchester area, and began dealing in property back in the West of Ireland. By the early 1990s, the father of four was a wealthy man who maintained strong links with the old country, returning for pleasure or business at least ten times a year.

Between the coach-hire business and his property interests there, Wall became involved in promoting tourism in Ireland. Through these links, he frequently met visiting Irish politicians at functions. One of those he encountered in the late 1980s was the young Minister for Labour, who was tipped for big things. The two men became firm friends. Between Wall's frequent trips home and Ahern's visits to Manchester for football, their friendship grew.

Wall was present at the Four Seasons on the September night of the whip-around, and he had closer links to Ahern than anybody else present.

By November, he was thinking of extending his coach-hire business to Dublin. His trips across the Irish Sea would be more frequent. The obvious thing to do would be to buy a house where he could lay his head rather than going through the hassle and expense of regular nights in hotels.

As it happened, his buddy was also looking for accommodation. Ahern was keen to move on from St Luke's. His dig-out friends felt he needed a proper house. They had thrown him a few pounds to get himself sorted. But, it would appear, he was more inclined to rent than buy.

From Wall's point of view, a property in Drumcondra would

be just the job. A house in the area would provide social benefits, through easy access to the Drumcondra set that orbited Ahern and with whom Wall had become friendly. More importantly, the area was just down the road from Dublin Airport.

Wall and Ahern discussed their converging requirements.

"I mentioned to Bertie Ahern that I intended to buy a house and he said he intended to rent a house," Wall said. The two men agreed that if Ahern wanted to buy the property at a future date, Wall would make it available to him.

By the autumn of 1994, Ahern was at the centre of a government that was looking decidedly shaky. The two party leaders in the ruling coalition, Albert Reynolds and Labour's Dick Spring, were not getting on. Anything was liable to happen. Ahern needed to focus on the job at hand. Wall couldn't spare the time to scout around north Dublin for a part-time residence. Celia Larkin was the obvious choice to locate a suitable property.

She hit on the ideal home in late November. The Beresford estate, just off Griffith Avenue, was only a few years old. It consisted of semi-detached and detached homes of three and four bedrooms. They were comfortable but definitely not ostentatious.

Number 44 was on the market for around £140,000.

During one of his trips to Dublin, Larkin brought Wall to view the property, which consisted of a look at the house from the road. He would say later that he hadn't seen the inside of the house by the time he made a bid for it. "Now that might sound stupid, but that's not unusual for me," he said. "I am a man who has bought lots of things without ever looking at them. I bought four buses one day, two hundred miles away, without ever seeing them."

She told him that the property would require some work. In particular, a conservatory would have to be built. "I was aware that the dining facilities in the house were too small and that some form of renovation would be needed to facilitate that," she said. Wall had no problem with that.

On Tuesday, 29 November, Wall rang Gerry Brennan, Ahern's solicitor, who would also act for Wall in the purchase. He told Brennan to tender £138,000 for the property. The bid was accepted, and arrangements made for a £3,000 booking deposit to be paid.

* * *

While the prospective purchase would mean a change of home for Ahern, he had far bigger things on his mind that week. The Fianna Fáil–Labour government had collapsed in the wake of the revelation that a warrant for a paedophile priest had not been processed by the Attorney General's office. Dick Spring led Labour out of government. Reynolds resigned as Taoiseach, and all the indications were that the government would be re-formed under Bertie Ahern. Having been elected Fianna Fáil leader without a contest, he had arrived at the pinnacle of the party, just one step away from being leader of the country.

It had been a long road since the scruffy twenty-five-year-old beat the odds to get elected in 1977. In the intervening time, he and those closest to him had developed the most formidable electoral machine in the country. They had secured dominance of Dublin Central and, from the shadows, watched their man rise to the frontline of Fianna Fáil. Now the ultimate summit was in sight.

Celia Larkin, one of the most important members of the Drumcondra Mafia – albeit unpopular with the many of the circle – was present at the press conference after Ahern was made leader. When a reporter asked about her status in the new arrangement, party supporters booed but Ahern had been anticipating the question and responded that she was his partner.

Later that month at the annual Friends of Fianna Fáil function she was very publicly at Ahern's side. As a key member of the Drumcondra Mafia, she was ready to take her place as the official partner of the new leader of Fianna Fáil.

The vote to confirm Ahern as Taoiseach was to take place on Tuesday, 6 December. But, regardless of national events, he would never forget to keep the home fires burning: he was due to host his annual constituency fundraising dinner on Friday, 2 December.

Earlier that day, or possibly the previous evening, Micheál Wall opened the safe in his office in Manchester. As he dealt in a cash business, he usually had a large stash in the safe. All of this, he would later reveal, was the proceeds of income that had been taxed. Typically, he retained between £30,000 and £40,000 in cash. Most of the money was in twenty-pound notes. He took several bundles from the safe and placed them in his black briefcase.

Wall was taking a table at the Royal Hospital bash and inviting between eight and ten guests to attend. His intention was to take a bag of cash over the Irish Sea for Ahern to put towards the work on 44 Beresford. "It was an ideal opportunity that I was coming over and to make money available. I had the money in my safe," he said.

On the face of it, the amount he was carrying to Dublin appeared to be far more than would be immediately required for any work on the new house. Wall didn't see it that way. "I was bulking to make sure there was enough for whatever had

169

to be done," he said. "I took a ballpoint-pen figure of what might be needed and brought it with me."

He and his wife sailed that morning, arriving in the Aisling Hotel opposite Heuston railway station some time in the afternoon. Before they left their room to go to the dinner, he took around £2,000 from the briefcase to cover the evening's expenses. Then he placed his briefcase, still stuffed with cash, in the wardrobe.

The dinner went well for Wall, presumably making up for the one he'd missed out on in Manchester. This time around, Mick got fed. At some stage during the evening, he met Ahern. "I had a chat with him and asked to see him on Saturday to talk further about the house," he said.

The following morning, Wall drove out to St Luke's with his briefcase. He hadn't counted the amount of money that remained in it. He rang the doorbell and was shown in. The prospective Taoiseach-elect took him into the small conference room. Celia Larkin was in the building. She "popped in and out a few times", according to Wall. There was some general discussion, and then they got talking about the house.

Wall put the briefcase on the table and took out the bundles of notes. "As a round figure, I reckon there was £28,000 there because I had spent some of it," Wall said. "There would have been a couple of thousand of punts in that figure." He didn't get a receipt for the money. "We didn't count it," he said. "He didn't count it. I didn't count it. I just said it's roughly there and he suggested that he'd put it in the bank and either he called in Ms Larkin or she came in, but she became involved and we had discussed with her as well that she would take charge of looking after the money and looking after the work that had to be done. And it was suggested that they would put it in the bank."

Wall characterised the transfer of funds in a particular way. "I didn't give it to him. I made it available," he says. The distinction shows that the money wasn't for Ahern, but to go towards work on the house. Prior to the handover, Wall had paid a booking deposit on the house by cheque. Later he would pay the full deposit by cheque and the balance by bank transfer. He had said he always dealt in cash, but the money he gave to Ahern was the only cash he produced in his purchase of the Beresford property.

Presently, Wall left. A decision was made that evening on what to do with the cash. "The money was given to Bertie who gave it to me to lodge on the Monday," Larkin said. "And on the Saturday evening, it was decided that I would administer it. The renovation was to be under my management."

* * *

The following day Wall and his wife took the boat home. On the Monday, Ahern had to fly to Brussels on government business. Larkin called to St Luke's and picked up the cash, which had been placed in another briefcase. It is unclear whether the money had been left out for her to collect or whether she had access to the safe. She says she didn't count the money: "I never physically counted it or looked at it. My understanding is it was sterling." She made her way to AIB in O'Connell Street.

Philip Murphy dealt with her business. Apart from lodging the thirty grand, Larkin also organised the transfer of £50,000 from Ahern's account into a new account she had opened. This money was to go towards work on the house that Wall was purchasing. According to Ahern, he and his prospective landlord had agreed to share the cost of the work.

This version of events suggests that the new landlord and tenant of the house at Beresford intended to invest more than £80,000 in renovations on a relatively new property worth £138,000.

Celia Larkin emptied the briefcase of cash. The total amount lodged came to £28,772.90. She, Ahern and Wall all insist that the money was largely sterling currency, sourced from Wall's safe.

The surviving records dispute this. According to bank records, a total of £1,921.55 worth of sterling was bought by the O'Connell Street branch that day, 5 December 1994. Coincidentally, the amount lodged by Larkin was exactly the same as what could have been purchased on the day with $45,000, minus the five-pound fee attaching to foreign-exchange transactions.

This introduces the possibility that the lodgement was actually a round sum of dollars, rather than the sterling Wall says he accessed from his safe in Manchester. Ahern, Wall and Larkin all deny that they ever dealt in dollars, particularly a sum of this magnitude. Years later, when the matter arose in the planning tribunal, Ahern retained a banking expert to demonstrate that the money couldn't have been dollars. The expert raised questions about banking records, but he didn't definitively demonstrate that the money hadn't been dollars.

Maybe it was just another coincidence in a narrative littered with such chances of Fate. If it ever turned out that the money actually was dollars, it would raise the most serious questions about Ahern and where the money had come from.

* * *

Christmas 1994 couldn't have been all sweetness and light in the Ahern household. The crown that had been within his grasp on the weekend he had been given a suitcase of cash had been whipped away within forty-eight hours.

When he arrived back from Brussels on 5 December, a storm was blowing. The Labour Party was apoplectic over a controversy about when senior Fianna Fáil ministers information about a second paedophile priest.

At the last minute, plans to re-form the coalition collapsed. Instead, Labour went into power with Fine Gael and Democratic Left while Fianna Fáil headed for the opposition benches. Instead of assuming the role of Taoiseach on becoming party leader, Ahern was now leader of the opposition. Later he revealed that this was a blow from which it took him some time to recover.

Many politicians have spoken of the adjustment that comes with sudden loss of governmental office. For a while the small things impact – you have to drive yourself around after having had a driver at your beck and call. So it was that Ahern found himself behind the wheel on 19 January 1995. He and Celia Larkin got into the car in St Luke's and drove into town. They were on a mission. Just six weeks after the deposit of Mick Wall's £30,000 and the transfer of £50,000 from Ahern to Larkin, the time had come for change.

She was going to withdraw the fifty. It was to be returned to the safe in St Luke's. For whatever reason, Ahern was of the opinion that the money would be better in the safe than in the bowels of a financial institution. He offered a number of reasons for this highly unusual move at the planning tribunal. "I do recall that when I was not elected Taoiseach I had to make up my mind whether I would continue with the arrangement whereby I had agreed just a short period before to rent a house that wasn't going to be ready for a few months and maybe look around and stay in my own apartment or buy later on for myself, or whether I would actually give Micheál Wall the money for him, him or Gerry Brennan who were really managing things with Celia Larkin to look after the house, or whether I would just give him back the money and get out of the deal altogether. I think they were the range of considerations."

The reasons appear to be contradictory. He was taking the money out because he was either going to go ahead with the arrangement with Wall, or he was not. Later, he indicated that taking the money out would make it easier for Larkin to access it as she went about the work with the house.

However, a few months later this was shown to make no sense: in one instance Larkin had to request a bank draft to pay a suppliers' bill. Why didn't she just go to the safe and remove the cash that was supposed to be there for her easy access?

Back on the day in question, the pair drove towards O'Connell Street. One of them had rung ahead to the banker Philip Murphy, asking him to make the cash available. Ahern parked nearby. He waited behind the wheel as Larkin went into the bank.

Philip Murphy met her in his office. He passed over the parcel. He didn't count it out for her. She didn't count it out in the banker's presence. As with Mick Wall and his suitcase of cash in St Luke's, nobody felt the need to count out the money in the presence of both giver and receiver.

Larkin thanked Murphy, left, and walked around the corner to the car, where the leader of the opposition was waiting behind the wheel. She has no recollection of the deal going down, but accepts that Ahern and Murphy remember it. The pair drove back to Drumcondra, secure in the knowledge that Ahern was liquid once again.

The latest cash stash was destined for further drama. Some of it went towards Larkin's work in whipping 44 Beresford into shape. But, according to Ahern, more than £30,000 was converted into sterling. He explained that he was considering pulling out of the deal with Wall, which would require him to reimburse Wall for the £30,000 sterling that had landed in his lap in December.

In keeping with Ahern's apparent weakness for that currency, he decided that the reimbursement to Wall should be in sterling, just as he had received it. Therefore, he took it upon himself to use the cash from his safe to purchase it. This, he says, was done between January and June 1995. However, after he had bought the sterling, he changed his mind and decided to go ahead with the plan as originally outlined and he relodged the money to bank accounts. His explanation covers two large sterling lodgements to his and Larkin's accounts in 1995.

On 19 June, a total of £11,743.74 was lodged to a Larkin account. This consisted of £2,000 and the purchase of £9,743.74 in Irish punts, the proceeds of £10,000 sterling. Ahern maintains this sterling lodgement was the first tranche of the recycling of the Wall £30,000.

On 1 December, he lodged £19,142.92 to his account, representing the remaining £20,000 sterling from the Wall money.

To carry on in this manner might strike the average PAYE worker, or even business person, as bizarre, but nothing about Ahern's money during this period was straightforward. In any event, he maintains these two sterling lodgements were the proceeds of converting the money from his safe.

Once again, the available records dispute this version. For instance, there is no record of a large sterling conversion in the 38–9 O'Connell Street AIB branch in this period, and no record that accords with such a transaction has been located in any of the financial institutions in Drumcondra, the only other places Ahern says he would have done the business.

When faced with this dilemma at the planning tribunal, he offered another explanation. "What I believe I must have done, I must have given it to somebody to change for me because I think I would recall if I changed it myself," he said. "The only banks I think I would have changed it are in Drumcondra or in O'Connell Street. If I didn't change it there, perhaps in Drumcondra, I could have changed it in smaller amounts, but I doubt it. I think it's more likely I would have given it to somebody to change for me."

This scenario is in keeping with a trend: bizarre. Instead of converting his cash into sterling, he gave it to somebody else to do so in smaller tranches. This explains why no record of the conversion remains in any of the relevant banks.

Naturally, such a top-secret mission, requiring a high degree of trust, would only be undertaken by a close confidant. Who ran these errands? "The people I checked with in my office and the few people that I thought might have been likely, and the answer [from them] is that none of them did it," he said.

Maybe some intern, seconded to St Luke's to see how politics operated, was given the bundles of cash to change at various banks across the northside of Dublin.

Whoever the mystery person was, Ahern is adamant that the £30,000 sterling lodged in his and Larkin's accounts in 1995 was recycled money. He vehemently rejects the alternative explanation – that the money represented new lodgements to the accounts from other sources.

* * *

The strange turn of events over the purchase and renting of Beresford didn't end there. Gerry Brennan completed the purchase in early 1995. Wall took out a mortgage of £97,083 with ICS Building Society on the property.

Ahern moved in in June, under an agreement to pay £450 a month in rent. Wall's plans to expand his coach-hire business to Dublin didn't materialise, but he says he stayed often in the house, as per the original agreement between the men. The documents tracking the purchase of the property include no record of a conveyance fee paid to Brennan.

That year Wall's plans were curtailed by a serious road accident: on Easter Sunday he was a victim of a hit-and-run driver. He was confined to a wheelchair for six months, and required the aid of crutches for another six. In December, despite his discomfort, he made it to Dublin for Ahern's annual fundraising dinner.

In June 1996, Wall made an amendment to his will. He instructed that in the event of his death, his property at Beresford should be bequeathed to his tenant Bertie Ahern. In the event of Ahern predeceasing him, or both men's demise coinciding, the house should revert to Ahern's two daughters, Cecelia and Georgina.

Ahern would later claim that he knew nothing of this gesture until he was told of it by the planning tribunal in 2007. Wall has never given any more explanation than that Ahern was the tenant and he didn't want to see him done wrong. "I could have left it to the Sisters of Charity, I could have left it to me aunt in Timbuctoo," he said.

In January 1997, Gunnes auctioneers valued the Beresford property at £185,000. In May, Brennan drew up a new agreement for Ahern to remain in the house for another three years at an increased rent of £650 per month.

Later that month, a general election was called. Now Ahern had his chance once more to become Taoiseach. In the midst of the campaign, tragedy struck. On 24 May, Gerry Brennan committed suicide. His death was a shock to all around him, including Ahern. There had been no specific recent incident or detail of his business or private life that might have contributed to his decision. Those close to Ahern say it was one of the few times in his political life that he appeared at a loss to comprehend what had happened.

But the election was a triumph for Fianna Fáil, and Ahern became Taoiseach, in a coalition with the Progressive Democrats. By July, a month after assuming office, he had decided he no longer wanted to rent Beresford but to buy it in accordance with the option he had agreed with Wall three years previously. Following Brennan's death, the Law Society had appointed solicitor David Anderson to manage his affairs and sell the business. In the transfer of the house, Wall and Ahern retained different solicitors: Anderson acted for Ahern while Wall was represented by Hugh O'Donnell, from another Dublin firm. Anderson and O'Donnell were subsequently appointed district court judges.

Ahern agreed to pay Wall £180,000 for the property. This represented a small loss to Wall over a period when the market was extremely buoyant, but he had no problem with that. In the summer of 1997 Ahern at last had a place to call his own.

* * *

In 1997 there was a postscript to the house that Mick bought. On 4 December, Wall walked into the Eyre Square branch of Bank of Ireland in Galway, of which he was a long-time customer, and withdrew £50,000 in cash. He took £40,000 in twenty-pound notes and £10,000 in fifties. A decade later the planning tribunal was then focusing on the possibility that the house he had bought might actually have been the house he had fronted when in fact Ahern had bought it. Wall was questioned on the withdrawal and said, "At the time it was my intention to go to an auction in Meath in the coming weeks or months and it was my intention to buy a crusher," he said. "As it happens, I didn't go to that auction and I took the money back to Manchester. And I put it in my safe." A crusher is a mechanically propelled tool often used in large construction projects or in building roads. While Wall wasn't specifically involved in construction, he said he would have had use for one. "It crushes stone, aggregate, you name it," he said. "Crushers were pretty rare. I was told it was likely there would be a crusher at that auction or I may have seen a brochure."

The money was taken across the Irish Sea and lodged in a safe under a different jurisdiction that operated with a different currency. Strange but true, according to all those involved.

No hard evidence was ever unearthed to suggest that the relationship between Ahern, Wall and Beresford was other than they claimed it to be. But Wall's explanation for moving a large sum of cash in 1997 for a purpose for which it ultimately wasn't used occurs repeatedly in Ahern's narrative of his own finances.

In the early 1990s, Ahern says he exchanged more than £15,000 punts into sterling to purchase a property, but ultimately declined to buy it. The first dig-out was designed to pay Ahern's legal fees, but ultimately the cash just went into Ahern's bulging kitty. Fifty thousand pounds was transferred from an Ahern account to a Celia Larkin account in December 1994 to facilitate payments for renovations on Beresford. Within a month, this plan was revoked, the money withdrawn in cash by Larkin and given back to Ahern.

There was another occasion on which £20,000 was withdrawn and redeposited in a different currency. That involved money which flowed through one of the most unusual bank accounts to feature in Bertie Ahern's finances: in time the B/T account would raise all manner of questions, not least of which was: what exactly did B/T stand for?

16

WHAT'S IN AN INITIAL?

Like all good bank managers, Blair Hughes kept an eye out for valued customers. Through the early 1990s, he was in charge at the Irish Permanent Building Society branch in Drumcondra. Naturally, he knew Bertie Ahern. During his time at the branch he had attended a number of functions hosted for local business people across the road at St Luke's.

Through one of those gatherings, or in the course of other business, he came across Tim Collins. Hughes knew that Collins was an associate of Ahern, so whenever he spotted Collins in the branch, he would, with his best bank manager's hat on, amble over and talk to this valued customer. Sometimes, to demonstrate how valuable he considered his customer, Hughes would complete a lodgement or withdrawal slip for him, or hand the documentation to a teller to be dealt with post-haste.

As a result of his familiarity with Collins's business, Hughes became aware that his customer was operating an account under two initials, B and T. It was an unusual name for an account, and Hughes noted it. Years later, it would be contended that Collins was operating the B/T account on behalf of the Fianna Fáil organisation based in St Luke's. This was news to the bank manager: "I had no reason to believe that this account was operated for or on behalf of the Fianna Fáil Party, a local cumann, or that it related to a building trust," he said. He had assumed the initials stood for something specific. "I just made an assumption that B and T was Bertie and Tim. I had no evidence to say it was anybody else's account. It was just an assumption on my part," he said. Ahern and Collins would claim it was no such thing but, as with much else to do with Ahern's money, there is little in the way of records to back up their explanations.

* * *

On 6 June 1989 Tim Collins opened the B/T account with the Irish Permanent Building Society in Drumcondra. He was its sole signatory. He instructed that all correspondence relating to the account should be addressed to the branch, from where he would pick it up. In opening the account, he signed a declaration that it was a personal account. "I was never a member of Fianna Fáil," Collins said later. "I was a helper with Fianna Fáil."

Two years later, Collins and Des Richardson embarked on a joint business venture. They opened an account in connection with it and called it the D/T account. Richardson confirmed that D/T stood for Des and Tim. But Bertie and Tim are adamant that B/T didn't stand for their respective initials.

Ahern says he had absolutely no beneficial interest in the account. It was opened at a time when he had no bank accounts. If he had had an interest in the B/T account, he would have been obliged to declare it in the family-law proceedings. He has always maintained that the account had nothing to do with him.

Collins and Ahern say that B/T stood for "Building Trust". The building in question is St Luke's, which already had a trust: the St Luke's Trust. The only record of this Building Trust's existence is the bank account initialled B/T.

According to Ahern, Collins and Joe Burke, the B/T trust consisted of a committee, called the house committee, composed of five members, Collins, Burke, Jimmy Keane, Paddy Reilly (the butcher, rather than the plasterer) and Gerry Brennan.

Of the five members of this committee, only Collins and Burke were still alive when the B/T account came to public attention. Burke confirmed the trust's existence and his role in it. "The building trust basically initially was opened so that we would have monies for any ongoing repairs that would be required to St Luke's," he said. "There was a considerable amount of money that had to be spent on it because the structures of the house had to be built on a raft and at times it can move and different things. And the trust agreed that some money should actually be set aside somewhere, should defects arise in the building because of the construction of the building."

The members of this trust decided to open a bank account. Across the developed world, in instances like this, an account of this nature requires the signature of two individuals. They did things differently in St Luke's. The burden of trust was placed on one man's shoulders. "He [Tim Collins] was asked to open the account," Burke said. "And funny word trust because we had total trust in him because we didn't see any reason to have a second signature on it." But when work was carried out on St Luke's, the funds were accessed from another account, the O'Donovan Rossa account, which was patently a Fianna Fáil account associated with the local cumann.

Tim remembers the account slightly differently from his friend Joe: "The B/T account, and I will say this until the day I die, is a sinking fund in the event of anything happening to Mr Ahern, that the trustees left alive wouldn't have to pick up the tab, be left with any debt."

If the B/T account was as outlined by the three men, then it was a political account, which would receive political donations associated with running the political operation. It excludes any possibility of the account being for the personal use of anybody associated with it.

No records of the building trust remain. The only record that testifies to its existence and purpose is the bank account named B/T, which was run by a close confidant of Ahern, who wasn't a member of Fianna Fáil.

＊　＊　＊

Money poured into the B/T account. It was opened with a lodgement of £7,285.71, which included a £5,000 cheque made out to Bertie Ahern. Three cheques to the value of £5,000 each were lodged in the account in March 1990, June 1991 and February 1992. The donor of these monies is unidentified. Ahern and Collins say they can't recall who it was, or locate any records that might provide a clue.

On 25 August 1992, a cheque for £20,000 was lodged, and £1,000 of this withdrawn in cash. Ahern and Collins say that this money was the proceeds of a golf classic, a common form of political fundraising that gained currency through the 1990s. However, surviving records suggest that the first golf outing for Dublin Central was in 1997. A letter written by the director of elections for St Luke's, Paul Kiely, in the summer of 1997 mentioned a golf classic: "In the aftermath of a very successful general election campaign I am committed to ensuring that the constituency debt is eliminated as soon as possible," he wrote. "With this goal firmly in mind, we have arranged the inaugural Dublin Central golf classic."

If that was the inaugural classic, how could £20,000 received five years earlier have come from a golf outing? "I can't comment on that, you know," Collins said, when asked at the planning tribunal to explain the discrepancy.

On 26 January 1993, two cheques of £5,000 each were paid into the account. One came from J. & E. Davy, stockbrokers, wishing Ahern well in the general election, which had taken place the previous November when the cheque was dated. Fifteen years later the account would only be discovered by the planning tribunal when it followed the money trail left by the Davy's cheque.

Then, two months later, on 30 March, a total of £30,000 was withdrawn. This consisted of a "loan" sanctioned by the trust committee for a staff member. "It was a decision by the house committee and the officers to a member of our staff who had a private family difficulty," Ahern said. "It was an exceptional issue to deal with, a problem of three elderly people, and the officers made a decision to give the money in certain circumstances to help the individual."

Two of Celia Larkin's aunts and another elderly relative had lived most of their lives in a house in the North Circular Road, which was due to be sold. They feared for their future. Larkin approached the committee and asked for the loan to purchase the house. "The committee would have been aware of the difficulties my aunts were in and the stress and strain they were under," Larkin said.

There is no record of the trust being approached for a major loan.

"I don't have any recollection of an actual meeting of the trust taking place to approve it," Burke said. "But I remember it being discussed with me. I was appraised of a problem that Ms Larkin and her family were having and that we were in a position to help, I think it might have been mentioned short-term, and I said something to the region of, 'Well, if the money's there why don't we do it? It's only earning short, small interest,' and that Gerry Brennan, who was our legal guy, would look after the legal details."

There is no record of a loan being forwarded from this alleged Fianna Fáil account to Larkin.

"My understanding is Mr Brennan, who was the legal person in the trust, would have put this documentation in place and I did not question everything that was done legally because I am not a legal expert," Burke said. "It wasn't a nod and a wink, as we might say," he added.

Brennan was a member of this alleged trust, and he was also to act for Larkin in her proposed purchase of the house. Ordinarily, the two roles might present a conflict of interest for a solicitor. Unfortunately, Brennan was long dead when the matter came to public attention in 2007. For the second time in this narrative of finances, his friends showed him acting in a manner that was less than professional.

Despite this portrayal of Brennan, Burke wasn't attempting to show any disrespect to his late friend: "I still have the ultimate trust in the fine man that Gerry Brennan was, that any legal issues that would have arisen in relation to the trust, in relation to the transactions, that Gerry would have looked after it."

The house cost in excess of £40,000. Larkin bought it in her name and became the legal owner. There was no charge on the property against the loan. Brennan did not charge any fee for the conveyancing.

According to Ahern and Larkin, they never discussed the matter until after the loan had been approved by the committee. The pair had become "life partners", who shared not just their personal lives but large parts of their respective careers. Yet they never discussed a highly personal matter that crossed over into their professional lives in St Luke's and the Fianna Fáil Party.

After the deal was done and dusted, Larkin filled in Ahern on how her problem had been sorted: "I told him what the committee had said and that I was relieved to be able to find a solution to the problem," she said.

Says Burke of the loan: "At the time, no, I didn't discuss it with Mr Ahern."

Ahern was at the centre of political activity in St Luke's. The premises were bought for his political benefit. The money that poured into the B/T account was allegedly political donations raised for his benefit. Yet the highly irregular move of extending a major loan to a staff member, who happened to be Ahern's life partner, was not discussed with the man himself.

The money was eventually paid back in 2008 after it had come to the attention of the planning tribunal. Larkin borrow-ed from Ahern the €45,510 required for the repayment. She left a blank cheque at St Luke's on 4 February 2008 for Ahern to add the amount that was required. She then applied for a loan with the Irish Nationwide Building Society to pay back Ahern. On 4 March 2008, she was personally approved for the loan by the society's chief executive, Michael Fingleton. It was later reported that Larkin did not provide the building society with any of the documentation normally required to secure a loan. There was no record of her showing identification, proof of income, current-account statements or details of other loans for which she was liable.

Whether or not the "loan" would ever have been repaid had the matter not come to public attention is a moot point. Legally, there was not one scrap of evidence to indicate that the money forwarded to Larkin from the account actually was a loan.

* * *

On 26 August 1994, there was another major cash inflow to St Luke's. Across the road, Collins withdrew £20,000 from the B/T account, apparently to pay for building work that would stop St Luke's falling into the Tolka.

Joe Burke's background in construction rendered him the man for the job. There is no record of a decision by the alleged B/T trust to direct that £20,000 be withdrawn from the account. "St Luke's developed a damp problem, which we got an engineer to actually examine and report as to what should be done," Burke recalled. "And I was asked because of my experience in the building industry [to locate the appropriate firm to do the work]. But we were told that it would cost in excess of £20,000. I asked that I be given the money and that I would go about finding a builder to do the work. I was given the money. I think I picked it up from the office in Drumcondra."

Collins's recollection coincides with this. "My recollection is I brought it to St Luke's and left it in the office, and whoever was there I said, 'Make sure Joe Burke gets that,'" Collins said.

Once more, cash was king. Burke is clear on the reasoning behind this move. Anybody employed to do the job would prefer to see cash. "You know the old saying, it's always nice to see the colour of your money," he said. Burke collected the money and brought it home to his own safe.

But the job didn't get done. After discussing the structural problems with some unspecified builders, the trust members decided to long-finger the work as it was going to be a much bigger job that originally envisaged. The twenty grand had to be recycled. Burke returned the money to St Luke's for collection by Collins on 25 October, two months after it had been withdrawn. Except he returned the cash in sterling, rather than the punts he had received. "I think I left it back in Drumcondra. I had possibly told him [Collins] that I was about to leave it back. It was due."

He left the money at the office, possibly with Ahern's secretary. He didn't warn her of what was in the bulging envelope. "I'm always of the policy that if you tell somebody there is cash in an envelope they will fret and worry. If you don't tell them anything they will just think it is documents," Burke said.

Burke had an explanation for why he had left the cash in sterling: "At the time, in '94 to '95, I was doing a huge amount of pub refurbishing in Ireland. I remember at one particular time we had eight or ten pubs on at the time. We would have been buying a lot of memorabilia and salvage and that in England. Since I didn't have any bank accounts in England I would have been using cash. And when the question came to me did I give it back in sterling, I was kind of stumped as to say, did I or didn't I? But it's possible that I did."

Once more, in the course of the narrative surrounding Ahern's finances, an account received a large sum of sterling because money was being recycled, having been converted into sterling. Such was the explanation for Ahern's sterling stash of £15,000–18,000, and it was also his explanation for two lodgements of £10,000 and £20,000 in 1995. All this homespun foreign exchange was going on in Drumcondra. The alternative explanation is that there was no foreign exchange and all these lodgements were fresh entries into the orbit of Ahern's finances. Ahern and Burke adamantly deny that such is the case.

There was one other significant lodgement to the B/T

account. On 18 July 1995, £10,000 in cash was signed in. This, according to Ahern, was the proceeds of another golf classic. As previously stated, the official inaugural golf classic for the constituency was advertised two years later in 1997.

In total, lodgements to the B/T account in the period 1989 to 1995 came to £89,649.66. By comparison, Ahern's annual salary in 1993 was of the order of £63,000.

Activity in the account ceased in 1995, with a balance of £45,000 or so. There were a number of other relatively minor withdrawals from the accounts to the order of £2,000–4,000, which were attributed to hosting parties in St Luke's and paying for election literature. Both of these activities were generally dealt with out of regular constituency accounts.

By 2008, the accumulated interest brought the balance up to €47,657. When Celia Larkin's loan was repaid that month, the balance increased to more than €90,000.

In January 2008, officers of the O'Donovan Rossa cumann applied to have the account renamed the Building Trust account. Two officers were named as the new co-signatories. This was the first time since the account had been opened in 1989 that there was any indication that the money held was the property of Fianna Fáil.

The twist in ownership of the account threw up an irony. In recent years certain senior Fianna Fáil figures had misappropriated money from the party. Charlie Haughey, Ray Burke and Pee Flynn had trousered money intended as contributions to the party. Now, here was an instance of Fianna Fáil – in a technical sense – actually being reimbursed with monies that had always been intended for the party.

17

WHOSE MONEY IS IT ANYWAY?

Between December 1993 and December 1995, a total of £147,500 was lodged in Bertie Ahern's AIB accounts and other accounts associated with Celia Larkin. This doesn't include the £30,000 sterling – which might have been $45,000 – lodged in December 1994. His savings account in the Irish Permanent Building Society received in the region of £20,000 in this period as well as £15,500 sterling. The B/T account, in which Ahern said he had no beneficial interest, received £89,650 over a six-year period. Ahern and his associates claim that £20,000 of this was recycled money. In all, eighty-six lodgements to his accounts were examined. The sums flowing through his associated accounts – excluding B/T – in the two-year period exceeded £220,000, amounting to more than three times his salary. None of the lodgements to any of the accounts corresponds to a salary cheque from Ahern's positions as TD or government minister.

Ahern has always maintained that his unorthodox financial activity during this period was entirely as a result of his marital difficulties. He also says that the only money he received was the two dig-outs, in December 1993 and September 1994, totalling £22,500 and £16,500 respectively; and the Manchester whip-around in May or September 1994, which yielded around £8,000.

Long after he gave evidence on these matters, he added that some of the sterling he had acquired came from winnings on horses in the UK. He was unable to specify how much.

He maintains that everything else that passed through his own or associated bank accounts was recycled money or, in the case of Mícheál Wall's suitcase of cash, money that was "made available" to him in relation to proposed accommodation arrangements. This money merely rested in his account for a few months.

His dealings should be placed in context. The legal separation of his marriage occurred around November 1993. The extensive inflows to and outflows from his accounts took place over the following two years, which gives some support to his claim. The various strands of his narrative are also supported by the sworn evidence of a number of people. In total, fourteen witnesses to the planning tribunal in 2007 and 2008 gave evidence that sat easily into Ahern's overall narrative.

If the evidence given to the planning tribunal by these witnesses was totally accepted, it would lend huge weight to Ahern's claims of complete innocence in these matters. Four of the eight donors to the first alleged dig-out in December 1993 testified that it occurred in the manner Ahern had outlined. All four donors to the alleged second dig-out echoed his version of events. John Kennedy, Mícheál Wall and Tony Kett claimed they were present at the alleged whip-around in Manchester.

Wall backs up everything Ahern says about arrangements to rent and eventually buy his house in Beresford. Celia Larkin's

Coming man: Bertie Ahern "went out of his way to conceal his potential" in his early days as a TD.

"The most skilful, the most devious, the most cunning of them all." Charlie Haughey's line of praise for his protégé came back to haunt Ahern throughout his career.

Bertie Ahern's time as Lord Mayor of Dublin propelled him into the national consciousness as a rising star.

Family fortunes: The Minister for Finance poses for Budget Day photograph with daughters Georgina and Cecelia.

Joe Burke, a key member of the Drumcondra mafia, whom Ahern stuck by through thick and thin.

NAME	TABLE
JERRY BEADES	22
EDDIE BOHAN	27
JIM MC GOVERN	14
DERMOT CAREW	17
CHARLIE CHAWKE	1
LIAM COOPER	5
SEAN DUNNE	21
JOHN FINNEGAN	3
SEAN HEHIR	11
KEN MCDONALD	4
VINCENT MC DONALD	9, 10, 15
DAVE MC KENNA	12
BERNARD MC NAMARA	25
JIM MANSFIELD	30
JIM MILLER & BRIAN KEOGH	6
JIM NUGENT	7
NOEL O'CALLAGHAN	16
OWEN O'CONNOR	24
MICHAEL O'CONNOR	29
NOEL O'FLAHERTY	20
EAMON O'MALLEY	8
LIAM SMYTH	26
JOE SOROHAN	28
MICHAEL WALL	19
ROBERT WHITE	23

Guess who's coming to dinner? The table plan for the annual O'Donovan Rossa fundraising dinner in 2001 included the great and good of Irish business.

Dig-out pals: Des Richardson (right), one of Ahern's closest associates, organised the first collection of money for Ahern. Businessman David McKenna was one of the friends who gave a "loan" to the then Minister for Finance.

Tim Collins opened the B/T bank account in the Irish Permanent in Drumcondra and always maintained the initials did not stand for Bertie and Tim.

aking the flak: Despite being Ahern's life-partner, Celia Larkin was
ever fully accepted by many of the Drumcondra mafia.

Michéal Wall arrived in St Luke's one Saturday morning
with a briefcase containing thirty thousand pounds, most
of it in sterling.

Up every tree in north Dublin: Ahern claimed to have made strenuous efforts to find out whether his friend and mentor Ray Burke had received money in connection with planning favours. The controversy around Burke led to the establishment of the Planning Tribunal in 1997.

Tom Gilmartin made numerous allegations of corruption about politicians and public officials, only some of which could be substantiated. His allegations about Bertie Ahern led to the planning tribunal trawling the Taoiseach's finances.

On 2 April 2008, Bertie Ahern came to the steps of Government Buildings to announce that he was resigning as Taoiseach. Some of his ministers were reportedly tearful when he told them of his plans just before he emerged to inform the public.

End of the line: Maurice Ahern, Chris Wall and key Drumcondra strategist Dominic Dillane forlornly crunch the numbers at the count for the Dublin Central by-election and local elections in 2009. Maurice failed to win a seat in either election.

Tell us more: Despite an extensive investigation by the Planning Tribunal, many questions remained about Ahern's finances when he completed evidence in 2008.

evidence paints a similar picture. Tim Collins and Joe Burke testified that the B/T account had nothing to do with Ahern. Grainne Carruth, a secretary at St Luke's, gave evidence backing Ahern's version of some money movements, but ultimately she changed her story when confronted with records.

In the round, the evidence of all of the above people would suggest that Ahern was unwise, silly, definitely greedy in accepting money when he had no real need of it and, above all, naïve in his personal dealings. But it would also suggest that he had received the monies that poured through his accounts in exactly the manner he claimed. At such a conclusion, he would emerge with his reputation for honesty and probity largely intact.

It could be claimed that the strange behaviour illustrated a man who was careless in his personal financial dealings because he was entirely preoccupied with his professional life, looking after the nation's finances and, when he became Fianna Fáil leader, his party's welfare.

Ahern's lifestyle can be wheeled out in his defence. Unlike his mentor Haughey, he is not a Charvet-shirt man. He has modest tastes and enjoys inexpensive pursuits, such as attending sporting fixtures. By the standards of even fellow politicians, his home is inexpensive. If there was any suggestion that he had ever received large sums of money, nobody could ever claim that he wanted or needed it to support his lifestyle.

All of the above suggests that Fate has mocked the man described as the greatest Irish politician of his generation. Bad-luck hauled him into a public inquiry that had nothing to do with him, and dredged up a painful and messy period in his life, which he had long since left behind. He was done a grave disservice. He was hounded. His private life was used and abused, thrashed around in the public domain to inflict a wound on his political life.

* * *

But there are problems with the analysis as laid out above. The legal separation of Ahern's marriage occurred seven years after he had left the family home. He was long into a new relationship by the time his separation received the legal imprimatur. Since early 1992, he had been living in an apartment above St Luke's. He maintains that issues around his personal finances involve just a two-year period in his career. This may or may not be the case.

The first lodgement to his accounts was in December 1993. For seven years prior to that he didn't have a bank account. He says that during this period he accumulated around £54,000 in savings in two safes. Nearly two years after acknowledging those savings, he said he had also had savings – and winning bets on horses – in sterling, which amounted to £15,000–£18,000. This equates to a total of more than £70,000 he retained in cash until late 1993, a sum of roughly twice his net annual salary as a government minister.

While it is plausible that he did make such savings – despite paying maintenance for his wife and two children – there is not one scrap of paper to back up his account of this money. All we know for sure is that he dealt in cash during this period. As no records survive, we must take his word for the origins of that cash.

It is correct that the end of his fevered banking transactions came in late 1995. This was two years after the legal separation of his marriage.

It may be a coincidence, but the first real effort to bring transparency to politicians' finances was made in 1995. The Ethics in Public Office Act made it compulsory for them to declare their material interests and tightened the rules governing the use of political funds and bank accounts.

At this time, too, there were rumblings about the activities of Charlie Haughey. Rumours circulated about High Court documents involving the Dunne family of Dunnes Stores, which were supposed to contain explosive allegations about Haughey. As it transpired, Haughey's money issues surfaced in November 1996, and sparked off enquiries that persisted for twelve years.

By late 1995, Ahern was in situ as leader of Fianna Fáil. Every previous Fianna Fáil leader had become Taoiseach and a general election was due within two years at the most. His own experience would have shown him how personal matters could be used against him in a political forum. When he was a contender for the party leadership in 1992, his marital status was ruthlessly exploited by rivals within the party. Through the mid-1990s there were rumours, and at the height of the leadership contest in 1992 a newspaper editorial, about the status of St Luke's. He became aware of media enquiries as to whether or not the building had been bought in his name using party funds.

In 1997 his concern that these matters could be used against him prompted him to have a report on the ownership of St Luke's drawn up by Gerry Brennan and senior counsel David Byrne.

This is the background against which Ahern's banking activity, particularly the lodgement of large sterling sums, ceased in late 1995.

There are problems with all the large lodgements to his accounts. The first was the £22,500 lodged in December 1993, the alleged proceeds of the first dig-out, solicited by Des Richardson and Gerry Brennan without Ahern's knowledge, to pay his legal expenses. Four of the donors, including Richardson, back up his claim. Two are deceased. Another, Michael

Collins, was unavailable to testify at the planning tribunal. The final donor Padraic O'Connor gave evidence that, if accepted as true, would completely undermine the contention that such a dig-out ever occurred.

When separate sources were contacted during the research for this book, they indicated that they could never have imagined the late Gerry Brennan touting people he barely knew to contribute towards his client's legal fees. By all accounts, Brennan was a quiet man, who wouldn't have possessed the self-confidence – or hard neck – to seek out funds in this manner. Of course, this is hearsay and does not imply that he couldn't have acted as Ahern, Richardson and the others said he did – their portrayal of Brennan does his reputation no favours. As Ahern's solicitor, he would have been aware of Ahern's financial position, and would have known he wasn't short of money.

If Brennan did tout for money for his client, his professionalism would have been compromised. He would have been forced to reveal some aspects of his client's family-law affairs to potential donors. While he wasn't looking for money for himself, he was the solicitor who hired counsel to act for Ahern, and their fees were part of the bill in question. Brennan's death in 1997 meant that these issues couldn't be addressed when the matter became public a decade later.

But the biggest problem with the story of the first dig-out is one of the alleged donors, Padraic O'Connor. He says he wasn't party to any dig-out. His story is backed up by two colleagues he consulted about the donation at the time. Unlike the other donors, he was not a close personal friend of Ahern's. He would have been a most unusual person to target for a dig-out compared to, say, Tim Collins or Joe Burke, or even Chris Wall, none of whom was approached.

If Ahern and Richardson were to be believed, then O'Connor took company funds to make a personal donation to a friend, and when the matter became public, he denied his friendship and the intended destination of the money handed over to Richardson. O'Connor gave convincing evidence about his bone fides to the planning tribunal. If his version of events is to be accepted, then the whole edifice of the first dig-out collapses. Which raises a glaring question: if the £22,500 didn't come from a dig-out, where did it come from?

* * *

The whip-around in Manchester also throws up problems. Only one of up to twenty donors who contributed the £8,000-odd could be located. The organiser of the event, Tim Kilroe, is dead. Senator Tony Kett – who died in 2009 after the tribunal hearings were completed – said he was there but didn't contribute. Where are these fabulously wealthy Irishmen who saw it as their duty to throw a few pounds into the hat for the Irish Minister for Finance?

Unlike Manchester, all of the donors to the Beaumont House dig-out were located. Their story is by turns touching and ridiculous, even if it is the whole truth.

They threw together a few pounds to put a roof over Bertie Ahern's head. It was a spur-of-the-moment decision. There was no discussion on how much was required of each donor. There was no effort to include other close friends of Ahern's in this generous gesture. There is no record of any of them accessing funds.

They each hit on different sums to throw into the hat. There were two donations of £4,000, one of £3,500 and one of £5,000. The man who gave the most, Barry English, hardly knew Ahern and wasn't working in a cash business. He had cash at home, which he had kept under his mattress or in a biscuit tin or wherever, for eleven months since he had returned to the country from abroad.

Those are the bare facts of the second dig-out.

The biggest problem for both this dig-out and the Manchester knees-up is bank records. Ahern says that the proceeds from these two events constituted the bulk of a lodgement of £24,838.49 on 11 October 1994. Applying the exchange rate for the day on transactions up to £2,500, and subtracting the five-pound chargeable fee, this equates to exactly £25,000 sterling. The branch also recorded buying in excess of £27,000 sterling that day, when the normal daily level of trading at the time was around £2,000.

Ahern disputes this analysis of the lodgement. He retained a banking expert to show how an entirely different interpretation could be applied to it. He has never made public the alternative analysis offered by his expert – former banker Paddy Stronge.

If the bank's records are to be accepted at face value, the existence of the second dig-out and the Manchester whip-around are immediately called into question. If he didn't get the money from those sources, where did he get it? And why was it in sterling?

A similar problem arises in relation to the strand of the narrative relating to Mícheál Wall's suitcase of £30,000 sterling. The corresponding lodgement equated to $45,000, using that day's exchange rate. Could this be yet another coincidence? If not, what was the source of the dollars?

Elsewhere, there are recurring themes. Substantial lodgements of sterling are attributed to recycled money. Lodgements of £20,000 and £10,000 to Ahern and Larkin accounts in 1995 are dealt with in this manner. So is the £20,000 lodgement to the B/T account in October 1994.

The source of this sterling cannot be accounted for. In the Ahern/Larkin lodgements, Ahern says he sent an unidentified person out to buy the sterling in small batches. This person, ghosting through the banks of Dublin's northside, cannot be located. Neither can any records of his or her activity.

The B/T sterling lodgement of £20,000 in October 1994 came from Joe Burke, who got the money from his safe. This is again claimed to be recycled money, withdrawn from the same account a few months earlier. Again, the evidence of this stands in the splendid isolation of witness testimony, with absolutely no records to back it up.

There are other coincidences. Individuals who might have been expected to pop up in one section of the narrative are absent, yet they pop up elsewhere. A suspicious mind might conclude that this ensured no individual popped up too many times.

For instance, Tim Collins, who ran the B/T account, was a close friend of Ahern. Yet he wasn't part of either of the two alleged dig-outs. Mícheál Wall was a close friend of Ahern. Yet in Manchester, having admitted he was present, he didn't contribute to the whip-around. As we know, Wall popped up in Dublin a few months later with his suitcase of cash.

Then, there was the house that Mick bought. He brought £30,000 in sterling from the UK to contribute to a major refurbishment of a relatively new house. Nobody counted the money when it was handed over. A month later, when Larkin was withdrawing £50,000 from her account, as Ahern waited outside in the car, again nobody counted the money.

Wall's decision to will his Beresford property to Ahern in 1996 is also bizarre. Even more so was the stipulation that, should he and Ahern both meet their demise, the property should go to Ahern's two daughters. Whatever about a landlord attempting to ensure that a tenant who is a friend should not be thrown out on the street, his decision to include Ahern's daughters in the will is curious.

In practically every aspect of the narrative, Ahern has shown no records that back up his version of events. Yet where records have been located – mainly through banks – the files dispute what he has said.

Sterling is another recurring theme. For somebody whose income was exclusively from the state, a lot of foreign currency flowed through his accounts. As we know, he has attributed this to his frequent trips to see Manchester United, allied to his dealings with the UK-based Wall.

By Ahern's account, Tim Kilroe organised the alleged whip-around, and he facilitated the foreign exchanges in cars and bars in the early 1990s. His recollection of these events, like those of Gerry Brennan, would have been fascinating, but both men were dead when matters became public.

In the round, Ahern's narrative can be viewed as highly suspicious if it is examined in a particular way. It includes too many coincidences, too much recycled money, too many bizarre explanations for accumulating sterling, and too many bank records that suggest all is not as he claims.

None of which means he hasn't told the truth. It's just that if he has, then Fate has conspired in a devious manner to leave him with a highly patchy version of events from the days when the money flowed gaily through his various bank accounts.

18

A TAXING QUESTION OR TWO

The cameras rolled. The interview took place on 30 June 1993, in the auspicious surroundings of Dublin Castle, a venue that, fifteen years later, would be Bertie Ahern's Waterloo. The Minister for Finance was emerging from a conference in the castle and agreed to talk to the RTÉ news reporter. The hot issue of the day was a tax amnesty that Ahern had recently introduced.

The minister was obviously uncomfortable at having done the deed. He held no candle for the tax dodgers whose activity had cost the exchequer dearly. But he was a realist, who accepted what had to be done. "Once we have corrected the system, then you have to have a merciless view on this," he told the reporter. "People know my view for twenty years. It would give me the greatest pleasure to watch non-compliant taxpayers go to jail."

* * *

The 1993 tax amnesty remains one of the great mysteries of Irish political life. According to most of those involved, practically everybody was against it, except the Taoiseach of the day, Albert Reynolds.

Bertie Ahern had always maintained it was a principled matter, as far as he was concerned, that tax cheats wouldn't get rewarded with an amnesty.

The terms of the proposed amnesty were particularly generous. Five years earlier an amnesty had been introduced that required applicants to pay all tax due, absolving them merely from interest and penalties. The proposal being floated for the 1993 amnesty was that applicants need only pay 15 per cent on undeclared money, effectively allowing tax dodgers to get away with paying a fraction of what the compliant had paid on their income. However, introducing a second amnesty so soon after the first would also open up the possibility that this might be a regular occurrence, and thereby encourage tax dodgers to take their chances and hang on for the next.

The Labour Party, Fianna Fáil's then coalition partner in government, was also opposed to it. Labour had achieved power on the back of a "Spring tide" election in 1992, in which the party had increased its Dáil seats from fifteen to thirty-three. Its triumph was, to a large extent, attributable to the high moral tone set by leader Dick Spring, in opposition in the previous Dáil.

The ruling Fianna Fáil–Progressive Democrat coalition had been beset by a number of scandals during its period in office. Most surrounded Charlie Haughey, but even after his resignation in February 1992, the government was mired in scandal over the Beef Tribunal, which examined the relation-ship between government and the beef industry.

In this environment, Labour prospered. Then, in government, they descended from the high ground. Some of their political capital was squandered in going into government with Fianna Fáil, whom Spring had excoriated for the previous three years. More was lost when party ministers filled political appointments with family members. Early the following year, the tax amnesty hovered onto the political agenda. If Labour was seen to support it, the cost would be far greater slippage from the high moral ground.

Reynolds clearly believed in the practicality of introducing an amnesty. Media comment suggested that between £1 billion and £2 billion of undeclared money was swirling around the economy. An amnesty would entice tax dodgers to 'fess up for a fraction of what they owed. The exchequer could expect a boost of £200 million to £300 million. This was money that could be put to good use in delivering an ambitious social programme promised by the Fianna Fáil–Labour coalition.

It all made perfect sense to Reynolds. He was reported as telling a parliamentary party meeting in April 1993 that the amnesty would bring large amounts of hot money back into the state where it would benefit the economy.

An array of forces was ranged against him. Ahern gave his biographers, Ken Whelan and Eugene Masterson, three reasons why he had been opposed to the amnesty: "One, the Fianna Fáil Party was against it; two, the Revenue Commiss- ioners were against it; and three, I saw the tax amnesty as unnecessary because I had given all this power to the Revenue Commissioners to go after these evaders in the 1992 Finance Act. I just did not think there was any reason to give a massive discount and I underline it – a massive discount – of 15 per cent to evaders. We are talking about very substantial bills which involve very substantial people."

A memorandum to cabinet on 21 May 1993 emphasised

Ahern's and his department's opposition to any amnesty proposal:

> Having regard to the likely negative implications for aggregate tax revenues over the next few years, to considerations of equity and the integrity of the tax system, and to the advice from the Attorney General's Office that any incentive involving a remission of tax properly due would be open to successful challenge on grounds of unconstitutionality, the Minister feels obliged to recommend against any such scheme.
>
> Instead, he seeks Government approval to issue a statement, in order to dispel the persistent media speculation, which is detrimental to tax-collection, to the effect that, having considered the matter fully, the Government do not intend to introduce such an incentive.

Ahern wanted it shouted from the rooftops that there would be no amnesty. He had plenty of allies. According to an account by former Labour Party adviser Fergus Finlay, in his book *Snakes and Ladders*, some party personnel were as adamant as Ahern about the implications of any amnesty:

> Two people argued consistently and strongly against the amnesty from the start. One was Bertie Ahern, the other was William Scally, senior Labour party adviser.
>
> At private meeting after private meeting, William pointed out what should have been obvious. In accepting the idea of a tax amnesty, we were cementing the contrast between the high moral tone of our politics before the election and a sudden drop of standards afterwards.
>
> Dick Spring agreed with William. But there was a

complication. The one thing that had become clear, as the debate went on in government was that the Taoiseach was strongly in favour of the amnesty. The Taoiseach and his Minister for Finance, both members of the same party, were on opposite sides of the argument. If Dick took sides with one of them that would end the argument – whoever he sided with would win.

Dick decided not to take sides. He believed that the arguments put forward by Bertie Ahern had already got a majority in the cabinet, and there was no need to expend political capital on a confrontation with the Taoiseach. It would be infinitely better if the amnesty were quietly buried without any difference emerging this early in the life of the government between the partners.

So, there is no room for doubt. Everybody, the Minister for Finance, the majority of Fianna Fáil ministers, the Fianna Fáil Party – according to Ahern – the Labour ministers and their advisers, was opposed to the amnesty. The Attorney General feared for the constitutionality of an amnesty. The Department of Finance and the Revenue were both opposed.

Reynolds, on the other hand, saw it as pragmatism. Retrieving some money was better than getting none at all. At the other end of the spectrum, opposition Progressive Democrat TD Michael McDowell characterised an amnesty as "a charter for criminals".

One of the principal reasons why the Revenue opposed an amnesty was that its investigators thought they might be on the brink of catching some serious evaders who might owe up to £100 million. This fact would only emerge in 1999, during the Public Accounts Committee probe of bogus non-resident accounts. If an amnesty was introduced, these individuals would slip through the net into freedom. Their identities were never revealed as the amnesty made the Revenue's investigation redundant.

The proposal was debated in cabinet through April and into May of 1993. Ahern's version of what happened casts him as standing alone with the "little people" who pay their taxes against the apathy and expediency permeating the cabinet room. "I was opposed and I fought the amnesty through five cabinet meetings," he told Whelan and Masterson. "In the end I was left on my own. There was no Dick Spring and no Ruairi Quinn there to help me out. It was fourteen to one all the time."

The cabinet meeting scheduled for 25 May was to decide the matter once and for all. According to Finlay, a meeting of Labour ministers that morning was told by party adviser Greg Sparks that he had had a phone call from Ahern at one a.m.: "Bertie was absolutely resolute, and determined to ensure that the amnesty didn't go through. He had wanted Greg to tell him that the Labour ministers would support him and Greg had done so."

Three hours later the cabinet met. Reynolds called the item relating to the amnesty. Ahern said he was proposing it. No arguments from the Revenue or the Department of Finance were put forward. The Labour ministers said nothing. According to Finlay, the six ministers were in something of a state of shock: "None of the Labour ministers insisted on a point of principle. None of us knew what had happened. But the amnesty that the Minister for Finance opposed was put into effect a few weeks later by the minister who opposed it."

That evening the government adopted the Waiver of Certain Tax Interest and Penalties Act 1993. According to Finlay, William Scally wrote to Spring resigning from his position, so distraught was he at the turn of events. "He had given a lifetime's effort to the Labour Party, and had served a number of party leaders through thick and thin. It caused him intense pain to leave, and he wanted to do it quietly, without causing any trouble for the party. But he saw the tax amnesty as a fundamental betrayal of everything the party he had grown up with ought to stand for."

Ahern would later tell his biographers that he also thought of resigning: "It got very near to that. I didn't support it but in the end I was left with little alternative. Under the rules of collective responsibility, I had to go back to the Dáil and bring it in, which I did. That was my job." The most cunning, the most devious of them all actually considered resigning on a measure that he himself had proposed to cabinet. Strange, indeed.

He has never elaborated on why he proposed the measure, despite opposition from himself, his party, most of the cabinet, the Revenue and the department.

The amnesty generated €240 million for the economy, which, at a rate of 15 per cent tax as per the terms, implies around €1.6 billion of hot money was declared.

*　*　*

Eight weeks before the amnesty was adopted, a strange thing happened in Drumcondra. Celia Larkin was forwarded her "loan" of £30,000 from the B/T account. There is no record of anybody involved in that transaction checking the tax implications of the loan. For instance, there is no documentation characterising the transaction as a loan. In the absence of any documentation, a Revenue inspector informed of such a transaction might have decided to characterise it other than a loan. That in turn might have had Revenue implications.

Bertie Ahern has always said he knew nothing of this loan. We can only assume that if he had been in full knowledge of what was going down, he would have strongly advised Larkin and the St Luke's committee to go straight to the Revenue to ensure they were being compliant. It would have been in keeping with his commitment to stand with the "little people" who pay taxes.

When the "loan" came into the public domain in 2008, the Revenue launched an investigation into whether or not there was a tax liability on the transaction.

On 30 December 1993, three days after the deadline for declaration for the amnesty passed, Ahern lodged £22,500 in a savings account. The circumstances of how he came into the money are highly unusual and disputed, but let's for a minute accept that it happened as he claims.

The donors of the money – apart from Padraic O'Connor – had said it was a dig-out to help him with legal fees. He characterised it as a loan, which would most likely exempt the money from tax. If it was a donation, as characterised by the contributors, then tax was due. At the time, the threshold for exemption from gift tax was £11,447. For a man who was so principled in the matter of others paying tax, he didn't bother to check whether there was a possibility – if not probability – that he was being deficient in the area himself.

The following 30 January, he lodged a cheque for £5,000 to his Irish Permanent Building Society account. He has characterised this as a "political donation for personal use". He didn't contact the Revenue about it.

Political donations are exempt from tax. Personal donations are not. The Revenue would have had a great interest, from a philosophical perspective if nothing else, in political donations for personal use. Where do the political and personal meet? Is it a gift? Is it liable for tax?

The money was received in the same tax year as the first dig-out. In that year Ahern had, by his own account, received £27,500. He didn't declare a penny of it for tax.

In May or September 1994, they passed the hat around the Four Seasons in Manchester and handed him £8,000 sterling. Now, according to his narrative, he was receiving gifts from strangers to go with the loans he got from friends, all of which are relatively tax-friendly transactions. In September, he pulled in the second dig-out, worth £16,500.

Again, there are problems with these narratives, but let's invoke the benefit of the doubt.

The status of the Manchester money is dubious. The second dig-out would have presented the Revenue with a few issues, if anybody had bothered informing their tax office. Ahern characterised it as a loan. One of the contributors, Barry English, compared his donation to an act of charity. The money went into Ahern's personal account, rather than to one of the political accounts operated in the constituency.

Yet Ahern was not haunted by doubt. He didn't check whether the money might be liable for tax. As far as he was concerned it was a loan, although there was absolutely no documentation to support this.

Two years later, he gave an opinion on the obligations of government ministers receiving loans. In November 1996, the Fine Gael-Labour-Democratic Left coalition was in power. The Minister for Communications, Fine Gael's Michael Lowry, was in hot water. It had emerged that he had billed a major extension to his home to the retailing magnate Ben Dunne. Initially, Lowry claimed that the cost of the work had been a loan.

The leader of the opposition, Bertie Ahern, wasn't having any of it. He said that if the payments were a loan, there would have to be incontrovertible written evidence of that and of the arrangement for its repayment. "Financial gifts have to be declared for capital acquisitions tax purposes if they exceed the threshold," he said. "In principle, apart from token presentations in respect of functions performed at home and abroad, neither politicians nor officials should accept personal gifts of value from outside their family."

He said Lowry's explanations left a lot to be desired. "An incomplete, complex convoluted explanation, constructed after the event will have less and less credibility as time goes by."

Unfortunately, his clarity of thought on Lowry's obligations appears to have been absent while he was receiving large sums of money during a period when taxation was a burning issue, due to the amnesty he had introduced.

In 2002, following new legislation, all TDs were obliged to obtain a tax-clearance certificate to demonstrate that their tax affairs were in order. Ahern obtained his certificate without any reference to his receipt of large sums eight years earlier. Neither did he declare his obligation to repay a loan.

In September 2006, Ahern introduced the dig-out money to the public domain in an interview for RTÉ News with Bryan Dobson. "I know the tax law. I'm an accountant," he said. And later: "I've broken absolutely no codes, ethical, tax, legal or otherwise. I've checked that to the best of my ability." The following day, in an address to the Dáil on the matter, he said: "I checked with the tax authorities long ago."

By that stage, he hadn't repaid the "loans", which had been provided some thirteen years earlier. He hadn't informed the tax authorities. Later, when this became known, he would claim that what he'd meant was that he had informed people who were "authorities on tax", as in tax advisers.

His claims to have checked out the tax law and checked in

with the tax authorities were disputed by none other than the taxman.

On 6 October 2007, three weeks after Ahern's RTÉ interview and Dáil speech, a tax inspector for his area wrote to him. Caoimhin MacGearraidh asked about the claims he had made:

> You spoke at a function in Manchester in 1994–5 and you stated that you received £8,000 sterling. During the course of the Dáil debate on this issue on September 27 last, you stated that 'I dealt with this properly in terms of taxes.'
>
> Later, during the course of the same debate you stated, 'In Manchester, as I said, I dealt with a range of issues – namely my taxes.' I can find no record of this issue having been addressed previously and would ask you to let me know how and when the taxation aspect of this payment was dealt with.
>
> During the course of the Dáil debate on September 27 last, you stated that you 'checked the matter . . . with the tax authorities long ago'. I can find no record of the taxation issues or otherwise being raised with the Revenue.

The inspector also referred to the loans that Ahern had taken out with his pals.

> If there was no written documentation [in respect of any agreement], please outline the terms of any verbal agreements in relation to the schedule of payments, time limits and the rate of interest payable.

The inspector added that there had been no declaration from Ahern for the years in question.

Ahern's accountant Des Peelo wrote back. His client wanted to straighten things out and was asking that his declaration be treated as voluntary. Ahern was effectively asking that the broadcast interview should be treated as an admission to the Revenue that he had a liability and would address it.

A reply from the Revenue said it did not accept that the declaration had been voluntary.

Following his receipt of that letter, and having consulted his own tax authorities, Ahern decided to put money on account with the Revenue, pending the outcome of any investigation into his affairs. He came up with a figure of €70,000.

Over the following months, Peelo continued to be in regular contact with the Revenue over tax liabilities. It emerged that, among a number of disclosures he made at the time, he had mentioned the £5,000 "political donation for personal use" he had received in January 1994 as a liability.

The Revenue also computed liabilities arising from his accommodation in St Luke's from 1992 to 1994. Persons who get free accommodation from their employer must pay income tax on the benefit derived. Ahern, who claimed to know tax law, had completely ignored this liability at the time when tax-amnesty fever gripped the political village.

He also made what he described as a "voluntary disclosure" over liability arising from renting Beresford from Mícheál Wall between 1995 and 1997. Under tax law a tenant who pays rent to a non-resident landlord must retain the equivalent of the standard income-tax rate and remit this to the Revenue. The average person may not know this, but an accountant who served as Minister for Finance might be expected to.

Much of Ahern's correspondence with the Revenue leaked into the media in late 2007.

On 6 January 2008 he issued a statement in response to the coverage:

> I was perturbed to see correspondence relating to my tax affairs published recently in a Sunday newspaper. I am fully satisfied that absolutely no details of my dealings with them have been made public by the Revenue Commissioners.
>
> I have, however, already said publicly that I engaged with the Revenue Commissioners on some matters, which emerged in recent months. I made voluntary disclosure to the Revenue and I paid them money on account which I understand is the normal practice. This does not necessarily mean there is a liability arising.
>
> My tax adviser is in discussions with the Revenue Commissioners on these matters. That process will take its course and will come to a conclusion in due time, just as it would for any taxpayer engaged in a similar process. I firmly believe that I am in a position to answer any questions raised by the Revenue Commissioners, who deal similarly with all taxpayers, regardless of their occupation. That is as it should be.

So it went for the man who had declared his abhorrence of tax dodgers, his knowledge of the tax laws, and the scrupulous care of his own tax affairs.

PART III

THE PRAETORIAN GUARD

19

A GLAD HAND AND MANY HATS

It was early March in 1994, and a big occasion in the house of Niall Welch. An accountant based in Glanmire, outside Cork City, he was hosting a special knees-up. The Taoiseach, Albert Reynolds, was to attend a private dinner at his house, to which a lot of big noises in the Cork area would be invited. The purpose of the occasion was to raise funds for Fianna Fáil.

Those wishing to support democracy with the contents of their pocket would be enticed to do so by the presence of the Taoiseach. As men of the world – there were no women present – they would be free to discuss in a convivial and discreet atmosphere how the country was faring. And if anybody had any ideas for the betterment of society, sure, where better to air them than in the presence of the nation's leader?

There were around twenty guests, and catering was provided by the Imperial Hotel. Apart from Reynolds, there were two other party officials, and the man collecting the donations, Des Richardson. This left fifteen or sixteen, who might have felt compelled to cough up for the party. Ultimately only nine did, but it's unclear whether the others refused or had contributed in another way. The average donation was £5,000. There was dispute as to whether Welch suggested an appropriate figure to some of his guests, or whether they arrived at it off the top of their heads.

One of the guests recalled seeing envelopes thrown onto the table at the end of the night. Another, who had forgotten his cheque book, met Richardson the following morning at a city-centre hotel to give his contribution.

The dinner at Welch's home on 11 March 1994 would eventually come to the attention of the planning tribunal. Owen O'Callaghan was one of the principal guests and, because of his contacts in Fianna Fáil, had helped to organise the guest list; he contributed a handsome £10,000 on the night.

The occasion offers an insight into fundraising for Fianna Fáil at the time. A number of such private dinners for wealthy businessmen were held to tackle the party's enormous debt. The man who brought the concept to new heights, and who proved to be quite a prodigious fundraiser, was Bertie Ahern's old pal Des Richardson.

* * *

Richardson was a key member of Ahern's Drumcondra Mafia. He is also central to Ahern's narrative about the flow of money into and out of his associated accounts in the mid-1990s. He had become involved with the rising politician in the mid-1980s through a mutual acquaintance, Jimmy Keane. Richardson and Keane had grown up in the south inner city, the area from which another Drumcondra player, Gerry Brennan, also hailed.

One of the first fundraisers for the O'Donovan Rossa cumann was held in the Mansion House when Ahern was Lord

Mayor in 1987. Richardson demonstrated his flair for raising money by organising that event.

When St Luke's was purchased in 1988, Richardson was one of the trustees. However, he wasn't a foot soldier. He didn't wear out his shoe leather canvassing for the boss. "We never saw Des Richardson," one Drumcondra insider said. "Tim Collins and Richardson were never around the place."

Richardson worked in business and had a professional construction qualification, but by the early 1990s Ahern had seen that he might have talents Fianna Fáil could put to use.

In March 1993, Albert Reynolds appointed Ahern party treasurer. Some saw the appointment as a poisoned chalice, passed from the party leader to his only potential rival. The party was in debt to the tune of £3 million. "Albert gave him the job to soften his cough," according to one party grandee. Typical of the man, Ahern rose to the challenge. His first appointment was a full-time fundraiser: Richardson.

Unlike his predecessors, the new man was not a member of the party. "It was nearly a badge of honour with him," one party official remembered. "He wasn't a party man, he was a Bertie man."

He was employed on a contract basis at £5,000 a month, or £60,000 a year. By comparison, Ahern's salary as a government minister was £63,000. The terms of Richardson's contract also meant he would operate independently of the party. A suite at the Berkeley Court Hotel was hired on his behalf, out of which he worked. According to sources within the party, he was reluctant to use the party's Mount Street headquarters.

The arrangement was not unique. Previous internal party fundraisers, Des Hannafin and Paul Kavanagh, had used hotel suites to facilitate fundraising – they provided donors with discretion. Richardson's sole brief was to pay off the debt. His activities would be separate from party fundraising for current spending.

There was some tension with Headquarters about the specifics of his role. Richardson wanted a separate account to cater for his activities. The request made perfect sense. However, he also wanted control of the account to be exclusively in his and Ahern's hands.

There was resistance at Headquarters. Ahern was treasurer, but he was not at that time a trustee of the party. The solution was to open an account in the names of Reynolds and Ahern; it was managed by party official Sean Fleming at Head-quarters. The statements and account information went to Mount Street, rather than to Richardson who, despite his earlier misgivings, was comfortable with the arrangement.

Within a month, he had organised the first fundraiser at Dobbins Bistro in Ballsbridge. A hundred donors turned up, all shelling out £150. They enjoyed a fine meal, a few words from one of the party stalwarts, and most had a punt on the raffle. The result was around £12,500 for the party, plus another grand from the raffle. Richardson was out of the traps. He soon got into his stride, with various fundraising measures. This would include bringing the fundraising tent at the Galway races to new heights. In time, it would come to symbolise the close relationship between developers and Fianna Fáil.

Towards the end of 1993, Richardson found himself wearing three different fundraising hats. The day job had him working on behalf of the Fianna Fáil Party. He was one of the main organisers of Ahern's December constituency dinner, and he found himself looking for a dig-out on behalf of Ahern the man, as opposed to Ahern the politician. Surprisingly – when you consider that the two men were so close – Richardson believed that Ahern was strapped for cash: "I was helping out a friend . . . it was meant as a contribution to somebody who had fallen on hard times," he told the planning tribunal. But, as we now know, Ahern had large sums at his disposal at the time of the alleged dig-out.

Apart from organising and contributing to it, Richardson was the only donor who left a paper trail. All of the other donors gave cash because Richardson told them that Ahern would not accept a cheque. He contributed by bank draft, which, fortunately, Ahern didn't have a problem with.

* * *

The Cork knees-up in March 1994 was not an isolated incident. Other private dinners were arranged for wealthy individuals around the same time. One took place at the salubrious home of Ken Rohan, a wealthy property developer. He lived at Charleville House, a Georgian pile near Enniskerry, County Wicklow, which he opens to the public on sixty days of the year. For this he can claim a tax credit against his income for maintaining the house.

In the early 1990s, he had a problem. Some of the contents in the stately home had been bought by his development company and were borrowed by him personally. As far as the Revenue Commissioners were concerned, they should have been treated as a benefit-in-kind: on 17 November 1993, Rohan received a tax assessment that took account of this. If it was accepted, or the Revenue won on appeal, the possibility opened up that Rohan would be liable for up to £1.5 million in taxes for the previous twelve years.

He lobbied to have the law changed. The Georgian Society also lobbied, although it is unclear as to what exactly it believed a change in the law would deliver.

221

The Revenue Commissioner was opposed to any changes that would negate Rohan's tax bill. In a letter to the Department of Finance in August 1993, a Revenue official pointed out: "The provision of works of art by a body corporate for its directors or employees, where no market value rent is involved, constitutes a chargeable benefit-in-kind."

The Department of Finance was against any change to the law. An official drafted a response to Rohan's lobbying, outlining four reasons why there should be no change to the law and concluding: "In current budgetary circumstances I feel an extension of such a relief to what by any standards must be a relatively privileged group of taxpayers could not be justified."

The letter was never sent to Rohan. The minister, Bertie Ahern, didn't sign it, but instead made notes in the margin saying he wanted the law changed as Rohan had requested.

Coincidentally, Rohan had friends in high places. Though Des Richardson was busy raising funds for Fianna Fáil, he also found time to undertake some consultancy work for Rohan, for which he was paid a monthly retainer of £1,000. Richardson would subsequently insist that he knew nothing of Rohan's tax issues.

The dinner at Rohan's mansion in early 1994 was a high-roller affair. Des Richardson was in attendance. So was Taoiseach Albert Reynolds and the Minister for Finance, Bertie Ahern. There is no record of any guest contributing to party funds. Rohan himself has admitted that he contributed to the party, but there is nothing to suggest that he did so on the night in question, or that he advised others to do so. When the matter became public, there were suggestions that up to £250,000 may have been raised from ten donors, but these figures were never confirmed by Fianna Fáil.

Ahern has always maintained he didn't know who was

contributing to the party. The official line was that senior party figures were kept out of the loop on purpose, to ensure there could never be any conflict of interest with their legislative duties.

The 1994 Finance Act, introduced by Bertie Ahern, included a provision under Section 19 that changed the law as requested by Rohan and the Georgian Society. It had two unusual aspects: only one individual in the country benefited from it – Ken Rohan – and it was to be applied retrospectively, which effectively neutralised any efforts to pursue Rohan for back taxes. The only loser was the Revenue, and Rohan would save an estimated £150,000 per annum in the years ahead.

There is no evidence to suggest that Des Richardson's overlapping functions of fundraising for the party, consulting for a donor and being a close associate of the Minister for Finance had any influence over a highly unusual legislative measure.

In February 1999, when the story broke, two officials from the Department of Finance were wheeled out for the media to declare that there was nothing unusual in the measure that had been introduced.

* * *

In April 1994, Richardson found himself in Bertie Ahern's favourite city. He had been invited to attend a Manchester United match by an English businessman, Norman Turner, who, at the time, had serious interest in Ireland. He was involved in plans to develop a casino as part of a wider redevelopment of the old racecourse in the Phoenix Park. He was a frequent visitor to Dublin and was aware of some local opposition to the casino. One of his associates in the plans for the Phoenix Park site was Robert White, an old school friend of Ahern. Richardson didn't know Turner particularly well at the time, so what unfolded must have come as something of a surprise to him.

"We had lunch before the match," he said, and at some point, Turner turned to Richardson and told him: "I would like to make a donation to Fianna Fáil." He added: "You are doing a good job over there and I'd like to help out." With that, he took an envelope from his pocket and passed it to him.

"I put it in my pocket and he said, 'That's a confidential contribution, I don't want it recognized, I don't want it acknowledged, that's between you and I. Spend it on Fianna Fáil overheads, or pay a bill for Fianna Fáil.'"

Turner didn't request a receipt. The only evidence of its existence was a note recording it, which Richardson forwarded to Fianna Fáil Headquarters as part of a plethora of documents some six years after the money was handed over.

Back in Manchester, Richardson continued with his dinner and let the envelope rest in his pocket. He went to the match, enjoyed the socialising and subsequently went home. Just like his friend Bertie Ahern, he had no problem walking around Manchester with a sizeable amount of cash in his pocket.

The next day, in his office in the Berkeley Court Hotel, he finally got around to tearing open the envelope to find out what constituted the latest donation to the party. He pulled out ten thousand dollars.

He didn't profess any astonishment when asked about it at the planning tribunal. He just took it as another donation. Yet this was a cash contribution from a British businessman, handed over in Manchester, donated to an Irish political party, and it consisted of American dollars. Strange, but apparently true.

Richardson says he converted the cash the following month

to £6,780. He used it to pay for ongoing expenses as he went about his work, raising funds for Fianna Fáil. There is no record of how exactly it was spent.

Later that year, the plans for the Phoenix Park casino were binned. Ahern, who had been lobbied by Turner and attended matches with him in Manchester, always maintained that he was opposed to the casino development.

* * *

Richardson made serious inroads into the party debt, accounting for an estimated £2.5 million in funds in the first few years of his tenure. Party sources agree he was an able man for the job. Others remember him as secretive. "Very few knew too much about him," one party activist remembers. "He wouldn't let his right hand know what his left hand was doing. For a party fundraiser, you don't want a blabber, you need confidentiality and discretion and Des was discreet to the point of being secretive."

Whatever about his efforts at the day job, Richardson's energy left him with plenty of time for other business pursuits. Through most of his time with Fianna Fáil, he was also involved in a company called Berraway, which had been incorporated as a property development company in the early 1990s. Its shareholders were Éamon Duignan, a property developer from Meath, and the political lobbyist Frank Dunlop. The company shared its registered address with Dunlop's lobbying business in Mount Street.

Richardson had a controlling interest of Berraway with Duignan. Dunlop was a passive shareholder. The three men were involved in the purchase of property in Navan, County Meath, in the mid-1990s. In 1995, Duignan resigned as a director. Richardson subsequently confirmed to the planning tribunal that he had sole control of Berraway's bank account between 1996 and when it was dissolved in 2000. During that period, around £850,000 (over €1 million) passed through the account.

Berraway was the company through which Ken Rohan paid Richardson for his consultancy work. Arks Advertising, retained by Fianna Fáil during the 1997 general election, also paid money into Berraway. Richardson acted as consultant to Arks in the mid-1990s. Dunlop paid at least £25,000 into Berraway for consultancy work by Richardson, who also consulted for an outfit called Risk Management International (RMI), which specialises in countering fraud and kidnappings.

In 1999, the year Richardson stepped down from his fundraising role, RMI paid him £1,000 a month for six months. The company's chief executive, Cathal O'Neill, subsequently told a newspaper that Richardson's fee was for assistance in sourcing clients. RMI had some state clients, but there is nothing to suggest that Richardson had any influence in the retention of this work.

While fundraising for Fianna Fáil with one hand, Richardson appears to have been busy consulting with the other. Among other clients, he worked for A1 Waste, a controversial waste-disposal company, which was subsequently prosecuted for extensive illegal dumping in County Wicklow. He was also appointed to the board of Marlborough Recruitment, established by his friend and alleged digger-out for Ahern, David McKenna. Richardson took up an executive role in the company and was later appointed chairman.

* * *

Richardson and Frank Dunlop enjoyed a close working relationship, but their connection says much about the small world that exists at the interface of business and politics.

In the early 1990s, Dunlop was involved in extensive bribery of county councillors who were drawing up the Dublin County Development plan. Dunlop acted for a number of landowners who were seeking to have land rezoned, thus increasing its value by a multiple. He would later claim that some were aware that he was bribing councillors on their behalf, while others weren't. In 2009, Dunlop pleaded guilty to corruption at Dublin's Circuit Criminal Court. He was sentenced to two years in prison, the final six months of which was suspended.

There is no suggestion that Richardson had any knowledge of Dunlop's illegal activities. But plenty of irony attaches to their then relationship. Richardson was raising funds to pay off the Fianna Fáil Party debt, while Dunlop was passing bribes to party councillors to enrich his clients, many of whom were party donors. No doubt, with their wealth greatly enhanced as a result of rezonings, the landowners would have been feeling generous when it came to funding the democratic process that had indirectly contributed to their good fortune!

The irony was even more acute when seen through the lens of the fundraising dinner in Cork in March 1994, outlined at the beginning of this chapter. On the night in question, Richardson spoke a few words to let his guests know that Fainna Fáil was in dire straits and would appreciate contributions. He later revealed that Dunlop had helped him with the speech, having "kindly offered his services in terms of communication".

One of the dinner's organisers was Owen O'Callaghan, who was employing Dunlop at the time to lobby for rezoning for the Quarryvale site in west Dublin. O'Callaghan paid Dunlop over

£1 million in fees. Dunlop says he used some of that money, without O'Callaghan's knowledge, to bribe councillors.

Now, at the dinner, Dunlop's words were used to urge businessmen to contribute to the furtherance of democracy while his actions were doing the opposite.

Of course, Richardson, who was uttering Dunlop's words, had no knowledge of this. He, like most people outside the loop, thought Dunlop was just a dab hand at getting councillors to see the merits of his arguments and act according to the interests of his clients.

While Richardson was one of the Ahern's closest confidants, he wasn't the only one to find himself thrust into the public domain as a result of his business dealings. Tim Collins was another and, like Richardson, he was strictly an Ahern man rather than a "soldier of destiny".

20

THE MINDER IN THE SHADOWS

Tim Collins was a key member of the Drumcondra Mafia. Like Des Richardson, he was neither a party member nor a foot soldier known for tireless canvassing in the constituency, hunting down number ones. Years later, when shown the names of constituency officers in Dublin Central, the only one he recognised was that of Chris Wall. As with Richardson, Collins operated behind the scenes, rather than on the doorstep. He was the sole signatory of the B/T account, through which tens of thousands of pounds flowed in the mid-1990s and a "loan" of £30,000 was sourced for Celia Larkin. Collins said he was "minding" the account for Fianna Fáil.

This reflected badly on what was one of the most successful political parties in western Europe. Although it boasted more than 70,000 members, plenty of whom had solid financial or business backgrounds, the people in St Luke's felt it necessary to go outside the party to find a suitable minder for a party account.

Ahern and Collins go back to the mid-1970s. They became friends after coming into contact through mutual acquaintances. Collins was working as a flooring contractor. By the late 1980s, the two men were close enough that Collins became one of the trustees of St Luke's. Around that time, he got out of flooring and pulled an unusual number in an architectural firm.

His work had brought him into contact with an architect by the name of Tim Rowe. The two men decided to form a company together, the Pilgrim Group. Collins had no experience of architecture. "My function was sourcing bits of property and marrying them up with people who would maybe give us a job to design," he said. He was joined in Pilgrim by his old buddy from St Luke's, Des Richardson. Two of Pilgrim Group's directors were now also trustees of St Luke's, and close confidants of the man who would be Taoiseach.

In addition to the above brief, Collins also began to get finder's fees for locating sites for potential development. This might involve just having a nose to spot an undervalued site with potential, but included the ability to make an educated guess as to where sites had a good chance of rezoning, which usually resulted in the value increasing considerably. To cater for these fees, he set up a separate company, Collins Consultants.

Years later, at the planning tribunal, he would claim that he never had a formal arrangement with clients: "It was assumed that if anything ever happened to the land, I would get some fee for finding the site," he told the inquiry in relation to one particular land deal he was involved in. This was incorrect. Later in his evidence, he was shown a contract document that stated he was in line for a specific 2.5 per cent share of profits on that particular deal. He admitted his earlier evidence was wrong. He said he had forgotten about that deal. It was one of a number of memory lapses Collins experienced at the inquiry.

At one stage, it was put to him that he was having difficulty in telling the truth. Judge Alan Mahon intervened following an objection from Collins's lawyer: "There is a number of contradictions. There is very vague recollection. More than that, very poor recollection even to a greater extent than we might normally be used to. It is a matter for Mr Collins to give evidence accurately and truthfully. And he is just being warned. It is only fair to him that it be made clear to him." In the cases where Collins couldn't remember, the production of documents managed to jog his memory. By contrast, it is crystal clear about the B/T account. It definitely didn't stand for Bertie and Tim.

Pilgrim Group had an early success. In the late 1980s, the state training agency for the catering industry, CERT, moved from offices in Ailesbury Road, Dublin 4, across the Liffey to Amiens Street. The agency was then under the control of the Department of Labour, whose minister was Bertie Ahern. The chairman of CERT at the time was Jim Nugent, who would come to public attention in 2006 as one of the group who contributed to Ahern's alleged first dig-out.

CERT was moving into Ahern's constituency. It is common in Irish politics for ministers to take advantage of a situation to bring business into their own patch. What was unusual was that two firms of architects were appointed to oversee development of the Amiens Street premises. A leading Dublin firm was engaged, and so was the Pilgrim Group.

In the early 1990s, Collins developed a business relationship with Frank Dunlop. In a statement to the tribunal years later, Collins said he had no personal or business relationship with Dunlop. When a record of the extensive range of contacts between them was pointed out to him – including phone records and diary entries – Collins said he had meant he didn't move in Dunlop's circle.

Dunlop advertised himself as a public-relations consultant and lobbyist. On that basis, Collins went to him on behalf of at least four clients seeking to have land rezoned. Collins always maintained he had no idea that Dunlop's lobbying included bribing councillors. When he gave evidence on the matter, on 2 April 2006, the tribunal lawyer, Patricia Dillon, asked him about the kind of service he thought Dunlop provided.

Dillon: Did you ever ask Mr Dunlop, how successful are you in lobbying the councillors?
Collins: I did not, no.
Dillon: Did you ever ask him about how he went about it?
Collins: No.
Dillon: Did you ever ask him what interaction he had with councillors?
Collins: I did not, no.
Dillon: Did you ever ask him about how he went about lobbying the councillors?
Collins: I did not, no.
Dillon: Did you ever discuss political donations to councillors?
Collins: I did not.
Dillon: Did you ever discuss corruption with Mr Dunlop?
Collins: I certainly did not.
Dillon: Were you aware of allegations, that there were allegations floating around that there was corruption in Dublin County Council?
Collins: Well, I wasn't aware of allegations.

Dillon: Were you aware of newspaper articles about corruption and concern?
Collins: I was aware of paper stories, yes.
Dillon: What did you discuss with Mr Dunlop?
Collins: I discussed would he take on … would he take on the job.

In one of their business deals, Dunlop maintains that Collins was aware that councillors would have to be bribed. A consortium that owned a plot of eighteen acres in Cloghran, near Dublin Airport, wanted the land rezoned from agricultural to industrial use. According to Dunlop, Tim Collins introduced him to one of the consortium, businessman John Butler, in January 1993. Dunlop claims that Collins said at the meeting: "I know that you will have to do things with the councillors."

Questioned at the tribunal as to whether Collins stated explicitly that councillors would have to be bribed, Dunlop said: "Both he [John Butler] and Mr Collins said that they were aware that some councillors would require payment for their support."

Asked if Collins had stated explicitly that he knew Dunlop would be paying councillors, Dunlop replied: "We were three grown-up men sitting and talking about the development of land for rezoning purposes. We were not talking about bringing councillors out to lunch."

Butler and Collins deny vehemently that they were ever made aware that Dunlop was paying councillors for their votes. Collins said the allegation had hurt his family.

The land in question was bought for £210,000 in 1990. Following the successful rezoning in 1993, it was sold three years later for £1.6 million.

Everybody made a few bob out of it. Dunlop was paid

around £68,000 for his services. Collins Consultancy received £29,613 and Pilgrim was paid £19,700.

At the same time that Collins was sourcing land for clients and hiring Dunlop to lobby, back in Drumcondra, tens of thousands were flowing into the B/T account.

There is no suggestion and absolutely no evidence that there was any connection between Collins's business dealings and the health of the B/T account.

* * *

Tim Collins first came to public attention in the early years of the twenty-first century following a controversy about serious profits being made on land acquired by the state. The Battle of the Boyne site in Oldbridge, County Meath, is of huge historic significance. The battle took place in 1690 and is regarded as a defining conflict between Catholic and Protestant forces, which has resonated down through the centuries.

A number of efforts were made to develop the 450-acre site. In the mid-1990s, a consortium looked at the possibility of developing a hotel and leisure complex. Frank Dunlop and the controversial TD Liam Lawlor were among those involved. Then, in 1997, the site was bought for £2.68 million by the McCann family, which has a controlling interest in the fruit-importing firm Fyffes. Collins had introduced the family to the site. A company was formed for the purchase, under the name Deep River. Collins received a shareholding of 12.5 per cent of the company.

Less than two months after the purchase of the property, the Minister for Foreign Affairs, David Andrews, announced that the government was going to develop the site as part of the evolving Peace Process in Northern Ireland. This was fortuitous for the new owners. Their property had just increased in value.

In 2000, negotiations to secure the property were completed. The final purchase price was £7.85 million, three times what the owners had paid three years previously.

An investigation by the Comptroller and Auditor General the following year revealed that the site had been valued at £8.5 million by the vendor, and "between £4 million and £7 million" by the Office of Public Works's own valuer. There was no explanation for the huge disparities in valuation between the vendors and the OPW, or for the large spread of the OPW's valuation. How could a site be valued at anything between £4 million and £7 million?

A further unorthodox element to the transaction was the manner in which the state purchased the property. Instead of merely buying the site, the OPW bought the company that owned the site, Deep Water. The effect of this was that the vendors were exempt from paying capital-gains tax on the sale. This deprived the Revenue Commissioners – which, like the OPW, is a state body – of around £920,000 that would have accrued if the deal had been done in the normal manner.

This was the first, and one of the very few times, that the OPW had purchased a property in a manner that effectively facilitated tax avoidance.

According to the Comptroller and Auditor General's report, "The option of purchasing the lands directly from the company was never available to the OPW and negotiations were carried out on the basis that the acquisition would be by way of purchase of the share capital of the company."

There was no explanation as to why the OPW did not insist on buying the site in the usual way.

The tripling of the site's value and the exemption from tax

on the sale left Collins with a tidy sum of £600,000 for his 12.5 per cent of Deep Water.

When the matter came before the Public Accounts Committee later, Fine Gael's Michael Noonan was not impressed. "I find it peculiar that an agency of the state should assist in tax avoidance ... it does not seem right that the Office of Public Works should enter into arrangements involving the avoidance of tax. I am choosing my words. It was not illegal or improper, but it was, at least, peculiar. Many citizens would find it a little strange."

Collins's involvement inevitably led to questions as to whether Ahern had exercised any influence on any aspect of the initial purchase and extraordinary sale of the site. He vehemently denied any impropriety.

In the Dáil, on 14 November 2001, Ahern said he was very happy to reply to questions raised by Noonan about the matter. "I understand the site, which was sold on a number of occasions by previous owners, was bought in 1997 although I am not sure of the precise date. The Department of Foreign Affairs issued its first statement on 8 January 1998, which statement did not refer to the purchase of the site.

"It was at the end of 1998 that solicitors representing the owners of the site came forward to state that this site of historical value could be bought. I accept that the deputy is not making any allegations and that he raised this matter in a fair manner. Those who bring up this matter are adding one and one to get eleven just because I know somebody who worked for the company that ultimately bought the site. I am aware that is the issue and I am glad that it is being dealt with.

"I welcome the opportunity to put on the record once more that I had no knowledge of what was happening to the site until my adviser brought it to my attention that the solicitor representing the owners wished to engage with the state. I had no part in the sale as the matter was referred to the Office of Public Works and the Department of Foreign Affairs. The record and the officials concerned will show that I was not very enthusiastic about the issue, but another forum will look ultimately at that. I appreciate that Deputy Noonan is showing concern, but he has raised the question of my involvement and that of those for whom I am responsible.

"I had very little involvement and the involvement of others commenced after the sale of the site. I did not know at the time that somebody I have known quite well for many years was associated with the owners of the site. It was with some shock that I discovered much later this man's involvement because I understand how these matters operate."

His shock that his buddy Collins was involved in the deal brings to mind other controversies that swirled around St Luke's. According to Ahern's words in the Dáil, the two men never discussed that Collins was going to buy, and subsequently become the owner of, the historic site until late in the day – this despite Ahern's involvement in the Peace Process and his known love of history.

This was also the case with Richardson, when he was employed by Ken Rohan, who was lobbying the Department of Finance for a tax break when Ahern was the relevant minister. Ahern and Richardson never spoke of Rohan's dilemma, according to both men.

So it was with Celia Larkin's controversial £30,000 loan from the B/T account. She never discussed it with Ahern until after the deal was done. Neither did one of the alleged B/T committee, Joe Burke. All of which raises a pertinent question: what exactly did the Drumcondra mafia actually talk about?

* * *

A couple of years later, at the planning tribunal, Tim Collins couldn't remember crucial aspects about the deal that had netted him more than half a million pounds.

Patricia Dillon asked him about his business dealings.

Dillon: Would you ever, for example, have been given a share of a deal, a specific percentage share of a deal?
Collins: Never. Never in my life got a share of a deal or anything like that.
Dillon: Did you . . . were you ever entitled to a share in a company in relation to a land transaction that you brought to the table, as it were?
Collins: None whatsoever. No.
Dillon: You are absolutely clear about that?
Collins: I wish I was. But I certainly am absolutely sure, yeah.
Dillon: When I'm talking about a share. I'm talking about possibly a share in a company that might have had an interest in the land, for example?
Collins: Certainly not.

When the details of his major windfall were pointed out to him a few hours later, he remembered that he had forgotten about that particular deal.

Dillon: And how much were you paid for your 12.5 per cent, Mr Collins?
Collins: £600,000.
Dillon: And when you were asked earlier this morning had you ever been paid a shareholding, by way of a shareholding in land, you told the tribunal that the answer was no. And you were then asked were you ever

. . . were you ever paid your fee by way of being given shares in a company that owned the land and you answered no.

Collins: That's true, I did. And I was mistaken.

Collins was called as a witness a number of times at the planning tribunal. Principally, his appearances were related to his involvement with Dunlop and, later, with the B/T account, which didn't stand for Bertie and Tim.

On the last day of the tribunal's hearing, 29 October 2008, evidence taken from Collins was read into the record to accommodate him as he was in ill-health.

21

A JOE SHOW AND JOBS FOR THE BOYS

Nobody will ever accuse Bertie Ahern of quietly and coldly dropping his old friends when he became successful and powerful. Quite the opposite. Although there are some in Fianna Fáil who believe he should have been more ruthless in distancing himself from some of the more controversial members of his circle, Ahern has been loyal to a fault. With a couple of additions – and precious few falling by the wayside – the people he had around him when he embarked on his extraordinary political journey still by and large make up his circle of friends.

One of his most enduring relationships during that time has been his friendship with builder Joe Burke. Although there would be strains between them during the three and a half decades that followed their meeting as neighbours in the Pinebrook estate in Artane, Ahern and Burke would stick by each other through thick and thin. This was never more apparent than when Ahern turned up with Burke by his side at Fairyhouse Racecourse for the Irish Grand National at Easter

2009 – a very obvious show of solidarity with a friend who had been through the mill over the previous year or so.

Burke was never renowned for canvassing voters, and there have been suggestions that, in later years, he was no longer part of Ahern's inner circle of confidants – indeed, that he had never really been "a player at a high level". But, for all that, the Donegal man has never been too far away from the action in St Luke's.

As well as being one of the pioneers around Ahern for his breakthrough in the 1977 general election, he was – unlike Tim Collins and Des Richardson – a member of Fianna Fáil, even getting elected as a councillor on Dublin Corporation for the party in 1985. When St Luke's was acquired, he was one of the trustees in whose name the building was held. He was also chairman of the house committee of St Luke's and was involved in fundraising activities for the cumann, including the annual dinner at the Royal Hospital Kilmainham and, later, Clontarf Castle. Since the early 1980s, the constituency office account in AIB Bank – which was operated by a finance committee – was in the names of Burke and Ahern.

Burke might not have had the political nous of a Chris Wall or been as successful in business as Richardson and Collins, but there is no mistaking his place on the St Luke's podium – even if he seemed, at times, like a lightning rod for controversies that would prove highly embarrassing for Ahern.

During his spell as vice-chairman of Dublin Corporation's planning and development committee in the late 1980s, Burke earned a reputation as a strong advocate of building houses and roads. "He was very forceful on planning issues. My recollection is that he chaired most meetings," says a fellow councillor.

However, in the 1991 local elections, Burke lost his council seat. While the point has been made that, ironically for such a close friend of Ahern, he had little appetite for the grind of local politics, it was probably more significant that he was now up against two sitting Fianna Fáil TDs in the Clontarf ward – Ivor Callely and Ahern's former nemesis in Dublin Central, John Stafford.

It was around this time that he moved into pub refitting. His refurbishment work included two of the Drumcondra Mafia's favourite watering-holes, Fagan's and the Beaumont House. Burke developed a reputation for doing the work quickly and without frills and for putting in low bids.

A young architect, Philip Sheedy, who would be at the centre of one of the biggest judicial controversies in the history of the state, did some work for him. Sheedy had received a four-year sentence for dangerous driving causing death while under the excessive influence of alcohol, but was released nearly two years early by Judge Cyril Kelly, who was not the original sentencing judge. Queries were raised about his premature release, and it subsequently emerged that Supreme Court judge Hugh O'Flaherty had asked the county registrar to put the case back on the list for hearing. The story caused a massive controversy when it broke in early 1999, prompting an official inquiry.

In an unprecedented development, Kelly and O'Flaherty were effectively forced to resign by the Fianna Fáil–Progressive Democrat government headed by Ahern. Despite this, Ahern's partner Celia Larkin was one of a stream of well-wishers to visit the O'Flaherty family home in Ballsbridge on the day of his resignation.

However, the real political fall-out came for Ahern when the *Sunday Tribune* revealed that, prior to Sheedy being released from prison, the Taoiseach had made representations on his behalf to secure day release for him – Ahern emphatically denied he had ever enquired about early (as opposed to day) release. Ahern had informed his Tánaiste and PD leader Mary Harney about this, but a serious rift developed between the two when Ahern appeared publicly to dismiss her concerns and denied that Harney had asked him to make a statement to the Dáil on the issue. Harney refused to attend a cabinet meeting and the future of the government was seriously threatened. Finance minister Charlie McCreevy, who was close to Harney, managed to bring the two sides back together. Ahern defused the issue by going into the Dáil to answer questions about it. Harney later told Stephen Collins for his book on the PDs, *Breaking the Mould*, "The closest the coalition came to breaking up was over the Sheedy issue. He told me he was going to go in and tell the Dáil all about the representations that had been made to him. When he didn't do it, I was bloody livid."

It also emerged, before the story on Ahern's representations broke, that Joe Burke had visited Sheedy in Shelton Abbey prison in October 1998, a few weeks before his release, and just a week before a High Court action was due to start against Burke for alleged breach of contract over work on a pub. The case was put back to January and Sheedy, who by then had been freed, was in court to appear as a witness.

There is no suggestion that Burke's visit and Sheedy's subsequent release were in any way linked. Burke insisted that Ahern had known nothing about the case before the controversy about the early release broke or about his visit to Shelton Abbey. "I absolutely never spoke to him about it, and he didn't mention it to me," Burke said. In his statement to the Dáil on the Sheedy affair, Ahern said he had made a routine inquiry, through his private secretary, following correspondence from Sheedy's father, also Philip, who was an employee of Fás. The response from the Department of Justice was that it was too early in Sheedy's sentence for day release. Ahern says that once this response was received the matter was dropped; he did not press it and no political pressure was subsequently applied to get Sheedy released.

There is no evidence that Ahern had any involvement in Sheedy's release although the point was regularly made in the aftermath of the scandal that there was never a satisfactory explanation as to why the two judges and the registrar had acted as they did. The controversy faded away, although it flared up again a year later with the government's ill-advised – and subsequently abandoned – attempt to appoint O'Flaherty to the European Investment Bank.

At the height of the controversy in 1999, Ahern attempted to play down Burke's political influence. The Taoiseach said that, despite how people had sought to portray him, Burke was a "fairly good builder" but he was not Ahern's closest adviser or confidant, the leader of his constituency organisation or the political mastermind behind him. Ahern claimed that Burke had not canvassed since 1991 and did not even attend meetings of the organisation.

Responding to a jokey query from Labour's Pat Rabbitte, across the floor of the house, as to whether he would put Burke on a prison-visiting committee, the Taoiseach said: "I do not think that would be advisable. He was on the Port and Docks Board and I think the former minister, Mr Wilson, would have appointed him – it was that long ago. He is a good friend and would have helped me with social nights and other fundraising measures but he is not a political heavyweight of any kind."

Yet three years later, this political lightweight, whom Ahern did not think it advisable to appoint to a prison-visiting committee, was given the extremely plum job of chairman of the Dublin Port Company. The appointment was made in the wake of the calling of the 2002 general election, by the then marine minister Frank Fahey, after Burke had apparently asked Ahern for the job.

Despite his less than flattering portrayal of Burke in the Dáil three years earlier, Ahern strongly defended the appointment, arguing Burke had "a number of attributes", including his wife's family, which was "very involved in the port, is from the port and lived in the port". Perhaps if they had lived beside the Phoenix Park, Fianna Fáil would have run Burke for the presidency.

Burke remained as chairman for seven years. However, he stepped down from the board in early 2009, three years before his second term was due to expire and just months after Fine Gael had questioned his continuing involvement after a High Court ruling restricted his role as a company director for five years unless certain capital funding conditions were met.

The High Court restriction order had been sought by the liquidator of Burke's pub refurbishment company, which went into liquidation in 2006. Justice Kevin Feeney put a stay on the restriction order in the event of an appeal and also noted in court that Burke had acted honestly in the conduct of the company's affairs.

Burke had argued the order was not warranted as there was no allegation of dishonesty and he genuinely believed he could raise adequate finance to help the company overcome losses sustained following the March 2004 smoking ban. However, the judge found he had acted irresponsibly in not arranging for the preparation and filing of accounts, including audited accounts, for the company for 2004 and 2005; in failing to enquire about the true financial position of the company; and in allowing the company to trade and build up tax debts when it was insolvent.

The restriction order did not legally inhibit Burke from serving on the board of Dublin Port as it had sufficient capital funding to meet the terms of the Companies Act. However, reports said that the Minister for Transport Noel Dempsey indirectly made it clear to Burke that his position was untenable and he should stand down. Burke subsequently announced his intention to stand down.

Burke's private life also went through considerable turmoil. His marriage of thirty years ended in 2004. In early 2008 he was at the centre of a complaint from a woman who had returned with him and her friend to a house in Malahide after celebrating New Year's Eve in a city-centre nightclub, although Burke vehemently denied any wrongdoing. The house in Malahide was owned by Barry English, a fellow member of the twelve alleged dig-out apostles. Neither English nor any of his family was present in the house on the night in question.

The twenty-three-year-old woman had made a 999 phone call just after five thirty a.m. on New Year's Day. According to reports, shortly after that call Burke rang Malahide garda station and invited them to come to the house, where he strongly denied any wrongdoing.

The next day gardaí found Burke slumped over the wheel of his Mercedes car in Ringsend and he was taken to nearby St Vincent's Hospital. After he had been discharged, he was treated for a serious illness at a private clinic in south Dublin.

Later in 2008, after a lengthy investigation by gardaí, it emerged that Burke would not face any charges. In a highly revealing interview with the *Irish Independent*, he said he had stopped drinking since that night and apologised for the behaviour that had led to him being questioned by gardaí. He said he regretted the embarrassment he had caused to Ahern, his family and friends. He also said that his relationship with

Fianna Fáil senator Maria Corrigan, "the love of my life", had been a casualty of the fall-out from that New Year's Eve.

Ahern had nominated Corrigan to the Seanad in 2007 and Burke, in that interview with the *Irish Independent*, was upfront about his attempt to use his influence with Ahern to secure the nomination: "The Taoiseach had eleven nominations and some had to go to the Greens and the PDs, but if I said I didn't have a word in his ear everybody would know I was lying," he said.

* * *

Joe Burke wasn't the only one to do well out of his association with Ahern. In February 2007, the then Labour leader Pat Rabbitte asked in the Dáil was there "anybody in the Drumcondra retinue who has not been appointed to one agency or another"?

Ahern, in typical hangdog fashion, replied "A handful of poor people from Drumcondra are beleaguered because they have known me for forty years but that is how it is." He claimed he had appointed to state boards more "card-carrying members of the Labour Party, who were paraded in prominent positions at that party's conferences" than residents of Drumcondra.

If that is true, then the card-carrying members of the Labour Party have done remarkably well because the list of state appointments from Ahern's circle of friends and associations is a long one.

Five of the twelve men Ahern identified in 2006 as donors to him in the two dig-outs have served on public boards – Burke, Des Richardson, Jim Nugent, David McKenna and Padraic O'Connor. Ahern's close friend and solicitor Gerry Brennan, who was allegedly involved in organising a dig-out, was appointed to the board of Telecom Éireann in November 1992.

Where Burke's elevation to the chair of Dublin Port probably proved the most contentious, Padraic O'Connor's appointment by Charlie McCreevy as chairman of ACC Bank in 1999 is probably the least, given his background in the Department of Finance, the Central Bank, IBI Treasury and as managing director of NCB Stockbrokers.

Des Richardson, who has become a successful and wealthy businessman, was appointed to the board of Aer Lingus in November 1997, serving until November 2002. Aer Lingus would traditionally have been seen as one of the most attractive state boards to serve on because it entitled directors and their families to concession-rate travel. He also served a term on the National Authority for Occupational Safety and Health, a forerunner to the Health and Safety Authority.

Jim Nugent served three terms as chairman of the state tourism training agency, CERT, although his initial appointment predated Ahern's presence in government. He was also appointed to the board of the Central Bank in February 1998, serving until February 2003.

David McKenna, who during the 1990s ran the high-profile publicly quoted recruitment firm Marlborough, was a member of the board of Enterprise Ireland from March 1999 to March 2001. He was estimated to be worth more than €60 million at one point, but Marlborough Recruitment collapsed in 2002.

The appointments were by no means restricted to the dig-out donors. Celia Larkin was appointed to the National Consumer Agency (NCA) in 2005. This proved highly controversial, with the opposition accusing Ahern of engaging in party-political cronyism. The controversy flared up again in May 2009 when fellow board member Eddie Hobbs quit the agency after Larkin reportedly rejected his calls to stand down over a loan she had received from Irish Nationwide. This was the loan that had been fast-tracked and personally authorised by the building society's chief executive Michael Fingleton, and Hobbs claimed it reinforced perceptions of cronyism, whether they were valid or not. He said the revelation of the loan was the "straw that broke the camel's back" and that he was not the only board member to be concerned about Larkin's presence as a director; the loan revelation and previous disclosures at the Mahon Tribunal had "raised question marks in the public mind" and were "damaging to the public perception of the NCA".

By the time of this controversy, Larkin had received over €55,000 in fees and expenses from her role on the NCA board since 2006.

Chris Wall, probably Ahern's closest political ally in Dublin Central, was appointed to the board of Aer Lingus in 1998 and served as a director until March 2009. After the 2007 general election, Ahern also nominated him to serve as a senator for the final weeks of the twenty-second Seanad, filling one of the seats vacated by senators who had been elected TDs. The so-called "weekend senator" appointments are highly coveted because they guarantee unrestricted lifelong access to Leinster House, including the members' bar and restaurant, and free parking.

One of those senators who had been elected as a TD was Cyprian Brady, who had run Ahern's constituency office in Drumcondra for years and had become an increasingly important figure in St Luke's. Brady was himself one of the Taoiseach's nominations to the Seanad in 2002 and served there until, in 2007, he won a seat in Dublin Central. Brady's appointment to the Seanad is understood to have caused some tensions in the ranks of the Drumcondra Mafia with at least one other key figure believing he himself was in line for the position. As it was, Brady got the nod and went on to greater things in the Lower House.

Tim Collins was appointed as a director of Enterprise Ireland in July 1998 but resigned from the board in early 1999 for personal reasons.

The late Tony Kett was co-opted onto Ahern's seat in Dublin City Council and was elected to the Seanad in 1997, 2002 and 2007.

His near namesake Tony Kenna, a low-profile businessman who enjoys a close relationship with both Des Richardson and Ahern, served on the board of Bord Gáis from 1998 until 2003.

Dominic Dillane, who became a central figure at St Luke's in later years, was appointed to the board of Fáilte Ireland in 2003. He lectures in tourism management at DIT Bolton Street. Another key St Luke's strategist, Paul Kiely, served on the board of CIÉ and Great Southern Hotels.

Long-time associate Paddy Duffy – who worked for Ahern in the Departments of Finance and An Taoiseach – was on the board of Fás for four years between 1988 and 1992. In June 1999 he was at the centre of a minor controversy when he resigned as special adviser to Ahern after it emerged that he was a director of Dillon Consultants, which had advised communications company NTL on its purchase of Cablelink from two state companies, RTÉ and Telecom Éireann. Duffy came under pressure to quit after the Tánaiste Mary Harney described as "totally unacceptable" and a "dangerous conflict of interest" that he was a director of the company.

Niall Ring, a well-known Fianna Fáil activist in Dublin Central until he won a seat on Dublin City Council in June 2009 as an independent candidate, served on the board of the IDA, while Ahern appointed Maria Kennedy, who ran Fagan's for a period, to the board of CERT in the late 1980s when he was Minister for Labour.

Ahern has given somewhat contradictory statements on his appointments of friends and associates to key state positions. In his Bryan Dobson interview on RTÉ in September 2006, he said: "I might have appointed somebody, but I appointed them because they were friends, not because of anything they had given me." But he later said he had appointed only a limited number of friends to key positions: "I have many friends who, with the greatest respect, lack the knowledge, expertise and experience to serve on boards. The number of those people whom one would appoint is limited." Anyone he nominated for a state board, he added, when another minister was making an appointment, "had the knowledge, expertise and experience required".

Ahern's comment to Dobson that he appointed people to state boards because they were his friends was referred to as part of a complaint by a member of the public to the Standards in Public Office Commission following Ahern's admission that he had received "loans" from friends in 1994. Under the commission's rules, state appointments "should be made on the basis of merit, taking into account the skills, qualifications and experience of the person to be appointed". After consideration, SIPO decided not to proceed further with the complaint because there was "no basis on which to initiate an investigation under the Ethics in Public Office Acts 1995 and 2001".

Whatever about the merits or otherwise of his state appointments, the perception among those in politics watching the Drumcondra Mafia from the outside is that, further down the scale, Ahern had always been good at "looking after" his friends and supporters. "It was a *quid pro quo*," is how one local rival put it. "Bertie was the meal ticket," is the blunt assessment of another close observer.

In a letter penned by him to a supporter in the early 1990s, uncovered during research for this book, Ahern assures the person that he has and will continue "to assist my better friends in obtaining employment" but says that there is a "difficulty" when officials have to be approached. Those comments certainly don't make him unique or suggest he had done anything improper. Many, if not most, TDs have succeeded in looking after their own. And Ahern was certainly no different from previous taoisigh in giving plum positions to supporters. But he was certainly the first to depend almost exclusively on a kitchen cabinet from outside Dáil Éireann: "He's the first leader of Fianna Fáil not to have friends in the parliamentary party. He doesn't frequent the Dáil bar or restaurant. He drinks in Fagan's and Beaumont House and the Goose with the Drumcondra Mafia. Those lads don't hang around Leinster House," says one Leinster House denizen. "Anybody worth their salt in politics has a group of hardcore supporters. They keep their eyes and ears open for anything their man needs to know. To paraphrase P. J. Mara, they make sure there's no one nibbling at his bum. If you look at Bertie's crew, Burke's done all right, Richardson's done all right, Collins has done all right. Their appointments to state boards open doors for them in business."

PART IV

THE SUMMIT

22

FAREWELL TO OLD FRIENDS

It was June 1997 and the net was closing around Ray Burke. For twenty-five years he had dodged and woven whenever scandal threatened to break over his head. Each time he batted away anybody who had the temerity to question his probity. The gardaí had been through his affairs with a fine-tooth comb. Three times they had conducted investigations into his life and work. He had emerged from it all unscathed, the man they couldn't hang anything on.

Now, though, things were different. The old certainties no longer applied. Charlie Haughey was in disgrace, his aura of invincibility torn from him by the mob. The newspapers were overcoming their habitual fear of the libel laws. A different atmosphere prevailed. Answers were being demanded. And the killer, the real sucker punch, was that it was all going down just as Burke was on the cusp of scaling a new peak in his career with an appointment as Minister for Foreign Affairs. Burke had been banished under Ahern's predecessor, Albert Reynolds. Now his friend was bringing him back in from the cold. But the mob was surrounding him just when he had thought it was safe to swagger back into government.

Within months, Burke's career would be over. The day he resigned, his north Dublin colleague Ahern would describe the circumstances of his exit as "the hounding of an innocent man". A tribunal would be established to investigate Burke's affairs. And, in time, that tribunal would come knocking on Ahern's own door.

* * *

The great unravelling had begun just over six months previously in November 1996 when the *Irish Independent* broke the story that government minister Michael Lowry had had an extension to his home paid for by supermarket magnate Ben Dunne. From such beginnings emerged the news that Charlie Haughey had received £1 million from Dunne back in the 1980s.

Haughey was by then nearly five years into a retirement during which his achievements in public life had gone through a serious revision. The cordite that had swirled around him for much of his career had been blown away. In its place there was a warm regard for somebody who, as he said himself, "had done the state some service". There were even strong rumours that he might have a run for presidency.

Then his carefully constructed edifice of elder statesman was shattered. Following the revelation about Dunne, more worms began appearing out of the muck. A tribunal was established under Justice Brian McCracken to establish the circumstances in which a serving Taoiseach had come into large sums of money.

Ahern began to distance himself from his old mentor. As

always, he went out of his way not to offend, but ensured that he got his message across. The prize of Taoiseach had once more loomed into view.

At the opening of the Fianna Fáil Ard Fheis on 18 April 1997, Ahern addressed the issues facing Haughey. He told the assembled faithful, "Certainly there would be no place in our party today for that kind of past behaviour, no matter how eminent the person involved or the extent of their prior services to the country." He went on: "Even if in the particular instance there were no favours sought or given, we could not condone the practice of senior politicians seeking or receiving, from a single donor, large sums of money or services in kind."

McCracken began his hearings. A general election was called in May. On polling day, Ahern emerged victorious.

In political terms, the 1997 election victory was probably his finest hour: he won power against all the odds. The Rainbow Coalition of Fine Gael-Labour-Democratic Left had been in power for more than two years and was perceived to be doing a good job. The economy was starting to surge ahead and the books were balanced. Despite this, they were no match for Ahern's presidential-style campaign on the hustings. In one notable photo shoot three coalition leaders were caught walking through an almost deserted Temple Bar. By contrast, Ahern was always surrounded by excited crowds, never more so than when he and Hollywood star Sylvester Stallone appeared together on a stage outside Stallone's restaurant on St Stephen's Green.

The campaign marked the birth of the "Bertie factor". Effectively, he was bringing to a national stage the attributes that had made him the undisputed top dog in Dublin Central. He put in a barnstorming performance, racing between con- stituencies and meeting as many people as was humanly possible. He crisscrossed the country by road and air, pumping every male hand, kissing every female cheek.

Ahern won the election not by default but by applying his considerable personal appeal to the campaign, allied to a ferocious appetite for the stump. In Dublin Central, the machine harvested its usual huge vote, securing 12,175 first preferences, which enabled Ahern to bring in running mate Marian McGennis on his surplus.

Throughout the campaign, he successfully distanced himself from Haughey's travails. But while he was bidding farewell to one mentor, he was sticking fast to another.

* * *

Ray Burke was first elected to the Dáil for the Dublin North constituency in 1973. His father, Paddy, had held the seat for more than twenty years and was retiring due to ill-health. Burke inherited his father's organisation, contacts and friends.

In his political life, his ways and means were not too dissimilar to those of the man down the road in Drumcondra. "Burke was an ambitious, populist politician of some ability. His loyalties lay with himself, his family and his family friends, his supporters and local party organisation, and his constituents, in that order," wrote Paul Cullen in his book, *With a Little Help from My Friends.* "He created his political machine with the support of the 'Mayo mafia' inherited from his father and felt little need to confide in circles beyond north Dublin."

In June 1974 the *Sunday Independent* published a story written by investigative journalist Joe McAnthony. Its basis was a document retrieved from the Companies Office, alleging that Burke had received £15,000 in relation to planning. The document had been filed by a company owned by two builders, Tom Brennan and Joe McGowan. The company was a vehicle to acquire lands near Dublin Airport, which the council was opposed to rezoning because of aviation dangers. The rezoning had gone through, and was supported by Burke.

By the standards of the early 1970s, all hell broke loose for a few days. Burke came out fighting. He implied that the money was paid in relation to his job as an auctioneer. At the time there was no obligation on politicians to declare commercial interests. Burke said there was no conflict of interest between his role as a politician rezoning land and as an auctioneer involved in selling it.

Throughout the affair he retained the confidence of his party leader and Taoiseach, Jack Lynch. In the fullness of time, it would emerge that Lynch asked the newly appointed government press secretary, Frank Dunlop, to put out the media fires. It was Dunlop's first encounter with the world of planning, but not his last.

The upshot of the affair was that Burke came out the other side of the storm intact. McAnthony, a respected and diligent reporter, was eventually forced to emigrate in search of work.

The gardaí investigated Burke over the affair and found nothing. They investigated him again in 1989, following more allegations. A third investigation took place four years later. Each time nothing was uncovered. In the 1989 investigation, Detective Superintendent Brendan Burns wrote in his report: "Newspaper articles were suggesting that bribery and corruption were endemic in the Planning Process. Whilst my enquiries were largely confined to the city and county of Dublin, I found this not to be the case." Time and the tribunal would prove him wrong.

There is no suggestion that the gardaí undertook their investigation with anything other than the utmost rigour. The problem was the constraints under which they had to operate. They had no access to bank accounts, and there was quite obviously no real political will to uncover any wrongdoing in this area.

Some observers of the planning process found it all too much to take. To them, it was obvious that money was changing hands, and they would have laid short odds on who among the councillors was pulling in the big bucks.

* * *

On 3 July 1995, hidden among the low-cost getaway offers and commercial notices that litter the back page of the *Irish Times*, there was a small ad entitled: "£10,000 Reward Fund". The money was offered for "information leading to the conviction or indictment of a person or persons for offences relating to land rezoning in the Republic of Ireland". It had been placed by a firm of Northern Ireland solicitors, Donnelly Neary and Donnelly. Such an innocuous notice hidden in a newspaper would ultimately cost Ray Burke his career, land him in jail, and, years down the line, unseat Ahern from his position as Taoiseach.

Two men were behind the offer. Michael Smith and Colm MacEochaidh were barristers who had a passionate interest in planning matters. They had decided to make the offer in frustration at the absolute absence of any accountability in the planning process. The small ad attracted the attention of James Gogarty, a seventy-seven-year-old retired engineer. He went to the solicitors' office and told them of his grievance over a pension with his former employer, Joseph Murphy, a millionaire Kerryman who had made his money in the UK.

Gogarty also said that Murphy's firm, JMSE, had paid Ray

Burke £30,000 to get lands in north Dublin rezoned. This had been done through Gogarty, who had gone to Burke's house in Swords and handed over the money in cash to the politician prior to the 1989 general election. Gogarty said another builder, Michael Bailey, had been present that day, and also Murphy's son, Joseph Junior.

The two barristers introduced Gogarty to a journalist, Frank Connolly. In early 1996 Connolly reported that a "senior Fianna Fáil politician" had received a large sum of money for a planning favour.

Sporadic stories followed over the next year, most of them inspired by leaks and rumours emanating from Gogarty. The matter hung around the edges of Fianna Fáil's campaign in the 1997 general election, but had no impact on voters. At one press conference, Ahern was asked about the rumours. No names were mentioned. Ahern said he had gone through the allegation in detail with the "member" concerned, and was satisfied that there was nothing to it.

The questions kept coming. In the week before polling, the Fianna Fáil director of elections, P. J. Mara, responded to an enquiry from Connolly, saying that Burke had received a political donation but there had been nothing untoward about the transaction.

Burke had been spokesman on foreign affairs in opposition and Ahern assured him that he was going to get the corresponding government portfolio. Over the following months, his career would begin to unravel. Of one thing there can be no doubt: Bertie Ahern did everything he could to protect his friend and colleague. This might have been for reasons of personal loyalty, or the desire that no scandal attach itself to the new administration. Whatever it was, his actions suggest that the last thing he wanted to find out was that Burke had done anything untoward.

Ahern and Mary Harney met in Buswells Hotel on 11 June to discuss appointments to the new government. When Ahern said he was going to appoint Burke to foreign affairs, Harney told him of the rumours she had heard. Her colleague in the PDs, Michael McDowell, had received a letter from Gogarty about the alleged JMSE payment. She asked Ahern to investigate it.

By then, Ahern had discussed the matter with Burke, who said there was no truth in it. Whether or not Burke admitted receiving the money as a political donation is unclear.

A few days later, Harney came back to Ahern. She had new information about Burke. Another source in JMSE, the husband of a PD election candidate, had informed her that Burke had received £60,000 for a planning favour. This man, Gay Grehan, was a second source, completely independent of Gogarty. Both sources had been employees of JMSE.

Ahern had also received a letter from Gogarty on the matter, although he has never specified whether or not he actually saw it.

If Burke had told him he had received the cash in question, then Ahern must have been suspicious. If he said he hadn't received it, what donation had Mara been referring to when he briefed Connolly during the election campaign?

Ahern reverted to type. He moved with caution, and purported to seek further information before making a decision. He detailed the party chief whip – and likely ministerial candidate – Dermot Ahern to go to London and meet Joseph Murphy Junior, the son of the JMSE owner. Dermot Ahern flew to Heathrow and met Murphy in an airport hotel. The bones of their meeting consisted of three questions: did JMSE give Burke money? Were any favours asked in return? Were any favours granted? Murphy replied each time in the negative.

Dermot Ahern travelled to London in good faith. What he didn't know was that his boss, who had given him his riding instructions, had already acquired much of that information.

Michael Bailey had told Bertie Ahern that Gogarty had given a "political donation" to Burke, which had no strings attached, on behalf of JMSE.

Ahern now had conflicting stories as to whether or not Burke had received a large wad of cash. He could have interviewed Gogarty. He could have interviewed Gay Grehan. Both might have been in a position to throw light on the affair. Instead, he did nothing. A cursory investigation designed to check whether Burke was fit to be appointed to high office was not completed. On 24 June Burke went with Ahern and the rest of the appointees to Áras an Uachtaráin to receive his seal of office. If the new Taoiseach and his Minister for Foreign Affairs thought that was the end of the matter, they were soon disabused of the notion.

A fortnight after the government was formed, the *Sunday Tribune* put names to the rumours that had been floating around: Ray Burke was the Fianna Fáil politician who had received £30,000.

When the continuing allegations were put to Bertie Ahern he said he'd been "up every tree in north Dublin" and hadn't found a thing. The party's general secretary, Pat Farrell, gave an interview to the *Irish Times* in which he stated: "The party leader has had the matter investigated and the investigation was satisfactory."

The following month, the *Sunday Business Post* added more detail to the story, citing JMSE as the donors of the money.

The media continued digging through the summer. By September, pressure was mounting on Burke to address the issue. On 10 September he made a speech to the Dáil, characterising it as a "line in the sand", which would bring closure: "The facts of the matter are that during the 1989 general election campaign I was visited in my home by Mr Michael Bailey of Bovale Developments Ltd, and a Mr James Gogarty," he said. "Mr Bailey was well known to me as he was a resident of north County Dublin and a long-time supporter of Fianna Fáil. I had not met Mr Gogarty previously but he was introduced by Mr Bailey as an executive of Joseph Murphy Structural Engineers – JMSE. Mr Gogarty told me JMSE wished to make a political contribution to me and I received from him in good faith a sum of £30,000 as a totally unsolicited political contribution. At no time during our meeting were any favours sought or given. I did not do any favours for, or make any representations to, anyone on behalf of JMSE, Mr Michael Bailey, Bovale Developments Limited or Mr James Gogarty either before or since 1989.

"If Mr Gogarty is the source of these allegations, then he is the author of a campaign of lies against me. I have also been the recipient of a number of anonymous threatening letters relating to these allegations. I have turned this correspondence over to the Garda.

"I am taking the opportunity to state unequivocally that I have done nothing illegal, unethical or improper. I find myself the victim of a campaign of calumny and abuse. It is totally unacceptable that this matter should be allowed to continue to fulfil an agenda which has nothing to do with election contributions or any other aspect of reasonable or reasoned political debate in public life. If any further untruths are published about me, I will take all necessary steps to vindicate my good name and reputation."

264

In time, the speech would be viewed as a litany of self-serving lies.

A few weeks later, *Magill* magazine published a letter from Bailey to JMSE, dating from 1989, promising to "procure" planning permission for lands in north Dublin.

By then Harney was pushing Ahern for a public inquiry. Ahern insisted that Burke's name not be used in the terms of reference. The initial advert posted in 1995 had prompted fifty-two allegations of planning corruption. If there was to be an inquiry, it would be an all-encompassing one, not a vehicle to be used against Burke alone.

The establishment of a tribunal to examine planning matters was announced in the Dáil. Burke was to stay on as minister through the inquiry, which, Ahern suggested, should complete its work by Christmas. (As it was to turn out, the tribunal sat for more than eleven years, with 917 days of public hearings, ending on 3 December 2008.)

Then, in early October, another Burke story hit the headlines, detailing how he had issued passports to a Saudi family under a scheme that awarded Irish passports in return for investment in the country. On 7 October Burke, finding his position untenable, resigned. That afternoon, Ahern spoke movingly in the Dáil about the political demise of his friend at the hands of assorted oppressors. "Those who choose politics as a profession know from the outset that they are putting their lives on the line in their determination to serve the public. They have to accept the criticism which attends their decisions and their every action.

"Their families too learn to take the brunt of stinging remarks, which often overstep the boundaries of civility and courtesy. In the case of Ray Burke, I see a much more sinister development, the persistent hounding of an honourable man to resign his important position on the basis of innuendo and unproven allegations.

"Some who would class themselves as protectors of basic civil rights have harried and hounded this man without according him the basic right of due process, which deems us innocent unless proven guilty. The according of due process is not just a basic right but the very essence of common decency."

More than a decade later, when the greatest politician of his generation would resign office over investigations into his personal finances, some of his supporters would decry the "hounding of an honourable man to resign his important position on the basis of innuendo and unproven allegations". Of course, the indignant supporters were very careful not to use those specific words.

*   *   *

The planning tribunal was established on 4 November 1997, under the chairmanship of High Court judge Feargus Flood. Following initial enquiries, and further allegations from the public, the terms of reference were broadened the following year.

The crucial term of reference, which was arguably inserted initially to ensure that Burke would not be the sole focus, was Section A (5):

In the event that the Tribunal in the course of its inquiries is made aware of any acts associated with the planning process which may in its opinion amount to corruption, or which involve attempts to influence by threats or deception or inducement or otherwise to com-promise the disinterested performance of public duties, it shall report on such acts and should in particular make recommendations as to the effectiveness and improvement of existing legislation governing corruption in the light of its inquiries.

This effectively gave the tribunal carte blanche to investigate anything resembling corruption that could be tied to the planning process. Over the decade that followed, it would result in a major investigation into planning corruption in Dublin City Council, which would uncover the activities of Frank Dunlop.

It would also lead to a major investigation of the circumstances surrounding the failed attempts of a truculent returning immigrant to develop two projects in Dublin. The man in question would claim that his failures were largely attributed to wholesale corruption. His name was Tom Gilmartin, and he would come to haunt the career of Bertie Ahern.

23

TOO MANY YEARS A-GROWING

All was quiet in the Printworks building in Dublin Castle. The personnel from the planning tribunal had departed for lunch. At one of the long tables reserved for lawyers, the former assistant city and county manager George Redmond ate a light lunch. Over at the press bench, a few reporters were leafing through newspapers and nibbling sandwiches. The actor and writer Joe Taylor, who performed re-enactments from the tribunal on radio, sat nearby. At the back of the cavernous hall, near the door, a uniformed prison officer loitered.

Redmond stood up and lowered himself to the powder-blue carpet. He began doing press-ups, belying his eighty-two years. He had been brought to Dublin Castle that morning from prison, where he was serving a sentence for corruption (the conviction was subsequently set aside). He was representing himself at the inquiry because, he said, he could no longer afford a lawyer. His questioning of witnesses was often rambling, sometimes straying from enquiry into long soliloquies of self-justification. At one stage, he asked the judge could he leave his position and move next to the witness box because he was having grave difficulty hearing the witness. The request was granted.

Back at the lunch hour, Redmond completed his schedule of press-ups. He sauntered over to the press bench, under the watchful eye of the prison officer at the back of the room. He approached a reporter from the *Irish Examiner*, Juno McEnroe.

Redmond asked the young man could he use his mobile phone. He explained that in prison he was only permitted three brief calls a day. He wanted to phone his wife.

Juno sympathised with his plight, but he wasn't in a position to help. The power was low on his phone and he couldn't risk being isolated from the Examiner's Office. Redmond shrugged, his face softening into the hangdog expression for which he had become noted over recent years.

Nearby, Taylor observed what was afoot. Six long years covering the inquiry had engendered in him a finely honed sense of the ridiculous. He reckoned he could get a sketch out of what he had just seen. And he had the perfect title for it – Juno and the Payphone.

It was early spring 2004. In the bowels of Dublin Castle the planning tribunal was plodding on to infinity. Outside, large numbers of the public thought it was descending into an expensive and pointless farce.

* * *

Through the first two years of its existence, the planning tribunal had stumbled and stuttered through James Gogarty's evidence. Then, in April 2000, the picture changed. A stuttering inquiry overnight became a focused light shining on widespread corruption. The crucial term of reference, which many believed was designed to deflect the focus from Burke, led into other dark corners. The tribunal was obliged to follow up allegations that were shown to have at least the possibility of substance.

One name kept recurring: Frank Dunlop. In April 2000, he was called to give evidence. At first, he denied any wrongdoing. Then he gave the tribunal the name of a councillor whom he believed to be corrupt. The councillor, Tom Hand, was dead. Throughout the decade of tribunals, dead men were blamed for a lot of crimes and misdemeanours.

The following week, the tribunal lawyer introduced a hidden bank account of Dunlop's. He was asked about suspicious movements of money into and out of it. He couldn't explain them and was asked to go home and consider his evidence.

The next day, Dunlop returned and began telling all about his life and times at the nexus of planning corruption in Dublin. The reaction in the media and politics was explosive. For decades, everybody suspected that corruption of this level had been going on, and now, finally, it was getting an airing. The tribunal had a second key witness.

The third key witness was, like Gogarty, a man scorned. Tom Gilmartin was from Sligo but had emigrated to the UK in the 1950s. He had made a success of his life, ultimately getting involved in property development. In the late 1980s, he had returned to Ireland with a headful of dreams. His experience in the booming UK economy had left him with an eye for potential development. He spotted a largely derelict site on Bachelor's Walk in Dublin city centre as ideal for major development. A retail element and a hi-tech bus depot for CIÉ were among the uses he could see for it.

Other forces were ranged against him, and in the end the Bachelor's Walk proposal never came to anything. According to Gilmartin, the Dublin city and county manager, George Redmond, was constantly putting up "roadblocks".

While he was in Dublin, he came across another site he reckoned was ideal. Quarryvale was at the junction of the N6 Galway road and the proposed M50 Dublin ring road. He set about exploring options, and attempting to buy up the land. He also began looking at how he would get the land rezoned to facilitate a large retail development.

Ahern and two of the Drumcondra Mafia, Joe Burke and Tim Collins, were to feature in the version of events that Gilmartin told the planning tribunal.

Gilmartin said he met Ahern four times in connection with his projects, and he had initially been under the impression that Ahern was "a straight man who wouldn't see him wrong".

Ahern, the local TD, appeared to be enthusiastic about the developer's plans. After Gilmartin initially made contact with him, Ahern put him in touch with his right-hand man, Joe Burke, then a Dublin City councillor. The meetings and conversations between Gilmartin and Burke would become a source of great contention in the evidence of both men.

One of the most serious allegations Gilmartin made was that Burke asked him for £500,000 on behalf of Ahern. Burke and Ahern deny vehemently that any money was requested from Gilmartin. Burke told the planning tribunal in 2008 that the allegation was "outrageous" and that he had "never solicited any money on behalf of Mr Bertie Ahern, nor has he ever asked me to".

Gilmartin says that Burke came to his office at Dublin's St Stephen's Green in September 1990 and, during a discussion on Quarryvale, mentioned a figure of £500,000. Gilmartin claims he initially thought he was referring to the deposit he paid for the land from the Corporation, but that Burke then referred to the "big bucks" he would make from Quarryvale.

Gilmartin further claims that Burke told him he could trust Ahern, at the time Minister for Labour, and asked would he not be prepared to pay the money because Ahern was looking after him?

Burke categorically denies this and says that no sum was sought by him on any occasion. He says his recollection is that the one meeting they had was about the Bachelor's Walk development and not Quarryvale.

Gilmartin has also said that, after the meeting at his offices on St Stephen's Green, Burke offered to drive him to the airport for his flight home, saying they would meet Ahern on the way. The two men drove in a pick-up truck to Fagan's and then to the Beaumont House pub, but couldn't find Ahern, at which point Gilmartin – much to Burke's chagrin – insisted on being driven to the airport lest he miss his flight. When the two arrived at the airport, Gilmartin claims he turned to Burke and remarked bitterly: "This is a great little country, isn't it?"

Burke dismisses this story out of hand. While he says he might have given Gilmartin a lift to the airport as he lived close to it, he never drove a pick-up truck, and added, "I was one of the few people who had access to the then Minister for Labour's mobile phone and I didn't have to drive around the city like a headless chicken looking for him."

Burke's version of events is backed up Ahern. The then Taoiseach told the Dáil that his friend balked at the massive nature of the Bachelor's Walk proposal. "Councillor Burke told him it would create grave difficulties for the council because it was in favour of the development in Temple Bar but was not in favour of the new bridge or the bus station on the Bachelor's Walk site." Ahern said that was the only meeting

Burke had with Gilmartin and that the former councillor was "quite adamant that he did not ask him for or about a contribution to Fianna Fáil, at my behest or otherwise".

Tim Collins featured elsewhere in the Gilmartin narrative. According to Ahern, one of the meetings he had with Gilmartin in Drumcondra was also attended by Collins. When the matter came to public attention, Ahern variously described his good and great friend as "somebody I know outside politics" and "one of my local supporters". In reality, neither description did any justice to the relationship between the two close friends.

Meanwhile, Gilmartin was busy attempting to get the Quarryvale project off the ground. A few miles away, Cork developer Owen O'Callaghan was in the initial stages of developing a designated town centre at Balgaddy in Clondalkin.

It soon became obvious to both men that there wasn't the market for two such developments. They came together to develop the Quarryvale site, which they agreed was the best option. Ultimately, Gilmartin opted out of Quarryvale and returned to the UK, having shipped major financial losses. O'Callaghan took over the project. Gilmartin has always maintained he was forced out because O'Callaghan was working in concert with the project's bankers, AIB. Both O'Callaghan and AIB deny this and point to the financial problems that Gilmartin had brought on himself as the real reason for his departure.

Later, Gilmartin would claim that he had been used and abused by various interests during his time in Dublin. He made numerous allegations against politicians, officials and O'Callaghan. Many of his claims would in time be backed up by independent witnesses. Other allegations were found to have no basis. Some of his more colourful claims concerned

Liam Lawlor, who was the local Fianna Fáil TD in west Dublin, and a man over whom a dark cloud hovered throughout his political career.

Gilmartin portrayed Lawlor as somebody constantly hustling for money, usually on the back of his political office. At one stage, Lawlor said he had been appointed a consultant to the Quarryvale development. "I wouldn't have that man consulting on a shithouse," Gilmartin told one of his business associates.

Gilmartin made allegations against George Redmond, and numerous TDs. It would come to light that he gave the then environment minister, Padraig Flynn, £50,000 in response to being told that a major contribution to Fianna Fáil would smooth the passage of his plans. Flynn trousered the money.

Gilmartin was also the source of an allegation that O'Callaghan claimed to have paid Bertie Ahern a bung of £50–80,000 to ensure that rezoning would be forthcoming for Quarryvale. Ahern and O'Callaghan have always denied that any money passed between them.

Gilmartin was contacted when the tribunal was set up. Initially, he was uncooperative. His experience of Ireland had left him bitter. He was convinced the tribunal would run into the sand and he didn't want anything to do with it.

That was until Padraig Flynn came down with a serious dose of foot-in-mouth disease. In January 1999, during an appearance he made on *The Late, Late Show*, the host Gay Byrne asked him about the allegation by Gilmartin that he had received fifty grand. Flynn wouldn't answer directly whether or not he had got the loot. Asked did he know Gilmartin, Flynn replied: "Oh, yeah. I haven't seen him now for some years. I met him. He's a Sligo man who went to England and made a lot of money. Came back. Wanted to do a lot of business in

Ireland. Didn't work out for him. He's not well. His wife isn't well. And he's out of sorts."

Over in Luton, Gilmartin was watching the show. He hit the roof. Flynn, who had been trying desperately to contact him since the allegations broke, was portraying him as unwell. The implication was that an ailment was contributing to Gilmartin's wild allegations. Within days, Gilmartin had reversed his decision to co-operate with the tribunal. He was coming home again. He was going to tell all. He'd bring down the government. It would be a long time coming, but within nine years he could claim that his allegation led to a process that ultimately saw a Taoiseach resign.

* * *

The high-water mark for the planning tribunal was the interim second report, delivered in September 2002. It detailed the extent of Ray Burke's corruption through his years in public life. Judge Feargus Flood found that Burke had received a bung, although ultimately the rezoning favour wasn't delivered. The judge found that Burke had received another bung of £35,000 from interests behind Century Radio, which had pioneered commercial radio in the country. The third major finding was that Burke had been in the pay of the builders Tom Brennan and Joe McGowan through most of his political life, and that they had given him his Swords home.

In all, eighteen witnesses were implicated in the findings. Burke was found to have received a corrupt payment. Business-men Joseph Murphy Junior, Joseph Murphy Senior (deceased), Michael Bailey, Oliver Barry, Jim Stafford, Tom Brennan, Joe McGowan and John Finnegan were deemed to have given or been complicit in giving corrupt payments. All of the above, with six other witnesses, were found to have hindered or obstructed the inquiry, and three more witnesses failed to co-operate with it.

The report was praised for its findings and the manner in which it was presented. For instance, it detailed the evidence of Joe McGowan, who had claimed that he had been involved in fevered political fundraising for Ray Burke in the UK. McGowan had claimed rather ridiculously that up to £125,000 that had passed from his accounts to Burke was the result of this political fundraising. The judge found that it was all lies.

None of those criticised in the report were ever charged with a criminal offence as a result of any investigation arising out of the report. Up to £35 million would be recouped in tax from a number of interests as a result of the inquiry into Burke's affairs. Mick Bailey and his brother Tom would eventually be shopped for €25 million in tax. Within two years, Burke would be sent to prison for six months after pleading guilty to tax evasion.

In an astute PR move, Flood ordered that the report be sold for €1 in the public interest. It became a bestseller.

On 10 October 2002, the Dáil debated the report. Taoiseach Bertie Ahern gave his verdict: "It has established the facts. Documents have been obtained through discovery, witnesses have been cross-examined and banks have been required to deliver up private accounts. Clear and conclusive findings of corruption have now been made. The report is a resounding statement of this state's determination to root out and expose corruption. In this republic nobody is above or beyond the law . . .

"The publication of the second interim report of the Flood tribunal is not the end, but only the end of the beginning of a long process. It is a process that will eventually succeed in restoring the trust and respect of the Irish people in the conduct of our public life."

By then, Ahern was in his second term as Taoiseach after a thumping general-election victory the previous May when Fianna Fáil came within a few hundred votes of winning an overall majority. He, like the Celtic Tiger, was at the peak of his powers. Fine Gael had been decimated in the election, losing many of their senior TDs. What was notable about the campaign was the complete absence of any reference to the ongoing inquiry in Dublin Castle. The tribunal simply didn't matter to the electorate. Within a few years, that would change, and Ahern's praise for the work and methods of the tribunal would be heavily revised.

In the wake of the report's publication, Flood became something of a national hero, and he wasn't one to shun the limelight. However, by then he was seventy-four and all the signs were that the inquiry had a lot of mileage left in it. Later that year, he recommended that others be appointed to sit with him.

The government attempted to find recruits in the ranks of the judiciary. Nobody would touch it with a bargepole. Judges had seen the travails to which Flood had been subjected. In addition, another long-running tribunal was under way at the far end of Dublin Castle. Michael Moriarty, regarded as a highly competent judge, was wading through resistance on all fronts in examining the financial affairs of Charlie Haughey and former government minister Michael Lowry. None of his colleagues could be persuaded to step up to a tribunal chair in the national interest.

In the end, new appointments had to be made to the bench to undertake the role. Three senior counsel were appointed Circuit Court judges, detailed to assist and ultimately take over from Flood. Alan Mahon was the most senior appointment, with the other two, Mary Faherty and Gerard Keys, appointed to sit with him.

By September 2003, Flood had retired and Mahon took over as chair of the three-person tribunal. The Flood Tribunal begat the Mahon Tribunal.

Public interest began to wane as the going got soft. A tribunal is designed to be a temporary instrument, which undertakes a public investigation to establish facts. The modern-day model was the McCracken Tribunal, set up in 1997 to investigate Charlie Haughey's finances in the first instance. That was done and dusted and the chairman had produced a concise yet detailed report in the space of six months.

But Mahon and his brother-in-inquiry further up the Castle's yard, Moriarty (son of McCracken), were dragging on. By 2003 and into 2004, Mahon was largely investigating alleged bribes to councillors of £1,000–5,000 dating from the early 1990s. The other focus was Gilmartin's allegations from the same period.

Mahon was beset by other difficulties. Lawlor and Redmond were both representing themselves and dragging out the hearings, whether by accident or design. In October 2003, Mahon himself issued a statement confirming that he had made a settlement with the Revenue Commissioners in the early 1990s for £20,000. The news was manna for the myriad interests intent on scuppering the inquiry. Comparisons were made between his settlement and the size of the alleged bribes under investigation from the same period.

On Saturday, 22 October 2005, Liam Lawlor was tragically killed in a car crash in Moscow. He had been a key figure in the tribunal's enquiries. He had been jailed three times for contempt of court after refusing to comply with orders of discovery.

The tribunal ploughed on, slowly making its way through witnesses, heading down to the Four Courts every so often to seek an order or defend itself from challenge. Outside, indifference grew. Now and again a high-profile witness would thrust the tribunal into the news, but otherwise it was a case of forgotten but not gone.

* * *

One aspect of the inquiry scurried regularly through the public psyche like a gnat: it was costing a fortune. In retrospect, the biggest mistake in setting legal fees was the failure to allow for the inquiry dragging on. A provision to reduce fees after fifty sitting days was not matched by any further reductions. As a result, those who began work for the tribunal were in the gravy. The "tribunal millionaire" became an envied and despised caricature of public discourse.

The full cost of the inquiry will not be known for many years, but a report of the Comptroller and Auditor General in February 2009 put the inquiry's own costs at €194 million. This does not include third-party legal fees, which could amount to a multiple of that. In addition, investigations by the Criminal Assets Bureau and the Revenue Commissioners in the wake of Mahon's enquiries have yielded around €50 million for the exchequer.

* * *

In December 2005, with frustration mounting about the costs and longevity of the inquiry, the Oireachtas amended the terms of reference. The tribunal would have to compile a list of the enquiries it intended to undertake and it would be confined to the items on that list. The A (5) term of reference, that allowed for any investigations into planning corruption, was effectively being binned.

The J2 list, as it was known, was completed on 28 April 2005. There would no new enquiries after that date. The tribunal was confined to those already under way. By then, its investigation into Bertie Ahern's finances had been spluttering along for six months.

* * *

Bertie Ahern's dealings with the planning tribunal dated from 1999. A Cork-based builder, Denis "Starry" O'Brien, contacted the inquiry and told lawyers that in 1989 he had paid Ahern £50,000 in the car park of the Burlington Hotel in Dublin. The money, he claimed, was handed over on behalf of Owen O'Callaghan.

It would eventually emerge that O'Brien was a forger and a liar, who bore a major grudge against O'Callaghan as a result of a failed business deal, but in 1999 the air around the tribunal was thick with allegations, and lawyers began to investigate the claim.

The following April, Frank Dunlop changed his evidence and admitted he was at the centre of extensive bribery in the planning process. In the fevered weeks that followed, the political temperature skyrocketed. There was a feeling abroad that big fish were about to be hooked.

That month, the *Sunday Business Post* published O'Brien's allegations, although it didn't name either O'Callaghan or Ahern. However, everybody who hadn't been on Mars for the previous year had a good idea who the principals were.

On Easter Monday, Ahern addressed the allegations at a

commemoration ceremony for the 1916 Rising: "I can say I never received one penny from Owen O'Callaghan, for myself, for the party, or for anyone else. I never got it in the Burlington or anywhere else. I never got money either from anything to do with Owen O'Callaghan."

O'Callaghan, for his part, blamed the allegations on "a serious personal, business or political vendetta against me". Both men issued libel proceedings.

Ahern confined his proceedings to O'Brien and didn't include the newspaper as a defendant. He brought the case to the Circuit Court rather than the High Court. Thus, the level of damages he might be awarded was limited to £30,000, but it meant that he could expect a quicker hearing, and the case would be decided by a judge rather than a jury.

He had to wait over a year to clear his name. In July 2001 he was awarded maximum damages in the Dublin Circuit Court after O'Brien effectively withdrew his allegation. Ahern told the court that on the day the offending article was published he had attended a football match. "I took more stick from the ordinary public that day than I did in my twenty-five years of politics," he said, to illustrate the effect the false allegation had had on his reputation.

He had other issues with Gilmartin, the most important being how much contact he had had with the developer when the latter was in Dublin in the late 1980s. In retrospect this was a minor issue, but for a while it appeared that it might damage the Taoiseach.

Gilmartin's scattergun approach to making allegations had rendered him toxic. When he had first emerged with them, he said he had had extensive contact with a number of senior politicians. Most remembered it differently, claiming they hardly knew the man. One of his crucial allegations was that he had been invited to an informal gathering of most of the cabinet in February 1989. Charlie Haughey, Ray Burke, Padraig Flynn, Bertie Ahern, Mary O'Rourke and Seamus Brennan were among those Gilmartin said were present at this meeting in Government Buildings.

He said that when he came out of the meeting, he was approached by a man who handed him a piece of paper detailing a foreign bank account into which he was asked to put £5 million. "You people make the Mafia look like monks," Gilmartin claimed he told this unidentified individual.

Burke, Flynn, Brennan and Ahern were all asked about the meeting, though none of them could remember it. Then Mary O'Rourke was asked and she could, because it had taken place around the time of her mother's death. Suddenly Gilmartin's credibility took a leap. He said he had spoken to Ahern four times about his projects, and that he had informed him of the "roadblocks" being put in his way by Redmond and Lawlor. He also claimed to have told Ahern about the £50,000 he had given to Padraig Flynn.

Initially, Ahern claimed to have met Gilmartin only once but then he revised this. He was adamant that Gilmartin never told him he had given money to Flynn.

When Gilmartin gave evidence in April 2004, Ahern's legal team attacked his credibility in a manner that drew rebuke from the chairman. Ahern's lawyer, Conor Maguire, referred to a 1977 District Court case in which the judge had described Gilmartin as "shifty". He also suggested that Gilmartin gave "dishonest evidence".

Mahon accused the lawyer of improper conduct, but he later withdrew the charge. There was little doubt that an attempt was being made to destroy Gilmartin's credibility. At the time, this appeared to be an extreme reaction to a man who had not made any allegation of significance against Ahern. Only later would it come out that Gilmartin was actually alleging Ahern had received a large amount of money from O'Callaghan.

Ahern gave evidence on 7 April 2004. He was in the witness stand for five hours and endured a torrid time at the hands of Gilmartin's counsel, Hugh O'Neill. He was asked repeatedly whether he stood over his own lawyer's attack on Gilmartin. Ahern didn't give a straight answer one way or the other.

Then O'Neill asked him about the meeting in Leinster House, which only Mary O'Rourke could remember: "I have to say to you that you must remember that meeting – chit-chat meeting or whatever, you must remember that. Here was a person that was of significance to you, it is someone you thought was important in so far as there was a person who could bring significant economic and employment benefits to the country or to Dublin. And I must put it to you that the meeting did take place, and that you attended it and that you remember it."

Ahern still had no recollection of it. He left the witness box bruised but unbowed. In the strictest terms his credibility was affected by his failure to dispel once and for all the notion that he had had extensive contact with Gilmartin and must therefore have been made aware of the activities of Lawlor, Redmond and Burke.

However, by then nobody really seemed to care. The workings of the tribunal were receiving a jaundiced appraisal from the public. The evidence from Mahon and Moriarty seemed to suggest that Ahern had just kept his head down while some of his colleagues were abusing their positions and enriching themselves. He didn't want to know and, some would say, who could blame him? In any event, *he* wasn't on the take, and wasn't he doing a good job running the country?

The tribunal wasn't finished with him, though. Gilmartin had alleged that O'Callaghan had told him around 1992 that he had paid Ahern sums of £50,000 and £30,000. He claimed that O'Callaghan had said that the latter payment was for the Minister for Finance's role in blocking favourable tax designation for a rival retail development at Blanchardstown.

On 15 October 2004, the tribunal wrote a private letter to Ahern, informing him of the allegation and the intention to conduct a private inquiry into it. If the allegation was found to have no substance, it would not proceed to public hearings. Therefore the matter would not come into the public domain. The letter outlined the tribunal's intention to seek an order of discovery on Ahern, which would oblige him to give access to his bank records. It wanted to see the colour of his banking. If no suspicious movements showed up in the records, he was out the door, free to leave all this tribunal stuff behind. Surely the life of a man well known to have simple tastes and little interest in money would be reflected in the simplicity of his bank accounts.

24

VICTIM ON A HIGH WIRE

The story broke in the *Irish Times* on Thursday, 21 September 2006. In a front-page report, public affairs correspondent Colm Keena wrote that the Mahon Tribunal was "investigating a number of payments to Bertie Ahern in and around December 1993, including cash payments". The details were sketchy, but the report said the amounts were between €50,000 and €100,000 in today's currency.

That day, Ahern was attending events in County Clare. Asked for a comment, he described the figures as "off the wall". Elsewhere in political and media circles there was much surprise at the revelation. Ahern had already been put through the wringer at the Mahon Tribunal over the extent of contact he had had with Tom Gilmartin. Now, out of the blue, he appeared to have money issues that warranted investigation.

The following day, he responded to calls for clarity by saying the report was the result of an "unfair, unjust leak". He immediately set a tone that his supporters adopted thereafter. The story was not the big sums of money he had received. The story was the leak. The subtext was that somebody was out to damage him, using the most grievous of tactics. He was being denied due process. He was a victim.

* * *

The concentration of emphasis on the leak was curious in one respect. Just four weeks earlier, on 20 August, the *Sunday Independent* reported on a leak from the Moriarty Tribunal, investigating Charlie Haughey's finances.

The lead story on the front page was headlined "TRIBUNAL RAPS AHERN OVER BLANK CHEQUES". The sub-head underneath declared "Taoiseach 'not unduly concerned' but opposition set to capitalise on rebuke". The report's author wrote that Moriarty was going to criticise Ahern for signing blank cheques for Haughey on behalf of the party. (Haughey was shown to have used party funds to support his lifestyle.) It was based on extracts of draft findings from Moriarty, circulated to parties who might be affected. It went on: "Mr Ahern is said by sources close to him to be 'not unduly concerned' by the nature of the tribunal chairman's criticism, which he believes to be 'minor enough'."

Clearly, somebody leaked the potential findings to the newspaper. "Sources close to" Ahern co-operated with the story. Journalists often use that phrase to describe a source who is talking off the record. Though there is no categoric evidence to suggest that Ahern leaked a file to a newspaper, it can't be denied that, as a career politician, he knew all about leaks and how to use them. A leak sprung in the dead of summer would take the heat out of the findings when they were officially released later that year. And when the spotlight was turned on his wads of cash, he was using the issue of leaks to present himself as the victim of a vicious one.

* * *

In responding to calls from the opposition to clarify the sources of the money, Ahern said: "I'm not answering what I got for my holy communion money, my confirmation money, what I got for my birthday, what I got for anything else. I'm not into that. I gave all the details of everything to do with my life to the tribunal, but I'm not under investigation for any of these things, including the unfair and unjust leak that's in the papers this morning."

It was the first time that Ahern introduced his first holy communion into an issue relating to the receipt of substantial sums of money when he was Minister for Finance. It wouldn't be the last.

It was also the first time that he claimed he had given everything to the tribunal. He would repeat this many times, but ultimately he would be shown to have been somewhat economical with the facts.

The pressure for disclosure mounted. Through the weekend, there were further calls from the opposition: "The Taoiseach may be justified in complaining about the manner in which this has come into the public domain," Labour's Joan Burton said on Saturday, "but this does not absolve him from legitimate questions that have been raised."

Ahern continued to point towards the leak of "confidential material which was made available to the Mahon Tribunal in the course of its enquiries".

He wasn't the only one concerned about the leak: Dick Roche was Minister for the Environment, the department responsible for the tribunal. He expressed himself "absolutely dismayed" that a leak had happened. "Some form of investigation will probably be needed to examine the Mahon Tribunal leak relating to the Taoiseach."

The story was now being given direction. Not only was there a leak, but it was a "Mahon Tribunal" leak. This inferred that the leak had come directly from the tribunal. Most of the public would have been unaware of the requirement to circulate documents to relevant parties prior to hearings, which routinely resulted in the springing of leaks.

Nobody was then aware that the tribunal had gone to the Four Courts to seek access to the Taoiseach's legal separation case of 1993. This was in pursuit of the tried and tested formula of "following the money". The potential for leaks was increased once the papers landed in the Four Courts. But the spin emanating from Ahern and his supporters kept implying that the leak must have come directly from the tribunal, rather than any other source. This, in turn, gave the impression that somebody in the tribunal was intent on damaging him. He was a victim of the unfettered power of the tribunal.

We now know that, behind the scenes, a completely different scenario had unfolded over the previous two years. The inquiry had repeatedly come across unexplained deposits to Ahern accounts. And the trail of correspondence would eventually show that he was being less than enthusiastic in responding to queries concerning them.

The Dáil was due to resume the following Wednesday after the summer break. There was no doubt what the foremost topic for discussion would be. Ahern decided he had to act before then. On Monday, word went out that the following evening he would be doing an interview with RTÉ's *Six One News* anchor Bryan Dobson, to be conducted not in the Taoiseach's office but in St Luke's.

The platform was well chosen for a politician who was personally popular with the electorate. He would speak to the people directly. He would not give primacy to the national parliament on what appeared to be a major issue. He would not speak through the media in a press conference.

His frequent interaction with the media was usually through the "doorstep" interview, where reporters were given the opportunity to fire a few quick questions at him as he was leaving an event. This narrowed reporters' scope for enquiry also meant that he was whisked away within minutes, particularly if the tone of questioning turned awkward. The frequent "doorsteps" provided an impression that he was highly accessible to the media. Now he would speak directly to the people from the place he felt most secure – St Luke's.

*   *   *

There was a little distraction on the morning of the interview. Junior minister Noel Treacy was contributing an item to *The Breakfast Show* on the radio station Newstalk 106. The presenter Ger Gilroy steered matters to the burning issue of Ahern's money.

He asked Treacy about the origins of the story in the *Irish Times*.

"The *Irish Times* did have information from other sources, but it's a well-known fact that the tribunal leaks like this. It's well known where the conduit is," Treacy said.

Gilroy then asked: "Really? Where's the conduit?"

Treacy replied: "Oh, it's very well known that this is a constant leaking for political purposes."

Gilroy: "And it's well known who the individual is?"

Treacy: "I think it is, yes."

Gilroy: "Can you tell us who it is?"

Treacy: "Oh, I wouldn't be able to say. I'm not going to make any comment about the activities of the tribunal."

So here it was, a government minister fingering an individual in the tribunal who was leaking information to do political damage to Ahern. And everybody knew who the leaker was. The direction in which Fianna Fáil was pointing the story was becoming clearer. It's the leak, stupid, not the money. The story is the leak.

Treacy, in following the party line, had broken one of the cardinal rules in spinning. He had been specific. He had ignored the imperative to be vague, to wave innuendo like a flag at a football match, to give the impression of knowing something more but being constrained from specifying it.

Before the day was out, he had received his own missive from the tribunal. Come on in and tell us all about who's doing the leaking.

Later that afternoon the cameras arrived in St Luke's. Ahern sat himself down opposite Dobson. The interview commenced.

In the short term, their conversation delivered Ahern from his oppressors. It was, in effect, his testimony to the people of Ireland, and particularly the voters of Ireland. Ahern's popularity was, to a large extent, drawn from his likeability. People trusted him. Women were attracted to him. His love of sport, his facility to articulate the emotional highs and lows of following a team, endeared him to men. His apparent dedication to the job was also a factor, but beyond that, people just liked him. As such, it was an astute decision to appeal directly to them. But he had to be honest with them. When somebody comes clean, there is usually understanding and often forgiveness. But the subject must come clean.

It would be well over a year before the entrails of the Dobson interview could be picked over, using information disseminated in the interim. And, observing it with 20:20 vision, it didn't make for good viewing.

Ahern began by laying out some of the ludicrous allegations that had been made against him, including "that I had bank accounts in the Netherlands, Antilles, Liechtenstein, Jersey, England, that I had £15 million in an offshore account". He didn't specify who had made these claims.

Throwing in the ludicrous stuff with the pressing issue is a technique of spin. It creates a context in which the viewer is set up to digest the substantive issue as being equally crazy.

He provided further background, including a comment that he had fully co-operated with the tribunal's various enquiries. This was incorrect, as would become apparent twelve months later when he began to give evidence.

Then he moved on to dig-out territory. More than once, he claimed that he had been on his uppers in December 1993 when the first dig-out occurred. Gerry Brennan organised a "contribution to help me because he knew of my financial state at the time". As has been established in this book, Brennan would have been aware that Ahern had around £70,000 available to him, and had secured a loan to pay off bills associated with his separation. None of this information was available to Dobson or the large TV audience viewing the interview. He named the dig-out people, including Padraic O'Connor. These were "friends at a time of need when they knew I was in difficulty". He said they had known he wouldn't be able to repay the "loan" for some time. The dig-out men were "close personal or political friends". O'Connor would claim, with some conviction, that he was neither.

Then he introduced his daughters, whose education he said he'd had to consider at the time. At this point in the interview he became emotional. In fact, he hadn't transferred money to his daughters' accounts until nearly six months after the dig-out.

Asked whether there were any documents to back up his claim, he responded: "There are no documents, well, other than, well, there is the documentation that all of these people have now given the tribunal." This suggests that the donors had documentation about the loans. In fact, none of them had so much as a scrap of paper to back up their stories.

Following queries from Dobson, Ahern said that the loans were debts of honour, although he hadn't repaid them yet. "To be honest, Brian, I would not have been able to pay it [back] until about 1999 or 2000." In fact, he could have paid it back three times over with the money available to him at the time. Yet he was implying that his financial situation was such that he was pinned to his collar for six years after he received the money. It would be more than a year before information emerged to contradict the assertions he made in the interview about his financial situation.

He also gave details of the Manchester dig-out. By introducing something that wasn't yet in the public domain, he was taking control of that element of the story. This is a perfectly acceptable tactic, if the story is true.

At the conclusion, he redirected the interview to what he claimed was the main aspect of the whole story. That terrible, terrible leak. "I don't know who leaked it, I don't want to be taking anyone's character, but somebody took mine, and in a very cynical way. But it's best that I just give the true facts and, you know, from the position of the Irish public, they've always been kind to me about being separated. They've always been understanding, and if I've caused offence to anybody, I think I have to a few people, I'm sorry."

It was a classic ending. The leaker was out to take Ahern's character, yet everything contained in the leak turned out to be correct. Ahern was giving the "true facts", yet time would show that his response to questions in the interview was a strange and elastic interpretation of the truth. And he used his marital difficulties to explain it all.

Pretty quickly, it became apparent that the interview had been a huge success. He had evoked sympathy in his audience for the plight of his family affairs. He had drawn from the deep well of goodwill he had built up with the Irish people. The general impression was that the public was uneasy about his acceptance of money, but they didn't see it as a hanging offence. In football parlance, it was a yellow rather than a red card. The interview had delivered for him, big time.

The same sympathy wasn't forthcoming in the political arena. The opposition smelled blood. The interview had raised a number of questions, and left many others unanswered. The opposition focused on two aspects of the affair. Was any tax paid on the money? And what was the mysterious wad picked up in Manchester?

The following day in the Dáil, Ahern dealt with the matter in Leader's Questions. In response to a query from Enda Kenny on the tax implications, he replied: "I know the law, although I am not an expert on every aspect. However, many years ago my tax advisers checked the issues in detail on the basis that it was a loan with interest . . .

"I receive an annual figure from my tax adviser. It was calculated over the entire period on that basis. I paid capital-gains tax and gift tax. It is not appropriate for me to spell out what I paid, but I assure the deputy that I did so following advice."

He has never produced a scrap of evidence to suggest that he consulted with tax advisers at the time of the loan. He hadn't paid any tax on the money. He didn't receive any annual figure from any tax adviser on it.

Later, Labour leader Pat Rabbitte asked for more details. Ahern replied: "Deputy Rabbitte asked me earlier whether there was documentation on the circumstances of these loans from the individuals concerned. There is comprehensive documentation and it is with the tribunal as well."

Again, there is not one scrap of documented evidence relating to the loans. When, in 2006, accountant Des Peelo produced a report for the tribunal on Ahern's behalf that listed the loans, his source was Ahern's word, rather than any record or documents.

The opposition kept up the pressure through the week. Apart from seeking naked political advantage, a number of entirely legitimate questions kept popping up. Even at that early stage, Ahern's narrative of his finances looked shaky in places.

* * *

The manner in which Ahern dealt with the issue of his private life and his finances during the Dobson interview chimed with an earlier episode in his life. In November 1998, *Bertie Ahern: Taoiseach and Peacemaker* was published. Authors Ken Whelan and Eugene Masterson had acquired Ahern's co-operation for the project but, typical of Ahern, it was unofficial. In effect, his fingerprints were all over the tome, but he kept his distance.

In the book, he addressed a matter that had dogged him for the previous five years. Scurrilous, unfounded rumours had circulated at every level of society that Ahern had been involved in domestic abuse. The rumours mined a nasty seam in Irish life, where people revel in believing the worst. Other public figures had been subjected to such treatment, but none had to endure it as much as Ahern. In the book, he was quoted as saying: "I know all the rumours and so do Celia and Miriam. I can do sweet nothing about these things. You can sound me out till the cows come home; you'll find no garda reports, no barring order, nothing. I'll tell you, there's not a whole many things in my life that I can 110 per cent swear on, because I'm no more an angel than anyone else in this life, but of the barring orders there is zilch."

The authors included the quotes, believing, with some justification, that Ahern was using the book to address the scurrilous rumours and put them to bed once and for all.

On Friday, 30 October, a series of radio adverts was aired promoting extracts in that weekend's *Ireland On Sunday* newspaper, which promised to reveal details about the rumours. Ahern's advisers hit the roof. There was no knowing what the public reaction to such sensitive material might be. A spin operation was initiated.

Over the following weeks, stories appeared in which "sources close to" Ahern asserted he had been duped by the authors: he had spoken off the record and shouldn't have been quoted.

Prominent Fianna Fáil TD Willie O'Dea penned a column in the *Sunday Independent* that amounted to an attack on the authors' integrity. In time, they would receive in excess of £50,000 in settlement of a libel action arising out of O'Dea's comments.

Two weeks later *Ireland On Sunday* published the original draft of the book, which showed Ahern's handwriting in the margins. He had made two corrections on the chapter where the rumours were dealt with. He had approved with a tick the use of his direct quotes.

With the evidence of his corroboration out in the public

domain, the spin changed direction. In an interview in the *Irish Independent* a week later, he claimed that he had seen an early draft, but by then it had been too late to change the copy containing his quotes. A week later that claim was thrown out when it emerged that references made about Northern Ireland had been excised after his adviser Martin Manseragh was shown the draft. It wasn't too late for Manseragh to make a change, yet Ahern had claimed he, who had had earlier access to the copy, couldn't change something he would regard as highly sensitive.

The manner in which he dealt with the affair was notable, and parallels can be drawn with how he would handle his issues at the tribunal from 2006 onwards. In dealing with the book, he made various claims about the authors that appeared perhaps to have some validity until further material entered the public domain – the published drafts – which showed him to have been less than frank.

Then he changed the story – that he hadn't time to alter the original draft – which sufficed until further material entered the public domain, which again exposed serious flaws in his claim.

Finally, he let it rest and wished away the controversy, which subsided, perhaps because of the public's desire to avert its eyes from anything involving the personal life of any public figure, particularly one as popular as Ahern. He would use this template in his dealings with the planning tribunal from 2006 onwards. Unfortunately for him, the final outcome would be quite different from that which occurred over the controversy with the book.

*　*　*

Much of the pressure surrounding the revelations about Ahern's finances was applied to Fianna Fáil's partner in government, the Progressive Democrats. Ethics in public office was a cornerstone of their philosophy. They had got rid of Brian Lenihan in 1990 over the possibility – which was never fully established – that eight years earlier he had inappropriately phoned the president's office over a constitutional matter.

In 1992 the PDs had signed Charlie Haughey's political death warrant over a variety of scandals in which he had been mired. Now it looked as if another Fianna Fáil leader was dragging standards below the acceptable PD threshold.

By 2006, Fianna Fáil and the PDs had been in government for nine years. It had been a time of plenty for the country, and the PDs could claim that they had contributed to the enormous success of the economy, particularly since 2000. This analysis would undergo major revision following the property crash and credit crunch, which were still two years away. There had been controversies along the way, but each time cracks had appeared, Ahern and the PD leader Mary Harney sat down and ironed things out. On 13 September, two weeks before the Ahern story broke, Michael McDowell had been elected unopposed as the new leader of the PDs.

If the party was in an invidious position over Ahern's money, then McDowell was doubly so. During his time in politics, and particularly since he had been appointed Minister for Justice in 2002, McDowell was a divisive figure. Some saw him as a no-nonsense politician who got things done. To others, he appeared to be the most right-wing politician to emerge in decades.

During his ministerial tenure he clashed with the opposition, the trade unions, the gardaí, prison officers and judges. He had also conceded a number of U-turns in policy, which his supporters put down to an overriding zeal to get things done.

Now he was at a crux. Two weeks into the job, would he be the PD leader to break up the happy home of coalition? He knew that even if he walked his party out of government, Fianna Fáil could continue with the support of independent TDs until after the general election, which was set for the following May.

He also had to consider the implications of pulling out in light of the party's chances of re-entering government with Fianna Fáil after that election.

McDowell reined in his customary instinct to talk fast into the nearest microphone. He didn't push the matter, but behind the scenes he let his unease be known.

Talks at various levels between the two parties ensued. It was agreed that it would be appropriate for Ahern to offer up an apology of sorts.

On 3 October, when the matter was raised again in the Dáil, Ahern used the opportunity to issue his apology. "The bewilderment caused to the public about recent revelations has been deeply upsetting for me and others near and dear to me. To them, to the Irish people and to this House, I offer my apologies." He also reiterated that he had received no other monies than those he had revealed in the RTÉ interview. "My savings were totally out of my income, from my TD salary and my salary as Minister for Finance," he said. Again, this was inaccurate. He failed to mention winnings on the horses, which wouldn't be revealed for another eighteen months. Neither did he reveal his "political donation for personal use", which he had used to open one of his numerous accounts.

The opposition was not satisfied. The following day, Rabbitte asked Ahern once more about Manchester. Only one person had come forward to identify himself as being present at the dinner. John Kennedy had said he was there and that his contribution was personal rather than political. The twenty-odd multimillionaires in the Manchester Irish community could not be located.

McDowell had asserted that Ahern had told him privately he would provide a list of these individuals. Rabbitte asked Ahern whether this could be expected.

"I stated that I have attended many functions and social events in Manchester. To try to piece together a list of every person who attended each individual event from the time I first began going to Manchester as a councillor, a deputy and a backbencher is impossible. I cannot do it and will not be able to do it. I have explained this to the House, to the public and everywhere else. I have no problem getting a list of people but I cannot reconstitute a list. That is the position."

Nobody had asked him for a list of every person who attended every event he had been invited to in Manchester over the years, just as nobody had ever asked him for details of his first holy-communion collection.

The PDs were happy. At a parliamentary party meeting later that day they passed a motion that Ahern was "not unfit to continue in office as Taoiseach", which was as far as they could go in approving his fitness.

Later that day the cat was thrown among the pigeons. An RTÉ investigation revealed that Mícheál Wall, from whom Ahern had bought his house, had admitted being at the Manchester dinner. In the fevered atmosphere of intrigue that prevailed, the latest nugget offered more potential for serious damage.

The following day Ahern tried to steady the horses. He told the Dáil that he had paid the full market price for his home. It was too late for the PDs, though. The Wall revelation was a bridge too far. McDowell went into something of a sulk. For more than twelve hours no senior figure in the party was contactable, an amazing situation for a political party in the modern media age. It looked for a while as if they were ready to pull the plug.

Fianna Fáil sources were not as reticent. The word was sprayed out into the media. There would be no head from the party this time. If McDowell wanted to leave government, off with him. The numbers were such that Fianna Fáil could limp to the next election with the aid of independents.

By the weekend, McDowell had resurfaced. Word was put out that an accommodation had been reached. The PDs weren't going anywhere.

On 10 October, McDowell issued a statement ahead of a joint press conference with Ahern. It began: "Since details of the Taoiseach's personal financial affairs supplied to the Mahon Tribunal were unlawfully leaked, it has been evident that the underlying intention of the leaker was to destabilise the govern-ment." Once again, the leak was the story. It wasn't McDowell's failure to ensure that Ahern adhered to basic standards. It wasn't the myriad unanswered questions about Ahern's money. It was the leak. The leaker and his leak must be defeated.

He had extracted from Ahern a commitment to legislate for tighter rules governing the acceptance of gifts. At the press conference, the pair accepted four questions from journalists, then turned to flee. As they left, McDowell was heard muttering to Ahern: "We survived that."

A postscript to the chapter was written the following morning. Noel Treacy was called to give evidence at the tribunal to identify for the judges the dastardly leaker to whom he had referred on the radio a few weeks previously.

It had all been a big misunderstanding, Noel told them. He'd gone on the radio early in the morning, and wasn't sure what he had been saying. "I have no evidence whatever to say that I have any knowledge of any person in the tribunal leaking," he said.

* * *

Two days later, the people gave their verdict. An *Irish Times*/TNS MBRI opinion poll recorded an 8 per cent rise in support for Fianna Fáil to 39 per cent, its highest rating since the previous general election. Ahern's own satisfaction rating was up by 1 per cent to a highly respectable 53 per cent, making him the most popular leader of a political party.

The poll also found that two-thirds of respondents felt Ahern had been wrong to take the two dig-outs and whip-around, but the obvious conclusion was that his actions from twelve years previously didn't warrant sanction and, if anything, had garnered sympathy.

The result was a major vindication for Ahern and signalled a turnaround in Fianna Fáil's fortunes just as a general election was coming into view. Support for Fine Gael and Labour both dropped. The people hadn't so much spoken as shouted from the rooftops: Bertie was all right by them.

The story that had emerged over the previous three weeks had been accepted: Ahern had admitted making a few mistakes twelve years previously, which had now ensnared him in the runaway train that was the tribunal. It would be another year before the real story would come out.

A month later the Fianna Fáil Ard Fheis provided a grave in which to bury the story marked "Leaks and Scoundrels". Communications minister Noel Dempsey told the gathering that opposition leaders had attempted a "character assassination" of the Taoiseach.

Ahern himself told TV3's Ursula Halligan that he had been the victim of an orchestrated smear campaign intended to drive him from office: "There was one group out to bury me. It was quite obvious who they were. I'm not going to personalise it but it was quite obvious who they were," he said. He was asked if he thought a "big bad enemy" was out to get him. "Yeah, I do. There was a sinister, calculated set-up. Somebody or some group tried to get rid of me, there's no doubt about that." One interpretation of his remarks was that he was referring to the *Irish Times* and elements of the opposition. He didn't attempt on that or any other occasion to address some of the glaring questions that remained about his money matters. Others, like the large sterling deposits, the foreign exchange in cars and bars, and the horses, had not yet entered the public domain.

At Christmas he daubed a few more strokes on the portrait of his victimhood. "From my perspective it was a hugely unfair period, but that is how the world is. But thirty years' experience in politics teaches you one thing: you fight your corner, you explain your position," he told radio reporters. "I was glad to be able to do that. There are always those in politics who have agendas. There are those who are personally out to get you all of the time. Some of them have been personally out to get me for twenty years. But you tell it as it is and you hope it works out for the best."

Politically, the main thing for Ahern was the forthcoming general election, and the prospect of a historic third victory. Everything else could wait until after that when, with a bit of a headwind, he could officially claim the title of the most successful politician since Éamon de Valera.

25

THE HIGHEST PEAK

It was to be one of the most extraordinary election campaigns in the history of the state. It began unexpectedly with a pre-eight a.m. trip up to Áras an Uachtaráin on Sunday, 29 April 2007, to get the President's signature on an order for the dissolution of the twenty-ninth Dáil before she left on an official visit to the US.

Although the *Sunday Independent* and the *Sunday Tribune* would be on the newsstands that morning predicting that Ahern would go to Áras that day, bleary-eyed journalists would have been unaware of this and therefore shocked to get dawn messages on their mobiles telling them to high-tail it up to the Phoenix Park.

The logic of Ahern's timing would be the subject of much debate over the coming days. Ahern suggested it was because he had not realised that the President would be out of the country but Mary McAleese later stated that she had informed Ahern some considerable time before of her plans to leave that Sunday morning. Most of the speculation centred on the fact that the Mahon Tribunal was due to open its public inquiry into Quarryvale – which would involve considerable scrutiny of the payments to Ahern in the early 1990s – the following day. Once the election was called, it was inevitable that Judge Mahon would opt to defer public hearings until after the general election – and so it proved.

But there may also have been another factor behind Ahern's decision to go that Sunday morning. That day's *Irish Mail on Sunday* (and the following day's *Irish Times*) carried further revelations about Ahern's personal finances – based on leaks of information given to the tribunal by the Taoiseach. The leaks revealed that businessman Micheál Wall had given £30,000 sterling in cash to Ahern in December 1994 and the money had been placed by Celia Larkin in an account in her name. This was to be used to fund work on a house in Beresford, Drumcondra, owned by Wall but rented by Ahern and later purchased by him.

Ahern had made the decision to go to Áras by Saturday afternoon but, by that stage presumably, the Taoiseach would have been aware of the story that the *Mail on Sunday* was preparing to run the following day. Whatever the reason for the early Sunday trip to the park, the fresh revelations in the newspapers reignited the controversy over Ahern's finances and dominated the first fortnight of the campaign, threatening to scupper Fianna Fáil's hopes of being re-elected.

For the first few days Ahern resembled a rabbit caught in the headlights. At a press conference later on that Sunday, at Fianna Fáil's campaign headquarters of Treasury Buildings, he read out a short statement to the assembled media but then promptly disappeared through an opening in the backdrop before any questions could be asked. He appeared again when refreshments were being served to make polite small-talk with members of the press, but the mood was awkward and tense.

Aside from a brief explanation on the Monday that the money related to "a stamp-duty issue", Ahern's line over the coming days was that he would make no comment on the issue of his finances, but would make a full statement to the Mahon Tribunal at the appropriate time. At one impromptu "doorstep" press conference, there was an extraordinary incident: Ahern buttoned his lip and gazed off into space rather than answer a question from a journalist on the issue. The silence persisted for an excruciating seven seconds until a party handler said: "Next question."

Gone was the strutting Ahern of the previous two election campaigns, when he had blitzed the country, chest out, pumping hands as he went. "Ratty", "narky" and "taciturn" were just some of the words used to describe him in the media. He seemed curiously disengaged from his party's national campaign, concentrating largely on events in his own constituency. The Fianna Fáil campaign seemed to be stuck in a variation of Groundhog Day in which the questions never changed and the answers weren't forthcoming.

On the Thursday of the first week of the campaign, Fianna Fáil launched its election manifesto in the historic Round Room of the Mansion House. But despite a promise to abolish stamp duty for first-time buyers, the assembled media had little or no interest in it. Questions quickly focused on the matter of Ahern's finances, but he swatted them away. Then the well-known journalist Vincent Browne grabbed the microphone. With his characteristic mixture of insight and bloodymindedness, he proceeded to interrogate Ahern on the question of the money from Wall.

Initially, Ahern cited tribunal confidentiality, but Browne wasn't having any of it. Ahern's credibility was in question, he said, because of his explanation that he was willing to put up

£50,000, along with Wall's £30,000, for the renovation of a house that had cost less than £150,000, was only three or four years old and that he was purporting merely to rent.

An unexpected thing happened. Although Ahern was under the cosh of sustained questioning, his body language began to change. He almost looked relieved to be able to face the charges head on. He began to give answers: it had been Wall's money and Wall's house. All the bills relating to that money were given to the tribunal. If I have money and want to do something with my own savings, what is wrong with me doing that? It was my money, Ahern insisted.

There was no shortage of "loose threads" in his version of events but, for the first time in the campaign, he had robustly come out fighting and defended – as PR expert Terry Prone put it a few days later – his right "to do whatever the hell he wanted with his own money". Gone was the tetchiness and maudlin countenance. "He was straightforwardly mad as hell, sure of his facts and concentrated on ramming them straight down the Browne neck," Prone added.

But while there was a feeling that Ahern had perhaps turned a corner, there would be a couple more twists in the coming days.

During that week stories were continuing to appear in the media, revealing more information about Ahern's dealings with the tribunal. The PDs were getting decidedly windy. For the opening days of the campaign, PD leader Michael McDowell – no doubt mindful of how badly his party's prevarication had looked the previous autumn when the Bertie-gate saga first broke – was sticking to the line that he did not want to turn himself into a "mini-tribunal". It was the responsibility of the Mahon Tribunal to investigate, and the PDs wanted to concentrate on the real issues of the election.

However, on the Friday, when asked if he would form a new coalition with Fianna Fáil or would he need greater clarity from Ahern on his finances, McDowell stunned everybody. He said he needed time to "reflect" on new material about Ahern's finances: "This is material now coming into the public domain that changes the position. I believe that there are a number of things on which I would want to reflect."

The "new material" consisted of documents he had received through his special adviser from a journalist with the *Sunday Independent*. They were believed to comprise a copy of the full transcript of a recent interview between Ahern and the tribunal lawyers about the Taoiseach's house. McDowell was said to be "shocked and horrified" by it because it had convinced him Ahern had not given him the full picture the previous autumn. Back then, it would emerge in the coming days, Ahern had told him about the purchase of his house in Drumcondra from a Manchester businessman, but said it was "an arm's length transaction on commercial terms for the full value". He shared what he had discovered with Mary Harney and Liz O'Donnell. The three decided to sleep on the matter and consult with other party colleagues before deciding whether or not they could continue in government with Ahern and Fianna Fáil. The unprecedented prospect of a party pulling out of government after a general election had been called looked very real.

On the Saturday, while out on the campaign trail, McDowell passed up the opportunity to play down the gravity of the situation, describing it as serious and confirming that a meeting of senior PD figures would take place that afternoon. The media went into a frenzy that they were on the brink of withdrawing from government. Fianna Fáil figures were privately resigned to this happening. On RTÉ *Six One News*, while chief reporter Charlie Bird stressed that there was "no smoking gun" in the new material McDowell had been given, the totality of the information had alarmed him.

However, not everybody among the PDs – most notably party president Tom Parlon – was thrilled at the idea of a last-minute withdrawal from government. The feeling among some was that it was too late and would be seen as a meaningless gesture; it would cost the party transfers from Fianna Fáil and leave it without any coalition options, potentially rendering it irrelevant come polling day.

Backed by a majority of the parliamentary party, Parlon's view held sway, and by late Saturday night, the word was coming back that the PDs would be staying put. At a press conference the following morning in Dublin's Morrison Hotel, a solitary McDowell did not announce the PDs' withdrawal but instead called on Ahern to give a "comprehensive and credible" account of his finances in a statement before polling day.

The flip-flopping was a PR disaster for the PDs and raised old questions about McDowell's political judgement. Virtual annihilation awaited the party on polling day.

* * *

However, for Ahern and Fianna Fáil, things were looking up. An opinion poll in that day's *Sunday Business Post* showed an increase in support for Fianna Fáil. And on that day a crucial meeting took place in Treasury Buildings between Ahern and the three most senior Fianna Fáil ministers – Brian Cowen, Dermot Ahern and Micheál Martin. They and party strategists believed it was necessary to get out Ahern's side of the story.

At that meeting, it was agreed that the Taoiseach would make a full statement on his finances. Only the four men involved know for sure what else happened. There have been attempts to portray it as an opportunity for the three ministers to lay down the law to Ahern, with particular emphasis on the fact that the meeting took place in Fianna Fáil Headquarters, not St Luke's. However, the location of the meeting might have had more to do with the fact that the four ministerial cars could drive straight through unnoticed by any waiting media into the underground car park. Cars parked outside St Luke's might have attracted an unwelcome photograph in the following day's papers.

Two weeks out from election day, a poll in the *Irish Times* showed the putative Rainbow Government of Fine Gael, Labour and the Greens on course for victory, with Fianna Fáil down at 36 per cent. Nearly three-quarters of poll respondents said they believed Ahern still had further questions to answer on his personal finances.

The following Sunday he moved to address those concerns with a long statement on the series of financial transactions surrounding his Drumcondra home during the 1990s. It said there was no evidence to back up Gilmartin's allegation that Ahern had been given money by developer Owen O'Callaghan and that all of the claims had been "borne out of spite and malice" and were part of a "changing and unreliable story".

Ahern said Mícheál Wall had bought and paid for the house and later sold it to him at market value. The cash he had had from Wall was towards the refurbishment of the property, related expenses and stamp duty. He himself had put forward £50,000 towards the work on the house, of which only £30,000 was spent. Ahern said his lifestyle was "as simple as it is honest" and concluded: "I have done nothing wrong and I have wronged no one." The Taoiseach also confirmed to reporters that, in the previous six months, he had made a voluntary payment "on account" to the Revenue, relating to the payments and gifts he had received in the early 1990s. Aside from that revelation, and the implication that the tribunal had got its sums wrong in suggesting that the cash amount given by Wall could equate to $45,000, there was precious little new in the statement.

However, as far as Ahern and Fianna Fáil were concerned, it had the desired effect – perhaps because it is impossible to sustain any sense of crisis in politics for more than two weeks. Or maybe it was because the opposition parties felt hamstrung by having dropped in the polls the previous autumn when they had gone for Ahern over his finances. Whatever the reason, the issue of Ahern's finances virtually disappeared for the remainder of the campaign. The economy became the central issue and Brian Cowen, as finance minister, played a key role by repeatedly getting the better of opposition representatives in TV and radio debates.

Two days after his statement, Ahern had the chance to show all his statesman qualities when he made an historic address to both Houses of the Westminster parliament. A Fianna Fáil party political broadcast, aired that week, included endorse-ments from Tony Blair, Bill Clinton and George Mitchell. How could Enda Kenny, with a CV that totalled two and half years as Minister for Tourism, compete with that?

Neither, it turned out, could Kenny compete with Ahern in the head-to-head television debate a week out from election day. Although the media were sluggish in calling it decisively for Ahern, subsequent polls showed the public were in no doubt. Ahern opened nervously, while Kenny apppeared confident. However, Ahern clearly outpointed Kenny in the section on health – supposedly the government's Achilles heel – and after that the Fine Gael leader hardly got a look in.

The following Monday – just days before the election – the latest *Irish Times* poll showed a surge in support for Fianna Fáil with the party back up at 41 per cent.

Ahern went to bed on election night after the polls closed. Emotionally drained and physically exhausted, he apparently did not wake until after four o'clock the following afternoon. The first person he spoke to was his bestselling-author daughter Cecelia, who broke the good news to him about his party's stellar performance. Fianna Fáil had marginally increased its share of the first preference vote from 2002, although it ended up winning three seats fewer. It remained to be seen which parties would make up the next government, but Ahern would clearly continue as Taoiseach, in a third successive term. It was an extraordinary turnaround. As political journalist Harry McGee noted on his blog, Ahern "didn't win an overall majority but, psychologically, it was a landslide".

* * *

In Dublin Central, Ahern had secured his usual massive number of first preference votes, 12,734 – almost two quotas. He also succeeded in bringing in Cyprian Brady, who for most of the previous twenty years had run his constituency office. Brady received just 939 votes – less than three per cent of the total vote – just under half the 1,725 votes that the third Fianna Fáil candidate Mary Fitzpatrick attracted.

However, it was Brady, not Fitzpatrick, who was the Drumcondra Mafia's anointed one. He secured 2,403 of Ahern's surplus compared to Fitzpatrick's 1,362, putting him 255 votes ahead of his running mate after the second count. By the time the fifth count was announced, Brady was still 169 votes clear, meaning Fitzpatrick rather than Brady was eliminated. Her transfers effectively guaranteed Brady the seat.

But while Brady was living proof that it was good to be Ahern's running mate, Fitzpatrick represented the other side of the coin. It wasn't necessarily anything personal – although that would change as the accusations began to fly – but she had become yet another victim of the Ahern machine.

Five years previously, Fianna Fáil had squeaked through, pipping Sinn Féin for the final seat by a few dozen votes, to win two out of four in the constituency. It had done this with a ticket of Ahern and Dermot Fitzpatrick, Mary's father. In the run-up to the 2007 general election, it had seemed obvious that another two-person ticket was the best way to hold the two seats. Mary Fitzpatrick, who had performed strongly in the local elections, was the obvious candidate. She was young, female – important given Mary Lou McDonald would be the Sinn Féin candidate – and geographically well placed at the Navan Road end of the constituency, far from Ahern's Drumcondra base.

However, the Drumcondra operation felt this was Cyprian Brady's time. Cyprian is the older brother of Royston who, only a few years earlier, had been expected to be the Brady on the ticket alongside Ahern in Dublin Central. Royston was regarded as "the new Bertie". Despite – or perhaps because of – this, relations between him, Ahern and the rest of the Drumcondra Mafia (including his brother Cyprian) broke down in the wake of Royston's unsuccessful bid for a seat in the European Parliament in 2004. The fall-out was poisonous, with serious disputes over who was responsible for unpaid bills in relation to the campaign.

Royston had been a front runner in the European poll, but lost the election after a series of controversies, including an allegation that he had incorrectly claimed his father's taxi had been hijacked by loyalist terrorists on the eve of the Dublin bombings in 1974. Unfortunately for Royston, it came to light not long after the election that his father's taxi had indeed been hijacked at that time.

A couple of days before this fresh information about the hijack emerged, Ahern was asked about Royston's claim in the Dáil and rather coolly replied: "If the Lord Mayor of Dublin [Brady] has anything of note to say he should reply to the letter he received from Mr Justice Barron (who was investigating the Dublin bombings) and give that information. I am not aware of whether he has any information that would be useful." He later added: "The Lord Mayor of Dublin was two years of age when this happened so his memory of any information would not be very good."

In later interviews, Royston would claim that, following an RTÉ interview about the money owed after the election, in the March or April after the Euro elections, he was summoned to a meeting in Dublin's Herbert Park Hotel by an unnamed "powerful Fianna Fáil individual", where he alleged he was "basically threatened" and told in no uncertain terms not to be talking to the media or he would "find it very hard to get work in this town". The meeting, he said, ended with him being told that if he stopped shooting his mouth off to the media, all the outstanding bills from the election would be paid through the raffle of a car. He told one interviewer: "I never ever received any more bills or solicitors' letters after that. All suppliers were paid. It was as simple as that."

With Royston *persona non grata* and out of the running to be a candidate in Dublin Central, Cyprian was certainly in the frame. But could he defeat Mary Fitzpatrick at a convention and, given his relatively low profile, would he get enough votes to take the second seat for Fianna Fáil?

The prevarication over who should be on the ticket for the election went on for eighteen months. Different rules applied to Dublin Central than to other constituencies, senior Fianna Fáil figures would admit privately. Sure, the Fianna Fáil Party constituency committee, which included heavy hitters like Brian Cowen and P. J. Mara, discussed Dublin Central. But nobody was in doubt as to who would have the final say. No constituency was polled as often by the party. The word was, no matter how the numbers were done, Cyprian Brady wasn't going to win the seat. He wasn't registering with voters. It was clear Fitzpatrick was needed on the ticket.

But that did not result in what seemed the logical two-person ticket. In the "interests of the party", Fitzpatrick was persuaded by Ahern to agree to go with a three-candidate strategy. Her supporters believe that was her biggest mistake.

The convention was finally held in March 2007 in St Luke's. There were five candidates up for the nomination: Ahern, Brady, Fitzpatrick, Tom Stafford and Chris Wall, Ahern's political right-hand man. Stafford withdrew his candidature at the start of the meeting and the remaining four candidates withdrew upstairs to the apartment to await developments.

While they were away, an announcement was made that Wall's candidature was being withdrawn. As they were walking down the stairs to rejoin the meeting and learn their fate, Ahern was overheard remaking to Fitzpatrick: "You've no idea of the friendships I've had to pull to get this for you."

Although Fianna Fáil had agreed its ticket of Ahern, Fitzpatrick and Brady, there was little fanfare that night. Ahern didn't even pose for photos with his two running mates. Not that photos of Ahern and Fitzpatrick would be particularly prominent at any stage during the election campaign. In contrast, there seemed to be shots everywhere of Ahern and

Brady. In Ahern's traditional Easter message from Drum-condra, he made no mention of Fitzpatrick in the ten-page colour newsletter. Ditto with a four-page leaflet at election time, which was full of photos of Ahern and Brady.

However, the real antagonism only surfaced in the final days of the campaign. Just hours before the polling booths opened, 30,000 letters were distributed to homes in Dublin Central. The letter was signed by the Taoiseach and headlined in red with the words "IMPORTANT NOTICE". It asked the reader to "support the party strategy" – also in red – in maximising support in Dublin Central by voting "in this area" 1 Ahern, 2 Brady and 3 Fitzpatrick. Why it was necessary to use the words "in this area" is not clear when the letters were sent to every home in the constituency.

Fitzpatrick and her people were furious at the drop and believed it cost her the election. Given that there were only 169 votes between her and Brady when she was eliminated, she might have had a point. The Dublin City councillor didn't pull her punches when she was interviewed for an RTÉ documentary that was covering the contest in the constituency between three high-profile female politicians, Patricia McKenna, Mary Lou McDonald and herself. "I never thought they were the Legion of Mary. I never thought they were going to do me any favours. I thought my insurance policy was that they needed a second seat, so I didn't think they would go out to completely undermine me and shaft me," Fitzpatrick told RTÉ's Ann Marie Power.

She was withering in her assessment of Brady's perfor-mance: "He had 900 votes after twenty years, supposedly, of loyal service, working the constituency, blah, blah, blah – and all he could deliver was 900 first-preference votes."

Ahern's team rejected any suggestion Fitzpatrick had been

shafted, claiming that others had stood down to clear the way for her to win the nomination at convention time. Chris Wall argued that Fitzpatrick had first contravened an agreement by dropping a leaflet in her ward asking for number one, which she had been asked not to do. "Having then done it, she therefore effectively set in train a motion which she wasn't going to be able to stop," Wall said.

Fitzpatrick angrily rejected this: "So they'd seen my canvass card for three weeks and then, all of a sudden, it was an issue? It's not an issue. That isn't why they did it. They did it because they wanted to hammer me." To try to pretend, she added, that "they did that letter out of retaliation for a colour flyer from me that probably wasn't picked up because it looked like one of my canvass cards, I don't buy it. I don't accept it. And that doesn't explain why the [Dublin] Central [Fianna Fáil] newspaper that they put out earlier in the campaign made no mention of me; why the education colour leaflets that they put out throughout the constituency made no mention of me and why in any properties that they had eight-by-four billboards in they couldn't accommodate any of my billboards . . . They didn't want me to get elected."

Her outburst went down like a lead balloon with the Ahern machine. They would not forget. Now it was personal. Two years later there was another convention in Dublin Central to pick a candidate to contest the by-election precipitated by the death of Tony Gregory. Although she was the Headquarters choice, Fitzpatrick was defeated by Ahern's septuagenarian brother Maurice.

Fitzpatrick and Maurice also went head to head in the local elections, held on the same day as the Dublin Central by-election, in the Cabra-Glasnevin ward. And in a definite case of history repeating itself, Bertie Ahern issued a letter to voters in the ward, five days before polling, asking them to vote for his brother Maurice in the by-election, and in the council election he eschewed the traditional alphabetical order to put Fitzpatrick's name after the third Fianna Fáil candidate, Seaghan Kearney.

In an interview with RTÉ Radio about the latest Ahern letter, Fitzpatrick denied she was in any way seeking a sympathy vote and insisted all she was looking for was "a level playing field". The very success of the Drumcondra Mafia had ensured there hadn't been a level playing field in Dublin Central for the previous twenty-seven years. The message was clear: don't mess with Bertie's machine.

So it went in his finest hour, the general election success of 2007. The most successful politician of his generation basked in the glow of the unlikeliest victory. On the night of the count, in an interview with RTÉ's Mark Little, he was asked whether he had any worries about his forthcoming appearances before the Mahon Tribunal.

"Not at all," he said. If he could, he'd deal with the matter the very next day. The image was of a man with nothing to fear from the investigation into his finances that was about to go public. Nothing could touch him now, as he stood on the highest peak of his career.

His apparent confidence was such that many accepted he was likely to sail through the hearings in the autumn. Wasn't he the Teflon Taoiseach? Nothing unwanted was going to stick to him. He was going to go out at the top of his game, untainted by anything minor the tribunal might discover.

Come September, it wouldn't take long for the foundations of such opinions to tremble and shake.

PART V

THE FALL

26

CASTLE DAYS

A full house in the Printworks building. It was just like the old days. The planning tribunal was box office again. And why wouldn't it be? It was starring Bertie Ahern, the first politician since Éamon de Valera to win three consecutive general elections. It was 13 September 2007, the first day of the long and slow unravelling of Ahern's money tales.

Originally he had been scheduled to appear in late July, but that had had to be cancelled because of delay on the tribunal's part and the complicated evidence in which Ahern's legal team was attempting to show how some banking records didn't tell the full tale.

Crucial to Ahern's narrative are the dig-outs and Manchester whip-around. The lodgement of £24,838.49 on 11 October 1994 was, he maintained, the proceeds of the £16,500 dig-out from friends, and the £8,000 gift from the Manchester millionaires. As outlined earlier, the bank record for the day suggests that the lodgement was probably £25,000 sterling. If the tribunal accepted this, Ahern's story would crumble and he would be liable to answer all sorts of questions, relating to perjury and the circumstances in which he had come to have £25,000 in sterling.

In July, his legal team attempted to show that the records could be misleading, if read in a different way, only for another expert witness to blow their theory out of the water.

*   *   *

Once it was decided that there would be public hearings, the tribunal had to divide them up into different sections as the situation was so complex. The first item on the agenda was the foreign-exchange transactions that accounted for five large lodgements to the accounts.

Ever since the story had broken nearly a year previously, Ahern had stated and implied on numerous occasions that he couldn't wait to get into the tribunal. Now he was there. His opportunity to clear up all the misunderstandings was at hand. Following the spectacular general-election victory, the perceived wisdom among senior Fianna Fáil figures was that the tribunal was now largely irrelevant. It wasn't long before that view underwent major revision.

Soon after ten thirty a.m., Ahern strode in and took up his position beside his lawyers. Des O'Neill, the tribunal barrister, was on the front row of the lawyers' benches from where he would do his questioning. O'Neill was a veteran lawyer who had been called to the bar in 1970. He became a senior counsel in 1999, the same year that he had joined the tribunal. A patrician figure, he would amass more than €5 million in a decade with the inquiry, and would achieve some fame for his polite yet doggedly forensic questioning of Ahern.

Ahern was represented by Conor Maguire, another senior counsel with considerable Fianna Fáil connections. In some circles he had been tipped for appointment as Attorney General, but his role as Ahern's personal lawyer during the hearings effectively ruled him out.

Ahern was called as a witness and made his way to the stand. He was reminded that he had already sworn to tell the truth, the whole truth and nothing but the truth during his previous appearance in 2004. He asked to read a statement, which would be a departure from tribunal procedure. After a brief exchange of lawyerly views, he was given the go-ahead. He started by referring to the allegation that had brought his finances to the tribunal's attention. Gilmartin's claim that O'Callaghan had paid him a bribe had been based on nothing but hearsay, he said, and went on: "I have been in politics for thirty years. I have never in that period been offered any money from anyone in exchange for political or other favours or taken money for that purpose. I have endeavoured to serve the country to my utmost. I have no interest in personal gain or benefit and never had."

He reiterated that all the lodgements to his accounts were as he had already told the tribunal in private session, much of which had leaked out to the media. Then he introduced his banking expert, a former Bank of Ireland executive Paddy Stronge, who would back up his claims. He denied that the bank records implicated him in any wrongdoing.

It was a fine statement, replete with the tone of the victim, which had informed most of what Ahern had had to say on the matter over the previous year. It also provided him with a slight advantage in that, contrary to usual practice, none of the other parties, including the tribunal, had had sight of it beforehand.

If tribunal lawyers had read it, they might have objected to the assertions about banking records as they would turn out to have been based on little more than an opinion offered by a former senior banker.

When Ahern was done, O'Neill brought him through the paper trial that had started in October 2004, and persisted for nearly three years up until that very day.

The upshot of a day's reading through correspondence between Ahern's legal representatives and the tribunal was that the picture Ahern had carefully painted of having bent over backwards to co-operate with the tribunal was ruined. It emerged that he had signed an affidavit in 2005 that omitted the vital information that he had transferred £50,000 from his account to Celia Larkin's.

In March 2006, the tribunal threatened that it would move to public hearings if Ahern didn't respond to questions. By then, the inquiry had been looking for answers for eighteen months. A letter to Ahern's solicitor summed up the tribunal lawyers' frustration: "The tribunal believes that it has afforded your client, Mr Ahern, every opportunity and sufficient time to allow him to provide meaningful assistance to the tribunal and every opportunity to consult with you and other professional advisers, in relation to the requests for assistance made of him to date."

A month later, accountant Des Peelo compiled a report on Ahern's finances and submitted it to the tribunal. Peelo had formerly worked for Charlie Haughey. The source for his report was Ahern's word. Was Ahern now attempting to suggest that sums weren't his strong point? Or was he deploying the politician's tactic of handing over responsibility to somebody else, and therefore removing himself from the front line? In any event, the Peelo report turned out to be grossly inaccurate. It made no mention of sterling deposits, the key to Ahern's finances. The inaccuracies were no reflection on Peelo, as he was merely working off information verbally supplied by Ahern.

When O'Neill put it to the witness that he hadn't given full information, Ahern agreed. "I accept that, yes," he said.

Afterwards, outside, a spectacle that would become routine unfolded. Two groups had gathered near the door from which Ahern exited. When he appeared, one group shouted insults, while the other, led by Chris Wall and new TD Cyprian Brady, loudly applauded their hero. Ahern, as always, kept a smile plastered to his face.

The following day, O'Neill forensically examined the Manchester whip-around. Ahern's story began to go down side-roads. During his tearful Dobson interview, and afterwards in the Dáil, he said that the whip-around was made because his strapped circumstances were known to Tim Kilroe, who had arranged for the hat to be passed around. Now, with his accounts out in the open, he dropped the poverty plea. At the time of the whip-around he had had around £70,000 available to him. Detail began to blur. Ahern said now that he wasn't sure whether the event had taken place in May or September/October 1994. No private room was booked. The bar where the cash was handed over had not been privately reserved for the party. He couldn't identify who had been present other than the three individuals who had come forward.

The effect of this evidence was that it would be even more difficult for the tribunal to confirm independently whether or not a function as described by Ahern had actually taken place. He had no recollection of lodging the cash, along with the £16,500 dig-out money, on 11 October 1994.

He had been scheduled for two days' hearings, but by the end of the second it was obvious that more time was required. Ahern left the witness box battered and bruised, the foundations of his public stance trembling in the face of O'Neill's examination.

* * *

The commencement of Ahern's testimony meant that the battle he was waging against the tribunal opened up on two fronts. In Dublin Castle he was being subjected to a cold parsing and analysis of allegations and claims. The process relied on forensic examination of witnesses and the production of documents where possible. It involved establishing facts.

Outside the castle walls, the main concern for Ahern and his supporters was to win the battle of perception, as expressed by public opinion. The media reported the tribunal's proceedings. The evidence attracted negative comment principally, though not exclusively, from the press. By any objective standard, the first two days of hearings hadn't cast him in a positive light.

In order to counter this, government ministers and other party figures rushed to defend their leader. (Opinion polls during the period Ahern appeared at the tribunal showed that around 30 per cent of people actually believed his evidence. Coincidentally, this figure also represents what was then understood to be the Fianna Fáil core vote.) The brief for those supporting him, although not articulated, was clear: counter any negative perceptions of Ahern by attacking elements seen as hostile to the Taoiseach. This required deft footwork. There is no problem in a minister attacking elements of the media that present analysis adverse to the leader's interests. Attacking a tribunal set up by the Oireachtas is another matter. It would bring the executive into direct confrontation with an instrument of the Oireachtas, set up to investigate matters of corruption without fear or favour. If any member of the executive had a problem with the operation of the inquiry, it should have been a matter for the Oireachtas, and thrashed out in its forums. At least two government ministers would find themselves at sea in constitutional terms over the following months.

The second front was not just confined to members of the party. By the autumn of 2007, Ahern had one of the state's most influential newspapers on his side. The *Sunday Independent* has long been the biggest-selling broadsheet newspaper in the Republic. It pioneered a form of journalism in which comment was to the fore, often trenchant, sometimes targeting individuals personally, and usually well written.

Prior to the general election of 2007, the *Sunday Independent* began to position itself as supportive of Ahern. Former government press secretary Mandy Johnson, speaking on the RTÉ programme *Conversations with Éamon Dunphy* the following year, outlined what happened. "The relationship started just pre-election 2007," she told Dunphy. "The *Sunday Independent* took the view that the vast majority of Irish people felt what Bertie was going through was unfair and they wanted to give him a voice during the election campaign to put his side across."

The relationship survived the election and prospered. Eoghan Harris, one of the leading lights at the paper, was appointed by Ahern to the Seanad in August. And then when September came around with Ahern in Dublin Castle, the *Sunday Independent* scaled the ramparts to defend their chosen one.

On a commercial level, it made sense to take Ahern's side in the affair. Most of the media comment cast him in a bad light, mainly because the evidence did. Standing with him allowed the paper to project itself as defending a downtrodden Taoiseach against the ravages of the demented media.

Editorially, there was some balance in the paper through columnists Alan Ruddock and Gene Kerrigan. Both were consistently critical of Ahern on the basis of his evidence and the facts that were emerging in the public domain. Tellingly, their contributions were rarely flagged on the front page, which tended to be dominated by pro-Ahern stories, many compiled on the flimsiest of bases.

On Sunday, 16 September, two days after Ahern's first stint in the box, the headline on the lead story on page one read: "ALL OUT WAR: AHERN TAKES ON TRIBUNAL". The subhead underneath read: "O'Dea accuses tribunal of acting outside its remit in public trawl of Taoiseach's finances". The first line of the story read: "In a dramatic escalation of the confrontation between cabinet and the Mahon Tribunal, a government minister last night accused the inquiry of acting outside its terms of reference in its inquiries into the financial affairs of Taoiseach Bertie Ahern." The minister in question was Willie O'Dea, who occasionally wrote a column for the paper.

The tone of the story, flagging a "confrontation between cabinet and the Mahon Tribunal", suggested that the executive of the government was locked in battle with the inquiry. This is not about Ahern having to explain where he got the pots of money, the tone suggested, it's about the cabinet defending its integrity. The story went on: "It is now expected that other government ministers will follow Mr O'Dea's lead and aggressively attack the tribunal before it resumes its public sittings this Thursday."

Through the months that followed, the *Sunday Independent*'s front page consistently produced stories that cast Ahern in a favourable light and the tribunal, or witnesses hostile to Ahern, as acting unfairly.

Whatever about how newspapers decided to tell the story,

O'Dea, the Minister for Defence, had claimed that the tribunal was acting outside the law. He was obliged to bring this to the attention of the Oireachtas as soon as possible. He did nothing of the sort. When asked about the matter by reporters, he refused to comment further on it. He had done his bit, defended his leader, sent out into the public domain the impression that the tribunal had gone off the rails. And impressions, not pesky matters like constitutional duties, are what it's all about in the world of spin.

* * *

The following week, the tribunal moved on to the £30,000 that Mícheál Wall had handed over to rest in the account of Celia Larkin. O'Neill brought the witness through the lodgement of the money and the Bonnie and Clyde routine, when Ahern had waited outside in the car as Larkin entered AIB empty-handed and came out with her parcel of legally acquired cash.

The other issue that was explored that day and the following Monday was Ahern's claim to have changed £30,000 into sterling before making lodgements to accounts in June and December 1995. In those months he made two, totalling around £30,000. The tribunal discovered – through banking records rather than from Ahern – that both were preceded by the exchange of sterling. This raised a burning question: where had he got the sterling? Ahern claimed he was merely changing Irish currency into sterling in order to return the money Wall had given him the previous December. In other words, this was recycled money, rather than a new wad coming from somewhere else.

The only problem is that absolutely no records could be found of large sterling transactions in any of the banks Ahern dealt with for the time in question. In the witness box, he changed his story. He was now saying that somebody else had been sent out from his office to purchase the sterling at some point between January and June 1995, and that the exchange must have been in small quantities, which explained why there was no record of it. He couldn't identify who this person was.

This opened a new strange twist in his narrative. The lawyer O'Neill was fascinated.

O'Neill: I take it, Mr Ahern, that there are very, very few people that one would entrust £30,000 in cash to go off and purchase £30,000 sterling with?
Ahern: Limited.
O'Neill: In anybody's circle?
Ahern: Limited.
O'Neill: Yes. You have checked with each of those people I take it and each one of those people is not in a position to say to you that they have a recollection of your giving them £30,000 to go out and buy £30,000 worth of sterling?
Ahern: Well, the people I have checked with are within my office and a few people that I thought might have been likely and the answer is none of them did.
O'Neill: So none of the people who come to mind as being the people who you would give that type of money to for the exercise you have just described have confirmed to you that they did so. Is that right?
Ahern: That's correct.

Once more, there was not a scrap of paper to back up Ahern's claim. Once more, an individual at the centre of his narrative was either dead or had disappeared into the ether.

At the conclusion of his fourth day in the witness box, Ahern dealt with the bank records that suggested he might have deposited £25,000 sterling on 11 October 1994. He produced a report from his banking expert Paddy Stronge that said Stronge had read all the documents and come to the conclusion that no deposit of £25,000 was made that day. There was no explanation of how he reached this conclusion. We just had to take his word for it.

Later when the tribunal sought to examine Stronge's correspondence with Ahern on the matter, Ahern went to the High Court to prevent any viewing of the material.

On 26 September, the Dáil resumed after its summer break to the sound of a vote of no confidence in the Taoiseach. During the election campaign the previous May, the opposition parties had been reluctant to attack Ahern over his finances because their market research showed that he remained hugely popular and the tactic might backfire. Now, in the wake of Ahern's shaky opening days at the inquiry, they were emboldened to attack.

Opposition leader Enda Kenny said Ahern had not told the truth to the Irish people and had not co-operated with the tribunal. Labour leader Éamon Gilmore said Ahern's story about where he'd got the money was "cock and bull". Cowen spoke on behalf of the government, saying the people had spoken at the previous year's election and their wish was to allow the tribunal to investigate these matters. The motion was defeated.

The following Sunday the *Sunday Independent* weighed in again: "KENNY WRONG; THERE WAS A DIG-OUT", the splash headline read. The subhead went on: "Businessman demands apology and identifies others who attended the Manchester dinner". The story concerned John Kennedy, the only

Manchester millionaire to come forward to confirm that the 1994 whip-around had occurred. Another nineteen or so Manchester-Irish multimillionaires couldn't be located. The story pointed out that Kennedy had received a CBE from Queen Elizabeth II and was a Papal knight. He told the paper of his memory of the night. "Tim Kilroe said, 'I don't know if you know it but Bertie has parted from his wife, he's the Minister for Finance and he hasn't a bob.'"

If the claim was accurate then the whip-around was nonsensical. By the autumn of 1994 Ahern had been parted from his wife for more than seven years. As has been established, he had a lot more than a bob at the time.

Kennedy identified others who might have been present, but nobody else from Manchester ever came forward to confirm the dinner and whip-around for the strapped minister.

In other quarters, the spin descended into the ridiculous. On Newstalk FM, Minister for the Gaeltacht Éamon O'Cuiv brought up the spectre of the country's long tradition of emigration to explain the Manchester whip-around. "With emigrants there was a culture of supporting people in need [back home]," he told the station's *Lunchtime Show*. O'Cuiv was comparing the relatively wealthy Minister for Finance with impoverished farmers from an earlier era.

Elsewhere on the airwaves, Minister for Agriculture Mary Coughlan gave her interpretation of the word "co-operation": "I think it's important to say that Justice Mahon did indicate that the Taoiseach was more than facilitating with anything he was requested to do," she said. Mahon had said nothing of the sort.

Also on Newstalk, junior minister Conor Lenihan didn't find the Taoiseach's poor memory in relation to major life events at all strange: "I believe the Taoiseach," he said. "I wouldn't remember depositing fifty in cash or receiving a suitcase with thirty sterling," he said.

Perhaps it was just how the other half lived, but the message from the party faithful, from senior ministers down, was clear: Bertie Ahern had done no wrong. He was a victim of circumstances, both his own unfortunate marital difficulties and, in recent days, the power of a runaway tribunal. He need have no fear but the party was going to continue to stand behind him. It would take more than a few unusual-looking transactions to raise eyebrows among the faithful. There would be no wobbles in the party's support for him.

27

WOBBLES

In November 2007, the tribunal began to examine the dig-outs from friends in December 1993 and September 1994, which had been cited to explain two large deposits to Ahern's accounts. In December 1993, he had lodged £22,500. In October 1994, he had lodged £24,818, which he had said was made up of a £16,500 dig-out and £8,000 sterling from Manchester. This lodgement equated to £25,000 sterling.

The contributors began appearing in Dublin Castle. First up was publican Charlie Chawke. He was followed by Jim Nugent and David McKenna, all from the first dig-out. All gave broadly similar evidence. From the second dig-out, Dermot Carew, Barry English, Paddy "The Plasterer" Reilly and Joe Burke did likewise.

When Paddy Reilly was in the box, tribunal lawyer Henry Murphy put it to him that the whole affair was fiction: "You're making it up. Isn't that right, Mr Reilly?" Murphy said.

The witness was put out. "No, that is untrue. And, by the way, Mr Murphy, do not accuse me of lying, please. I did not come in here to be accused of lying, so do not attempt it, Mr Murphy, do not attempt to do that."

Later in his evidence Reilly, who had achieved some fame since he was introduced to the public in the Dobson interview more than a year previously, said: "I will defend myself."

What exactly he had to defend himself against was unclear. After all, he was only being asked to recount a friendly dig-out for a down-at-heel mate.

Barry English, who had hardly known Ahern when he had handed over five grand, was equally sure of his memory of the occasion. As usual, there was no paper trail, no withdrawal of cash from a bank, nothing that might independently support the evidence put forward.

The two crucial witnesses were Des Richardson and Padraic O'Connor. Richardson had organised the alleged dig-out. Included in the monies was a draft for £5,000, which Richardson said was from O'Connor, who was then chief executive of NCB Stockbrokers. As we know, O'Connor says he had nothing to do with a dig-out, that he made a political donation on behalf of his company at Richardson's request. If O'Connor's evidence is accepted, then there was no dig-out, raising the question as to where exactly the money had come from.

Des Richardson told the inquiry that the idea for a dig-out had come from Gerry Brennan. "I sat down with Gerry Brennan one evening, had a chat about the situation and picked out friends who could probably afford it," he said.

Then Richardson was asked about Padraic O'Connor. He claimed he had approached O'Connor on much the same basis as he had the others, although he personally wasn't friendly with the stockbroker. He said he asked for a hand-out for Ahern's legal fees. O'Connor complied. There was a procedural cock-up in issuing the cheque for £5,000, which was drawn on O'Connor's employer's account, NCB.

After the tribunal began making its enquiries, Richardson rang O'Connor and asked to meet him at the Berkeley Court Hotel in June 2005. Richardson explained that Ahern was being asked to trawl his finances. "Do you remember that five grand you gave me?" O'Connor told it as he remembered. The money had been a political donation from his company to Ahern's constituency operation. They parted.

The following year, in June/July 2006, Richardson requested another meeting, this time at the Radisson SAS in Stillorgan. They went over old ground. O'Connor had no doubt about the money in question. They parted. O'Connor was the only person involved in the alleged dig-outs whom Richardson met in these circumstances.

It wasn't until June 2006, twenty-one months after it had made initial enquiries, that the tribunal was told by Ahern that O'Connor had been involved in a dig-out.

O'Connor gave his evidence a week after Richardson, on 28 November. He said he wasn't approached to help out a friend in need. He had known Ahern personally in the early 1990s. As a former economist at the Central Bank, he had advised the Minister for Finance on the currency crisis that was blowing at the time. His contact with Ahern was sporadic and he didn't meet him outside the work environment. "I suppose it's flattering to be described as a friend," he said. "I was not a close personal friend. Since I left NCB nine years ago, I perhaps met Mr Ahern maybe once or twice . . . I made no personal donation to Mr Ahern . . . There was no personal payment to Mr Ahern. There was no payment from me to anybody. There was a payment from NCB to the O'Donovan Rossa constituency."

He certainly wasn't part of any Drumcondra circle. He was

shown the names of the others who claimed they took part in a dig-out. "I know some of them. I've never associated with any of them. I don't believe that I've met any of them," he said. He had no recollection of Ahern ever thanking him, as Ahern had claimed. "The loan never happened so the thank-you can't have happened," he said.

He told the tribunal about the meetings with Richardson, which he found highly unusual. After informing Richardson of what he recalled, he said Richardson replied: "'That's your recollection, and presumably you will be asked and you will have to give them your recollection.' I wasn't told what the alternative version was about."

Crucially, O'Connor's testimony on what occurred in 1993 was backed up by two other former NCB executives, who gave evidence the following day. Chris McHugh and Graham O'Brien both confirmed that O'Connor had related to them that Richardson had requested a political donation for Ahern's constituency. Arrangements were made for the payment.

When O'Connor completed his direct evidence to the tribunal, he was briefly questioned by a lawyer acting for Richardson. There were no questions from Ahern's lawyers. In fact, his team was not even present during most of O'Connor's evidence.

Here was a man who was, by default, calling Ahern a liar, and whose evidence, if accepted, would have horrendous ram-ifications for the Taoiseach. If O'Connor was to be believed, there was no dig-out – certainly not one including him. This implied that Ahern got the money somewhere else and was going to some lengths to cover up its origins.

Here was a man whom Ahern claimed was a friend of his, who, Ahern alleged, had been asked to help him out by another friend, Richardson. Yet Ahern chose not to have O'Connor questioned, his evidence tested, his claim of kinship put under the microscope.

Instead of testing O'Connor in the tribunal, where facts are coldly analysed, Ahern chose to spin on his own patch. Less than an hour after O'Connor stepped down, Ahern was doorstepped by reporters coming out of a function in Cavan. What, the reporters wanted to know, did he make of O'Connor's evidence?

"I thought that Padraic O'Connor was a very good friend of mine. If he has changed his mind I can't do anything about that," Ahern said. There is no room for testing such a statement on a doorstep interview. You just throw it out there, and it grabs tomorrow's headlines, and impressions are formed by readers.

The following month, when Ahern was next giving evidence, O'Neill asked him why he hadn't cross-examined O'Connor on his evidence. "Well, Mr O'Neill, first of all, Mr O'Connor is a friend of mine. He has been a friend of mine through the 1990s. I may not have been in touch with him in more recent times.

"I was a friend of his in the 1990s, and his family and in-laws would be very good friends of mine. So if you are criticising me for not allowing my legal team to come down and cross-examine a person that I considered a friend and who was very helpful to me because of his professional advice to me in the 1990s, well, I … well, I think that's the point that you're making that I didn't do that. But I didn't do that. I didn't ask my legal team to come down and cross-examine."

It was a staggering answer. Ahern did not cross-examine a man whose evidence could destroy him, ruin his political career, because he considered the man to be a friend. No greater love hath any man than to lay down his career rather than challenge a friend.

On 2 December, the second story on the front page of the

338

Sunday Independent was headlined "NCB chief O'Connor was 'close' to Ahern". The story began: "Padraic O'Connor described himself as 'close' to Taoiseach Bertie Ahern in private testimony to the Mahon Tribunal earlier this year." It was based on O'Connor's testimony to the tribunal in private interview. Nowhere in the copy published did O'Connor actually say he was "close" to Ahern. But, then, facts were a casualty of the war in which Ahern saw himself immersed.

* * *

He was back in the box on 20 December. More questions about the origins of his money, more tittering in the public gallery, more wall-to-wall media coverage. Towards the end of the day, O'Neill outlined a complicated theory in an attempt to explain circumstantial evidence around the first alleged dig-out. He had shown that Ahern might well have known he would be getting money over Christmas, which would rule out a spontaneous dig-out. He suggested to Ahern that maybe he had managed to set up a situation in which he would be receiving a loan from the bank, based on the promise of money.

Ahern professed himself flabbergasted at the theory. "It is unbelievable, Mr O'Neill," he said. "And I really, really don't believe it . . . that you or anybody else would put that together other than trying to set me up or stitch me up. That is just unbelievable. Unbelievable!"

In fact, O'Neill's theory, while based on circumstantial evidence, was as believable as the stories of the dig-outs. However, one premise on which it was based was that Ahern was giving a completely untrue version of where and when he had been given the dig-out money. The implication therein is that he was lying.

Unsurprisingly, his response was outrage. Following his own response, there was a set-to between his lawyer, Maguire, and O'Neill, with Maguire claiming his client was being unfairly treated.

Outside the castle walls, the battle was joined. Within half an hour of the day's proceedings ending, the evening radio talk shows were being offered government ministers to come on air and defend their leader. The only stipulation was that they would not debate with another guest about the tribunal. They just wanted to express their own feelings.

That afternoon, Noel Dempsey, Seamus Brennan and Mícheál Martin appeared on radio shows to criticise the tribunal's examination of the Taoiseach. On *The Six One News*, Dermot Ahern did likewise. None had access to transcripts from the day's proceedings that early, but the government press secretary, Eoin O'Neachtain, had been present for Ahern's evidence.

The following morning, Dick Roche was on RTÉ's *Morning Ireland*. He accused the tribunal of "bias" and "badgering a witness". He referred to the "appalling treatment of the Taoiseach": "Every citizen has rights and when a powerful, powerful body like the tribunal tramples on the rights of a citizen, they diminish the rights of all citizens," he said. It was an a very serious accusation. He had implied that the tribunal was behaving illegally against a citizen, and not just any citizen, but the elected leader of the people.

Like Willie O'Dea, he didn't bring his concerns to the floor of the Dáil to debate whether the inquiry was now corrupt. Ahern didn't bring the matter to the High Court where dozens before him had sought relief. But the word went out over the airwaves. The Taoiseach is under attack.

Fine Gael senator Eugene Regan, who was also on the

programme, offered an alternative analysis of why half the cabinet was rushing onto the radio. "The evidence of the Taoiseach to date is quite unbelievable in relation to dig-outs and whip-arounds and Manchester dinners and so on. Are ministers going to interfere every time the tribunal gets close to the truth? They are trying to undermine the tribunal and its credibility."

Later in the day Willie O'Dea was manning the ramparts on the station's *News at One* programme. He brought up an old chestnut: "I'm waiting for the day the tribunal is going to go back to Bertie Ahern's first communion day and examine what he did with his first communion money and did he get it in notes or coins or did he put it in a piggy bank or a real bank or did he get a half crown from Owen O'Callaghan." He added that he was not attacking the tribunal, but merely raising questions as a citizen.

Ahern was into another day's evidence. That morning, another set-to developed between his lawyer Maguire, the judge and the tribunal counsel, O'Neill. Maguire claimed that O'Neill was working to an agenda. Judge Gerald Keys said he found such an accusation offensive. Relations between Ahern's team and the tribunal were deteriorating. But the man himself ambled up to the box, wanting only to be of assistance to the inquiry.

Proceedings thereafter reverted to tense politeness. The day was spent parsing the alleged dig-outs. At one stage, O'Neill asked Ahern how he felt about his personal solicitor going around asking people to help him out with his, Ahern's, legal fees. Wasn't his family-law case confidential? Would Brennan not be intruding on the solicitor-client bond of trust? Didn't Brennan know that Ahern had taken out a loan to cover the fees?

"He wasn't telling anyone any great secrets, to be frank with you," Ahern said. "I'm not going to condemn a person who isn't here. I mean, they were all friends of mine. In no way would he be divulging anything to anyone in an improper way."

At the end of the day, Ahern left the witness box wishing a happy Christmas to all the tribunal staff.

Over the holiday period, he gave the usual round of Christmas media interviews. On 6 January, the *Sunday Independent* published its piece under the headline: "BERTIE GOES BALLISTIC OVER PRURIENT AND PRYING TRIBUNAL". It was a reference to the 20 December hearing in which questions arose about the Taoiseach's bedroom. In examining a dig-out designed to put a roof over Ahern's head, O'Neill asked about his accommodation in St Luke's where he already had a roof. His former secretary, Grainne Carruth, had already told the inquiry that upstairs at St Luke's was private, that it was Ahern's personal domain. He didn't agree. "I think your question is, 'What was the apartment?'" he replied to O'Neill. "The apartment was the bedroom." So, Ahern had brought the tribunal into his bedroom, and when O'Neill attempted to test this evidence he was accused of prying and prurience. It was classic Bertie.

On the same day, he gave a radio interview to RTÉ's *This Week*. He told Gerard Barry that he'd been dealing with the same issue of whether or not he had received money from Owen O'Callaghan for eight years. "It's the same issue – that I got money from Owen O'Callaghan – that has led to investigating endlessly my marriage, my accounts, my tax affairs."

He was asked was it advisable that he had taken money from friends. "I would have been better off if I'd got a bigger loan from the bank," he said. Of course, this was nonsense. Even by his own account, his personal wealth at the time was such that he didn't require any loan. Were dark forces out to get him? "There has been an effort by a small group of people to, in whatever way they can, to do me damage. Anyone who has followed this closely can see how that system works. I have no difficulty with answering a tribunal. The difference with me, when it's me when I'm there, there's sixty or seventy media, full public gallery. It's played out in soap opera."

The song remained the same. He was doing his best to help out, despite the myriad forces ranged against him. A much simpler analysis might conclude that if he had just told the inquiry all the details of his extraordinary accumulation of large sums of money in a credible manner, all the questions might have gone away.

28

A TOPPLING OF THE CARDS

When the new year of 2008 rolled around, Ahern looked to have weathered the latest storms. There was no question of him coming under any pressure from within his party. The cabinet, as evidenced in the rush to the ramparts in December, was four square behind him. Throughout the country the party was also secure. There were no murmurings of discontent. Ahern's great skill in uniting the party soon after he assumed leadership in 1994 was now bearing fruit for himself in a most unlikely situation. No faction saw the tribunal evidence as an opportunity.

In any event, Ahern had already signalled that he would depart before the next election. The party had a lot for which to be grateful to him in electoral terms. This complicated business of money and St Luke's and a helping hand from friends, sure, the public didn't really grasp it and that was all that mattered.

The two smaller parties in government, the PDs and the Greens, knew from Michael McDowell's bitter experience that it was best to remain on the sidelines while Ahern's money woes were played out.

On a wider scale, the practice of politics was taking a hit. Up to that point, opinion polls were reflecting a view that between half and two-thirds of the public didn't believe Ahern's evidence. Yet, as seen in December, a whole slew of government ministers were prepared repeatedly to answer that they did believe it. They were also attacking the tribunal for the manner in which Ahern was being questioned. With the most senior politicians in the state behaving in this manner, there couldn't but be damage inflicted on the credibility of politics as a whole.

January dawned with further grief. A story broke in the *Irish Mail on Sunday* outlining Ahern's contacts with the Revenue Commissioners following his Dobson interview fifteen months previously. The correspondence showed that the Revenue had not been contacted about any possible liabilities on dig-outs or loans prior to Ahern's RTÉ interview.

An MRBI opinion poll in the *Irish Times* a fortnight later made uncomfortable reading for Ahern. More than three-quarters of those polled said they did not believe his evidence to the tribunal. This response from 78 per cent was up six percentage points on the last poll done two months previously. A total of 14 per cent said they believed he had given a full picture of his finances, which was down three points on the last poll.

The electorate was evenly divided on whether he should resign immediately over the issue, 44 per cent saying yes, and 46 per cent no. The big chasm was between the parties. Only 16 per cent of Fianna Fáil voters felt he should resign, while 77 per cent were opposed to the idea. By contrast, among Fine Gael, Labour and Sinn Féin voters, between 60 per cent and 71 per cent were keen that he should go.

The message was clear: fewer than one in five people in the country actually believed that the Taoiseach was giving truthful evidence under oath in an inquiry into corruption. Around half felt it was a resignation matter, while the other half felt it didn't matter.

Crucially, the base was solid. More than three-quarters of Fianna Fáil voters wanted him to stay and at least half actually wanted him to remain at the helm for the next election. There were only two explanations for the support emanating from the party. Either it reflected the legendary loyalty that it elicited from its members or large swathes didn't care that their leader had received large quantities of cash in dubious circumstances and was now giving incredible explanations. Either way, bar any further revelations, the party was secure behind him.

* * *

On 11 February, Ahern followed two dozen other prominent politicians and businessmen in asking the High Court to rein in the tribunal. Most of those who had gone to it over the previous decade were subsequently shown to have had something serious to hide. Some weren't. All claimed they were acting on a matter of principle as citizens.

Now the Taoiseach, the leader of the House of the Oireachtas, which had initiated the tribunal to clean up politics, was donning his Joe Citizen hat and asking the courts to protect him from the excesses of the tribunal. Ahern's lawyer applied to the court, claiming that the tribunal was acting in a manner that was "manifestly unconstitutional". There were three planks to the challenge.

The first was that Ahern was disputing the inquiry's right to question him on statements he made in the Dáil in the wake of the story breaking in September and October 2006. The principle involved here was that statements to the House are privileged, and under the constitution should not be answerable in any other forum. Ahern may have decided that, as a career politician, it was a principle of his that statements made in the House should not be answerable to any higher power in the name of democracy. Coincidently, any raking over the statements he made in the Dáil in those heady days would uncover what might charitably be described as inaccuracies, such as references to contacting the "tax authorities".

The second plank was a claim of client confidentiality over his correspondence with his banking expert Paddy Stronge. Ahern had employed Stronge to dispute the bank records that suggested he had made large sterling and dollar lodgements in 1994. Stronge had an eminent background at the Bank of Ireland. The only public result from his deliberations had been delivered in evidence the previous September, when his report declared that he was of the opinion there had been no large foreign-exchange lodgements as suggested by the records. There was no analysis of his deliberations. There was no detailed breakdown of how he had reached his conclusion. There was no explanation as to why the branch records might have been wrongly interpreted. He just stated that, as an expert, he thought Ahern was right.

Now Ahern wanted any correspondence between his legal team and Stronge to be kept from the tribunal. He could have decided on this course of action to protect citizens at large from a powerful inquiry. It might have been another matter of principle. Or maybe he just didn't want the tribunal to see the correspondence as it might weaken his case that the bank records couldn't be right.

The third plank of his challenge was to demand he be given access to the material used by the tribunal when it had put a hypothesis to him about how he had come into the dig-out money in December 1993. This was a reference to the theory O'Neill had put to him the previous December when Ahern had accused the lawyer of trying to set him up. O'Neill had presented a set of circumstances in relation to bank records to suggest that Ahern had been expecting money before Christmas 1993, and therefore his story of being presented with the proceeds of a spontaneous dig-out could not be true. Ahern now wanted to be shown all the records used to construct this hypothesis.

This element of the challenge appears reasonable, and when the matter came to court, a lawyer for the tribunal immediately said the inquiry was willing to supply that information.

When he was asked by reporters about taking the tribunal to the High Court, Ahern replied that he was just acting on the advice of his lawyers. Nothing to do with me, guv.

In the round, the challenge demonstrated that Ahern was no longer clinging to his public stance that he was co-operating with the tribunal as best he could to clear up a misunderstanding.

Whatever about the optics, the legal basis for his challenge was sound. The case was heard by the High Court two months later: it ruled in Ahern's favour on the two issues that were outstanding.

* * *

Ahern's next appearance was on 21 February, ten days after he had launched the High Court challenge. The dastardly Mr O'Neill brought him through details of transactions in his Irish Permanent account, and in the B/T account, which stood for Building Trust, definitely not Bertie and Tim. He asked about a £5,000 lodgement to the Irish Permanent account in January

1994. The witness couldn't identify the source of the money. He then said it was a "political donation for personal use".

"Why would you take money like that, Mr Ahern?" O'Neill asked. "In what circumstances would you not say, 'Sorry, I don't take money from you ... I'm not going to take gifts from you merely because I'm a politician'?"

Ahern replied: "Nowadays, you're not allowed to take it without total declaration, but if somebody gave you money and said it's for your use, then they are giving it to you as a gift. That's the only way."

The chairman asked him if he believed a political donation was a donation to him as a politician to be used to discharge political expenses, or a personal gift to be used to spend on holidays or a house.

He responded that sometimes individuals might give him a contribution for his personal use and if he lodged it to a personal account he still spent it on the constituency. "You'd still end up using it," he said. "I could spend €400 or €500 in any weekend around the country in draws for cars, for clubs, for organisations. I have to use my personal money to do that – every politician does."

He wasn't totally incorrect. Prior to the Ethics in Public Office Act in 1995, and various regulations established in its wake, some politicians were careless in how they dealt with political donations. It wouldn't be unheard of for a politician to put a donation in his or her personal account from which they would also draw money for the various events Ahern described.

However, £5,000 was a large sum for the times to be treated in that manner. The odd few hundred, maybe even a thousand, might find its way into a personal account, but five grand was in a different league for most other politicians.

There was also the problem of why he had put it into an account that wasn't a current account from which he would access regular withdrawals. He had lodged it in an account opened to buy a house.

In any event, the money, the way it was treated, the failure to declare it for tax, all might have been forgivable if these had been isolated incidents. Instead, they were just more bricks in the wall.

In further questioning, Ahern said that a number of lodgements to the Irish Permanent account represented salary cheques.

Later in the day, O'Neill moved on to the B/T account. When Ahern had prepared and signed an affidavit in 2005, outlining twenty-three accounts that touched on his personal or political life, he hadn't mentioned the B/T account. It had come to the tribunal's attention only when it had followed the money trail left by a political donation from Davy Stockbrokers.

Ahern said the account had nothing to do with him: it was all the business of this mysterious building trust. O'Neill asked about a withdrawal of £30,000 on 30 March 1993. Ahern said it had gone to a staff member to help out with the purchase of a house for elderly relatives, who would have had to buy the house they were renting or be evicted. "The aged people would have had to go to court," Ahern said. "They would have got a restricted use of part of the house." He added that they were frightened.

O'Neill asked had the loan been repaid. Ahern said it had.

"Do you know approximately when?" O'Neill asked.

"It would have been after the first tribunal letter, some time after the first tribunal letter," Ahern replied. The loan was repaid fifteen years after it had been extended and only after the tribunal had discovered the account.

The following day began with more hassle between Ahern's lawyer, Maguire, and the tribunal. Mahon, having sat through numerous occasions when it had been implied that the tribunal was acting unfairly, finally let rip. He told Maguire that the lawyer was alleging he and his two colleagues were corrupt.

Mahon: You are making an allegation that we are pursuing some sort of agenda. You are saying in effect that we are corrupt, that we are …

Maguire: I didn't say that, Chairman, and you know I didn't.

Mahon: You have said it. You have said it. You have used the term "agenda". If we are following the agenda that you have accused us of and in effect, we reiterate now. The effect of that allegation is that you are saying that we are crooks. That is what you are saying … that we are conducting a witch hunt. And how can that be interpreted as anything but an allegation that these three judges are off on some sort of a frolic of their own, out to do down people in a way which is unconstitutional, unfair and is in effect criminal?

Maguire: Chairman, you are putting a construction on matters which has not occurred. That … Let me finish, Chairman. I must have some right to continue my points.

First of all, in relation to an agenda. I have accused counsel for the tribunal of having an agenda. Now let's take that as being the first point and I don't make any apology for saying that.

Mahon: Why haven't you done something about it? If you were serious about that you would have taken that [to court]. That would be probably the most important point that you could raise by way of judicial review. You

351

could, you are a former chairman of the Bar Council. You should have, if you had views about the tribunal counsel that you are suggesting that you have, that is professional conduct on their part.

And the proper course was for you to make a complaint to the Bar Council. You know what those rules are better than anyone in this room. You should have gone to the High Court long ago and said this tribunal is engaged in an agenda.

It's the most . . . Of all the allegations that have ever been made against us, and many have been made, that is the most serious allegation because it is the one which, if it was established as being true, would completely undermine the work of the tribunal.

There was some applause in the public gallery. The exchanges went on for a few more minutes, but Mahon had made himself clear. The low-level sniping, which he obviously saw as designed for media consumption, had better end.

The judge had a point, even if emotional outbursts from the bench are a rarity. Maguire had stated that he believed the tribunal counsel was following an agenda, which was a serious charge. Yet he wasn't willing to bring the issue to the professional body or the High Court. If he believed that his client was being unfairly treated by an instrument of the Oireachtas, he was obliged to seek a remedy. Instead, his words were consumed by the media and thrown out to the public, raising barstool questions as to whether or not some people were out to do down poor Bertie.

The tactic reflected that of the government ministers, who had accused the inquiry of acting illegally. Instead of bringing such a charge to the appropriate forum, they had simply thrown it out for consumption as impressions of bias. Whatever about the battle inside the castle, the parsing and analysing of cold facts and testing evidence, those supporting Ahern beyond the castle walls knew how to mollycoddle public opinion.

Later in the day, Ahern was asked to which staff member the loan of £30,000 had been extended.

"Celia Larkin," he replied.

He said he had had nothing to do with the loan. It was a matter for the building trust committee, of which no record of its existence has ever been located. He wasn't even told about it until after the loan was granted. Larkin was now the owner of the property in which one of her elderly aunts still resided.

The day ended with a decidedly uncomfortable Ahern. The base maintained a united front against the world outside the party, but a few small rumblings could be detected. It was one thing to have tales of money going in and out of Ahern's account. Now it looked as if he was co-opting party funds for personal use, even if it was a hard-luck story on Larkin's behalf. (That, of course, was on the assumption that the B/T account was a party fund, and not a Bertie and Tim slush fund.)

It didn't look good, this Celia business. But worse was to come.

* * *

On 5 March the tribunal received information that changed everything. In attempting to get details of Ahern's lodgements to his Irish Permanent account, the inquiry had been informed by a bank official that records didn't go back as far as 1994. This was subsequently revised, and details of lodgements were delivered to the tribunal. The details showed for the first time that Ahern's secretary had made a number of sterling lodgements.

In evidence before Christmas, Carruth had informed the tribunal that all the lodgements she had made to the account were from Ahern's salary cheques. On 21 February, Ahern told the tribunal that the lodgements were from his salary cheques. Now there was evidence to suggest that these two statements, from different sources, could not be true.

The development was significant. In practically all the lodgements to his associated accounts, Ahern had offered an explanation, most of which appeared to have a dubious basis when tested. This was the latest, and perhaps the most serious.

The question that had haunted all his tribunal woes over money popped up again. If he hadn't got the money from where he'd said he had, then whence, or from whom, had it come? The question was informed by the new discovery involving, once more, sterling.

On 6 March, the tribunal wrote to Ahern to inform him of the new evidence. The implications must have been clear to him. Both he and his former secretary had given evidence independently that was now shown to be inaccurate. Carruth was due to go back to the tribunal to revisit the matter.

On the afternoon of 19 March Grainne Carruth stepped up to the witness box. Three months previously, on 18 December, she had been asked about the lodgements to the Irish Permanent account. "Bertie would hand me his cheques and ask me to go to the bank. I'd go to the bank and at his request if he wanted I would lodge money to his daughters' accounts in the Permanent TSB [Irish Permanent had taken over TSB in 2001] and then return with the money to him," she said. Asked had she converted sterling for Ahern, she said: "I never dealt in sterling." She made no mention of lodging money to Ahern's own account in the branch.

Later, she was asked by Judge Gerald Keys for clarification.

Keys: Do I take it from your evidence that the only banking input you had with Mr Ahern was related purely to his cheques arising from his salary. Is that correct?
Carruth: Yes, Judge.
Keys: Nothing else?
Carruth: Nothing else, Judge.

Now she was back in the witness box to explain why the records begged to differ completely. She stuck to her original line. "I have no recollection of any dealings with sterling whatsoever," she said.

"I have no recollection. I have no belief that I ever saw or handled or dealt in sterling," she said later, and again: "I made lodgements to the girls' accounts for his salary cheque ... I have no recollection of him having an account there at that time ... I have no recollection of sterling ever being in my hands."

Yet the records said that, on at least three occasions, she had brought large bundles of sterling, up to £6,000 worth, and lodged them to accounts on behalf of her boss.

Asked how she felt when she had received notice from the tribunal that she had handled large sums of sterling, she replied: "I shook for two hours."

At three fifty-five p.m., the chairman intervened. "I think in the circumstances it would be better to continue Ms Carruth's evidence tomorrow. And I think in the meantime Ms Carruth should look at the documentation again – talk to your solicitor so that you will be quite clear yourself as to what your position is in relation to the evidence you are giving and the evidence you have given in the past."

Carruth returned the following day, but there would be no singing. She stuck to her line, despite the evidence. "I don't believe I told an untruth. I tried to be as honest as I could at all times," she said. "I have to accept as a matter of probability in my dealings here yesterday that it was sterling and there was transactions done in Irish Permanent."

The judge asked her had her solicitor told her what the consequences were of telling a lie in a tribunal. She said he hadn't. O'Neill told her that a conviction on perjury or obstructing a tribunal could attract a prison sentence.

"I just want to go home, Judge," Carruth said. She broke down.

O'Neill asked her why she had changed solicitors. When she had first dealt with the tribunal two years previously, she was accompanied by Liam Guidera, who was also Ahern's solicitor. She was now represented by Hugh Millar.

She said her husband had found Mr Millar for her. She gave no further explanation for the change.

Why hadn't she got in touch with Ahern when she received documents from the tribunal demonstrating that she had given false evidence, and was now in a serious situation?

"Because my first priority was to get my children sorted and then, with his schedule, he was away and that, so I never thought … I never thought of it."

At one point, the evidence appeared fleetingly as if it might be heading towards a revelation.

O'Neill: Why is it that you did not contact Mr Ahern in relation to these matters that are of crucial importance to you and your family?

Carruth: Because I'm hurt.
O'Neill: Because why?
Carruth: I'm hurt.
O'Neill: You're hurt?
Carruth: And I'm upset.
O'Neill: And what is upsetting you about your evidence here to the tribunal today?
Carruth: Because it's taking me from my family and that's why I'm upset.
O'Neill: Is there another reason?
Carruth: I just want to go home.

The expectation of a revelation passed. Soon after, the judge called a break to allow Carruth a rest from what was highly emotional testimony. She returned to the witness box and finished her evidence before lunchtime. There was no great revelation, but irreparable damage had been done to Ahern.

Carruth was a young mother of three. When she had been employed by Ahern in the mid-1990s, she was in her twenties, working for sixty-six pounds a week. Yet she had been thrust to the front line to defend the grubby practices that had been afoot in St Luke's in those days. It didn't reflect well on Ahern.

The mood in the wake of Carruth's evidence was probably best summed up by *Irish Times* sketch writer Miriam Lord in the following day's edition:

Bertie Ahern must be a very proud man today. His Ministers must be so proud of him too. It's such a pity none of them could make it to Dublin Castle to watch Gráinne Carruth give her evidence.

They would have seen a woman, alone and trembling in the witness box, battling back the tears as she whispered in tones so anguished they were barely audible: "I just want to go home." It was so pitiful, it's just a pity Bertie wasn't there to see it.

He might have stood up and shouted like a man: "Let the girl go. It's me you want!" But that only happens in the movies.

The Taoiseach was unavailable to the media yesterday.

If he had been in Dublin Castle, he would have witnessed the distress of his former secretary, loyal servant to the last, struggling to maintain her composure in the face of strong but fair questions about his finances.

Over the following fortnight, Ahern kept an unusually low profile. He attended a football match in Parnell Park on Easter Sunday, but was generally unavailable for comment, not even one of his fabled doorstep interviews.

The noise emanating from his colleagues was not as reassuring as it had been up to then. Mary Harney said that Grainne Carruth's evidence was unsettling. No ministers rushed out this time to say that they found nothing unbelievable in it.

A Rubicon had been crossed. Ahern's explanations as to how he had come into unusual and large sums of money had never been watertight. However, this was the first time there had been a clear and indisputable conflict between his version of events and what the tribunal showed to be the facts.

The perception that Ahern had left his modestly paid former secretary swinging in the wind did not go down well in Fianna Fáil. Political commentators began to posit the view that if he could not come up with a reasonable explanation for the discrepancies he was finished as Taoiseach.

On 26 March, Cowen returned from holidays and a day later

made his way to Beresford where he had a meeting with Ahern about the tribunal evidence, as described in the prologue.

On Sunday, 30 March, Minister for Agriculture Mary Coughlan appeared on the RTÉ TV programme *The Week in Politics*. The presenter, Sean O'Rourke, asked her on a number of occasions whether she believed Ahern's evidence in light of all that had transpired. Coughlan, who was known to be close to Brian Cowen, didn't give a straight answer. She repeatedly talked around the question, refusing to go where she and all her colleagues had previously dived in. It was the first public sign of a crack.

Three days later, the Dáil was due to resume after the Easter break. Early in the morning, reporters were getting news of an unscheduled press conference. Soon after ten o'clock, Ahern came to the entrance of Government Buildings surrounded by his cabinet. In a speech that was otherwise becoming for one who had served in public office for thirty years, he reverted to type in relation to his dealings with the tribunal:

"The constant barrage of commentary on tribunal-related matters has and, I believe, will continue to dominate the political agenda at an important point for our country. We face uncertain economic times and challenges and we are soon to cast our vote on the Lisbon Treaty. The vital interests of Ireland demand that the national dialogue of our political system address these fundamental issues and not be constantly deflected by the minutiae of my life, my lifestyle, and my finances.

"The decision I am announcing today – like all other decisions that I have taken in a lifetime in politics – is solely motivated by what is best for the people. I have been reflecting on pursuing this course of action for some time. This is solely a personal decision. I have no doubt that a simplistic analysis will suggest that my decision has been influenced by most recent events at the tribunal. What I announce today is completely inspired by the desire to refocus the political dynamic in Ireland.

"Recent developments have not motivated my decision. For the record I state today that nothing could be further from the truth. I look forward to comprehensively dealing with these matters at the tribunal and robustly refuting any imputation against me."

He went on: "I want everyone to understand one truth above all else. Never, in all the time I have served in public life, have I put my personal interest ahead of the public good. I have served this country and the people I have the honour to represent in Dáil Éireann honestly.

"I have provided more details about my personal finances than any person in public life who has ever held office. While I will be the first to admit that I have made mistakes in my life and in my career, one mistake I have never made is to enrich myself by misusing the trust of the people.

"I have never received a corrupt payment and I have never done anything to dishonour any office I have held. I know that some people will feel that some aspects of my finances are unusual. I truly regret if this has caused any confusion or worry in people's minds. All of these issues arose in a period when my family, personal and professional situations were rapidly changing and I made the best decisions I could in the circumstances in which I found myself. I know in my heart of hearts that I have done no wrong and wronged no one.

"I look forward to the completion of the tribunal's work and I am confident that when it reports, the tribunal will find that I have not acted improperly in any way. Equally I will not allow issues concerning myself or my finances to divert attention from the important job of government at hand. I believe it is in the best interests of the government, my party and, most importantly, the people of Ireland that I set out the time-frame for my departure from office."

There was nothing simplistic in the analysis that his announcement was connected to the tribunal revelations. It was as plain as day that the recent evidence was the reason he was leaving.

In relation to his comment that he had provided more details about his personal finances than any person in public life who has ever held office, he failed to mention that the reason for such scrutiny was that he either couldn't or wouldn't answer simple questions in a plausible manner on how he had come into large sums of cash.

The following day, in a doorstep interview at University College Dublin, he was asked how he viewed the questioning of Grainne Carruth in the tribunal. "Lowlife stuff," he said. The implication was that the tribunal lawyers had behaved appallingly in testing what, on the face of it, appeared to be entirely false evidence. He himself, of course, bore no responsibility for putting his former secretary into the position in which she had found herself.

Weeks later, the outgoing Taoiseach was on his lap of honour, addressing the US House of Congress. RTÉ's Bryan Dobson collared him for an interview. He asked about Carruth, and why he hadn't contacted her prior to her attending at Dublin Castle.

"If they [the tribunal] had bothered to ask or tell me the information, I would have done that but that isn't here nor there."

But the tribunal *had* informed him eleven days before Carruth gave her evidence. That wasn't public knowledge yet, and Dobson wasn't in a position to challenge Ahern on the matter. It was a classic example of the manner in which the Taoiseach had spun the tribunal story since it had first surfaced eighteen months earlier. From the off, he had made statements – and appeared to be stating various things in his own inimitable way – which, when subsequently introduced to the public domain through evidence, were shown to be wholly inaccurate. The tactic had served him well, even seen him through a third general election.

Finally, however, the evidence had caught up with the spin, and his latest round of explanations about how the big bad tribunal was out to get him no longer stood up.

WHERE HAVE ALL THE CAMERAS GONE?

Bertie Ahern returned to Dublin Castle for the last but one round of torture on 4 June 2008. He was no longer appearing as Taoiseach, having formally left office a month previously. He had an assistant and his garda driver, but the retinue had greatly thinned out. So had the public gallery, which, while still relatively full, was not heaving, as it had been for previous appearances.

During that day's examination, he revealed for the first time his facility for backing horses. In explaining where the sterling lodgements made by Carruth had originated, he related for the first time his foreign exchanges in cars and bars with Tim Kilroe: "In or about the early 1990s, I contemplated an investment opportunity, being the purchase of an apartment to be constructed in Salford Quay, Manchester," he explained. It was for this investment that he had built up a pile of sterling cash, which came from Kilroe, in exchange for Irish punts, which came from his salary cheques back in Dublin.

He added that some of the cash had come from elsewhere. "As is well known publicly, I am interested in horse-racing and

over the years I have placed bets on horse-races. Over the period
of time in question and subsequently, I won various sums of
money. Some of these would have been paid in sterling."

It was a defence that might well have been true but had an
unfortunate echo. In Irish folklore, whenever the taxman asked
about the origins of unexplained money, the standard reply
was "I won it on a horse." This was the company in which
Ahern now found himself. Again, if this was an isolated
incident in his narrative, if it was a matter of a few thousand
in sterling that he had a problem explaining, he would be
entitled to some slack. Instead, it was part of a pattern.
Another coincidence, another trail that can't be picked up,
another batch of sterling from an unlikely source.

If he hadn't left high office by then, the latest revelations
would most likely have propelled him out. Saying he'd won it
on a horse – even though this was just one element of the
money – simply wouldn't have washed any more in the political
system at the end of a long, weary investigation of his unusual
finances.

Over three days, O'Neill examined Ahern on his building-
society account and the by now fabled B/T account. He
established that, despite the account's alleged purpose, none of
the eight significant withdrawals from it had been used to fund
building work in St Luke's. Ahern was adamant that the B/T
account most definitely had nothing to do with him. "This
account was not opened for me. I personally never lodged one
penny or cent into it and I never took one penny or cent out of
it," he told the inquiry.

The previous January, when the tribunal's inquiry into the
B/T account had been well under way, the constituency
organisation had retained PricewaterhouseCoopers to compile
a report on its existence. As with other reports, the consultants

relied chiefly on Bertie Ahern for their information. The only documentary evidence they received constituted handwritten notes by him.

In the same month, the constituency reclassified the account. It became officially known as the Building Trust Account. Tim Collins stepped down as a signatory and was replaced by two constituency officials. The B/T account was coming home to Fianna Fáil, in spirit if not in actual ownership.

Another summer passed, this one the first for eleven years in which Ahern wasn't serving as Taoiseach. It was his first summer in more than twenty years when he wasn't occupied by the problems and challenges of high office. (In 1995 and 1996, he had been leader of the opposition.)

On 15 September, he was back in Dublin Castle for his last stint in the witness box. It was just over a year since his first appearance, when his reputation had begun to crack. It was nearly two years to the day since the story of his dig-outs had surfaced. This time around, he finally got to address the kernel of the issue: had any of the batches of money flowing through his accounts come from Owen O'Callaghan?

Tribunal lawyer O'Neill brought him through three scenarios that raised the possibility of a connection between the two men. The evidence is entirely circumstantial.

Tom Gilmartin had said that O'Callaghan had told him at a meeting with bankers that Ahern had assured him there would be no tax designation for a rival shopping centre to Quarryvale at Blanchardstown, and that it had cost him £30,000. At that stage O'Callaghan and Gilmartin had been developing Quarryvale. Gilmartin was vague on dates and the exact circumstances of the meeting.

On 24 March 1994, Ahern met O'Callaghan in Government Buildings. At a meeting with bankers some time after that

O'Callaghan told them he had received assurance from Ahern that the tax designation would not go ahead.

On 24 April, Ahern met with a bank official in St Luke's and gave him £30,000 in cash to put into a special savings account. He says this money was from the savings he had accumulated in his safe. It was an odd deposit. He already had £22,500 in the special savings account. The maximum allowable was £50,000. Yet here he was putting in £30,000, which was more than the account was allowed to accommodate. The round figure coincides with the £30,000 Gilmartin alleges passed between O'Callaghan and Ahern.

In any event, the Department of Finance's advice was to deny designation to Blanchardstown, and Ahern acted on it.

Ahern and O'Callaghan vehemently deny that any money passed between them. Hypothetically, even if the developer had paid him money, Ahern had acted only as his department advised.

O'Callaghan was formulating plans to build a football stadium in Neilstown at the same time. On 2 August 1994, his lobbyist Frank Dunlop delivered a detailed proposal to Ahern's office. Six days later, Ahern made a cash deposit of £20,000 to his daughter's account. This, he says, also came from savings he kept in a safe at St Luke's. The large round figure does not coincide with the £50,000 and the £30,000 that Gilmartin alleges was a bribe.

O'Callaghan had a US investment bank, Chilton O'Connor, on board with his plans to develop the stadium. Chilton O'Connor was based in Los Angeles and looking at opportunities in Ireland. On 10 November 1994, their representative met Ahern to lobby for the stadium proposal. Ahern says he gave them short shrift. Yet subsequent correspondence suggests that the Americans were still under the impression that the project might find favour.

On 5 December, £28,772 was deposited to Celia Larkin's account. This, Ahern says, came from his pal, Mícheál Wall, who wanted to buy a house in Dublin, which Ahern would rent. The sum deposited equates to $45,000 using one of the exchange rates in the bank that day. It may well be a genuine coincidence that what equates to a large round-dollar sum ended up in an account associated with Ahern three weeks after a meeting with American businessmen.

The Americans involved denied that they had paid any money whatsoever to Ahern. In any event, O'Callaghan's plans for a football stadium were shelved. Again, in a hypothetical instance in which money was paid by the developer to the politician, there is no evidence to suggest that anything specific was actually done for it.

Earlier at the tribunal, the journalist Éamon Dunphy had given evidence. He was involved as a consultant with O'Callaghan on the stadium project. He claimed that O'Callaghan told him one evening that the problem with Ahern was you gave him the money but he didn't do what he'd said he would for it. O'Callaghan denies ever saying such a thing, and there is no other evidence to suggest he did.

The possibility that money passed between O'Callaghan and Ahern was thus explored by the tribunal, and the evidence elicited was entirely circumstantial. It would in all likelihood require other supporting evidence to conclude that it had actually happened.

"In forty years of politics, I burst a gut working for the public," Ahern said, from the witness box. "I never got a bribe, I never received money from Owen O'Callaghan, Frank

Dunlop, Chilton O'Connor or any of these people in any form."

At the conclusion of his evidence, Ahern addressed Mahon, and thanked everybody at the inquiry: "Well, Chairman, if I can just say to you, as I have said many a time, I spent a lot of time dealing with you all, and at times I have felt a lot of the issues from counsel for the tribunal, my good friend Mr O'Neill, were always picked out to try and trap me and trick me and everything else, but I'd like to end on a friendly note, but repeat that I never, in my public life, took a bribe, backhander or anything else, from anybody, not to mind the individuals.

"And I have no doubt that in the hard job you have to do, to take all of the evidence, I have had to deal with it for eight years, a concerted campaign by a few people about this issue, who did everything they could to damage me, but I did my best in front of this tribunal to tell the full truth."

With that he was gone. Outside, he was his usual courteous self in pausing for a few words with reporters: "Hiya, folk, how ya doin'?"

Who, they wanted to know, did he think had it in for him, as he had implied inside?

"Start at the start and work it all out," was all he would say.

The ambiguity was appropriate. His claim that he was being victimised was never substantiated, but his song remained the same. People were out to get him. His unfortunate marital circumstances were behind all his money woes. Nothing else to see here, folks, move along and don't ask awkward questions that go beyond the soundbite. Start at the start and work it all out.

EPILOGUE

ST LUKE'S, HOUSE PRIVATE

It began with an election in June. It ended with an election in June. In 1977, Bertie Ahern came from nowhere to win a seat. In nine subsequent Dáil elections, he would top the poll and get elected on the first count. In all three general elections he contested as leader, Fianna Fáil had come out on top – on two of those occasions, against all the odds. That extraordinary record of electoral success would come to a shuddering halt on the first weekend of June 2009. Ahern's name wasn't on the ballot paper in the by-election in Dublin Central or for the Cabra-Glasnevin ward in the local elections, but his older brother Maurice's was, and it was the Bertie brand that was being sold to the electorate.

The response from voters was emphatic and devastating. Maurice came in fifth place in the by-election, behind the Gregory camp, Fine Gael, Labour and Sinn Féin – all previously accustomed to being on the hind tit in Dublin Central during the three-decade-long reign of the Drumcondra Mafia.

The disappointment didn't end there. Maurice couldn't get

elected to Dublin City Council either, failing to get enough votes in the Ahern heartland of Cabra-Glasnevin and being edged out by Sinn Féin for the final seat in the five-seat ward.

Neither could the blame be placed on the unpopularity of Fianna Fáil. While nationally it did have a terrible election, in Cabra-Glasnevin the Fianna Fáil vote was about twice the level it was across Dublin. Mary Fitzpatrick, by now firmly identified in the minds of voters as an Ahern nemesis, got one of the best Fianna Fáil votes in the country. She topped the poll in the ward with 3,088. Maurice Ahern, despite his brother's endorsement, got less than half that. Three-quarters of the Fianna Fáil voters in Cabra-Glasnevin had opted not to place a '1' in the box beside the Ahern name.

It would always have been a huge ask to expect even the legendary Drumcondra Mafia to deliver the Dáil seat for Maurice. Governments don't win by-elections and certainly not in the teeth of the worst recession in decades. Given Tony Gregory's achievements in the constituency, the Gregory candidate would prove virtually unbeatable.

But to fall so badly short in both the by-election and the locals couldn't simply be put down to those factors. On RTÉ, former Taoiseach Garret FitzGerald opined that, after so long as a positive, the Ahern name was "now a negative". It was impossible to disagree. The strains were there in the legendary Ahern machine. While many of the Mafia faithfully put in the hard slog, there were reports of ward bosses refusing to canvass for Maurice.

In any event, the much-vaunted ward-boss system introduced by Ahern three decades earlier was not what it had once been. By 2009, most of the bosses were living outside the constituency. Some, like Paddy "The Plasterer" Reilly, remained in situ, but for the others distance meant they didn't have the local intelligence that had once been the hallmark of the machine.

Whatever was happening behind the scenes, in the June 2009 elections there was none of the visibility and intensity of Ahern campaigns in the past. Bertie went from door to door in support of his brother but, struggling badly with a leg injury, he was a pale shadow of the swaggering, thrusting Ahern that voters had become used to seeing on the canvass.

His condition was a metaphor for the disintegration of the once tightly knit group that had surrounded him and propelled him to power. Some had passed away, others had faded into the background, and one in particular, who had been integral to Ahern's rise in politics, was no longer around. Celia Larkin's influence over Ahern has often been underestimated, sometimes deliberately by the lads in the Drumcondra Mafia. The media often tended to focus exclusively on the couple's romantic attachment, ignoring her importance in his political life. Their relationship ended in mid-2003, not long before Ahern's daughter Georgina married pop star Nicky Byrne at a celebrity-laden wedding in France.

By then, Larkin had already left her official job in Government Buildings and set up a beauty salon in Drumcondra, just up the road from St Luke's. Now she was leaving him personally as well as politically. Only the couple themselves know the reasons for the break-up but speculation has always focused on the issue of one wanting to formalise the arrangement in marriage with the other resisting. In this case, it is generally believed that Larkin was eager to marry. Ahern, perhaps because of his strong Catholic beliefs and concern over the reaction from his family, was reluctant to change their arrangement. Either way, the relationship had run its course.

Larkin's role as the Taoiseach's partner, as opposed to his

wife, was not without its challenges. This was never more clearly demonstrated than in May 2001 when an invitation was issued in the names of Ahern and Larkin to Cardinal Desmond Connell, to attend a reception in Dublin Castle. It provoked controversy. The Church of Ireland Dean of St Patrick's Cathedral, Robert McCarthy, declined, saying Ahern was projecting his relationship with Larkin as quasi-marital.

The reception passed off without incident, although Ahern greeted the Cardinal with Tánaiste Mary Harney at his side rather than his partner.

It was an indication that, while society at large had accepted Larkin's role, the lack of a formal relationship meant that she was not accorded the full status of the Taoiseach's spouse.

Within eighteen months of the break-up, Ahern's political life began to unravel, with correspondence arriving from the planning tribunal over his cash lodgements. It is a matter of conjecture as to what positive influence Larkin would have brought to bear during this time, on the basis of her political nous so well displayed during Ahern's rise. Many in political circles believe he wasn't the same politician without her by his side.

After the break-up Larkin concentrated on her business interests, quickly opening a second beauty salon in Limerick, which prompted her to move to the fashionable County Clare village of Killaloe. Her relocation meant she was completely out of the picture as far as Drumcondra was concerned. She returned to the public eye during her appearances at the tribunal, which in turn prompted much media comment on her stylish appearance and über-confident demeanour. Today, she is a rare presence in the capital, preferring the more sedate surroundings of County Clare.

Larkin's old adversary in the Mafia, Chris Wall, was the last man standing during the 2009 elections. He was constantly at the side of Maurice Ahern in the canvass and was one of the few who braved the RDS during the count to provide support to the defeated candidate. He and his grown-up family still live in Dublin Central and he is still heavily involved in Fianna Fáil in the constituency.

The days when the plush Jaguar and Mercedes of Des Richardson and Joe Burke respectively could be seen parked outside St Luke's are long gone. Richardson did well out of the property boom, selling his home off the prestigious Torquay Road in Foxrock, south County Dublin, for €3 million. Since he stepped back from the front line of fundraising for Fianna Fáil, Richardson has been involved in a number of companies, including a software venture with his old friend and fellow dig-out sponsor Dave McKenna.

Ahern's successor Brian Cowen very tellingly brought the curtain down on one fundraising venture associated with Richardson: the Fianna Fáil tent at the Galway races. In the public mind, it had come to symbolise Fianna Fáil's connections with big business and particularly property developers, who had been nurtured by Richardson for the benefit of Fianna Fáil. But clearly Cowen had decided that this benefit was outweighed by the negative publicity and perceptions surrounding the tent.

Through all his tribunal ordeals, Ahern is understood to have remained very close to Richardson. As was heard in evidence at the inquiry, it was Richardson who sought meetings with Padraic O'Connor in 2005 and 2006 to clear up apparent "misunderstandings" about O'Connor's alleged involvement in the first dig-out.

While nearly all of the Drumcondra Mafia fared well outside politics, Fate wasn't as kind to Joe Burke. He was dogged by problems in his business and personal life. By 2009, he said in an interview, his personal problems were behind him. He was no longer running his own business but working as a project manager on a construction site in Dublin. Through it all he remained close to Ahern on a personal level, although there are suggestions that his political influence had waned in the latter years of Ahern's tenure as Taoiseach.

Tim Collins has also faded from the scene. In 2008, he was dogged with bad health that necessitated him providing evidence to the tribunal by commission rather than in person. Given the torrid time he had under questioning at an earlier appearance, it might have been a relief to him that he wouldn't be subjected to it again in public. Like Richardson, he also benefited from the property boom. His role as a land agent saw him make serious money from the sector. In one case, he was part of a consortium that made €2 million on a single deal in March 2002. It involved "flipping" a site, which means the consortium bought it from one interest and sold it to another immediately for a much greater price.

The site was that of the former Lyric Cinema off James Street in Dublin in the south city centre. The deal was perfectly legitimate, but it highlighted the vast profits that could be made by property agents and developers at the height of the property explosion.

Collins remains the one member of the Drumcondra Mafia around whom the greatest mystery lingers. His involvement in the B/T account was unusual to say the least, as was his role in St Luke's, particularly given his minimum involvement in constituency affairs.

Of the other central figures, Tony Kett sadly passed away in 2009 after a short illness. Paul Kiely is believed to have scaled back his involvement in the Ahern operation even before

Ahern's tribunal travails. Meanwhile, Cyprian Brady has an enormous challenge ahead of him if he is to continue as the standard bearer for the operation. Although he was elected to the Dáil in 2007, the performance of Mary Fitzpatrick in the 2009 local elections leaves her as the party front-runner in the constituency.

Brady currently uses St Luke's as his constituency base, but it's not like the old days. The heretofore omnipresent ministerial Merc parked at the kerb outside is now a rare sight. The bricks and mortar still exist, but St Luke's as we knew it is no more.

* * *

Ahern had been expected to be the exception to Enoch Powell's famous maxim about all political careers ending in failure. Unbeaten in general elections, he would go at a time of his choosing and, in his sixties, plump for the calmer surroundings of Áras an Uachtaráin – the first since de Valera to hold the positions of both Taoiseach and President.

Instead, he was effectively forced from the office of An Taoiseach and his presidential ambitions were left looking fanciful. Where had it all gone wrong? There is no question that the meltdown in the Irish economy had prompted some revision of his legacy of presiding over the greatest boom in the history of the state. But the original damage to the previously untouchable Ahern brand was done by what emerged down in Dublin Castle.

It is only right that it will be left to historians to write his legacy but it is inevitable that what happened in that two-year period in the mid-1990s, when large sums of money passed through his bank accounts, will feature large.

As will the men and women with whom he surrounded himself during his extraordinary political career. The question has been asked as to whether Ahern would have made it to the top without the Drumcondra Mafia. But the pertinent fact is that, deliberately or otherwise, he chose not to. None of the ten heads of government who preceded him or the one who came after him had a similar apparatus in their political careers. When the call came, they left their local operation in the constituency, seeking in national office the counsel of senior elected politicians or hired strategists and advisers.

This was never Ahern's *modus operandi*. For better or worse, until political death did them part, the marriage of a young, thrusting politician and a group of ambitious and wily associates – first consummated in the general election of 1977 – would endure throughout. It was never just Bertie Ahern. It was always Bertie Ahern and the Drumcondra Mafia.

ACKNOWLEDGEMENTS

The authors would like to thank their editor Ciara Considine, copy-editor Hazel Orme and everybody at Hachette Books Ireland. Thanks also to Noirin Hegarty, Diarmuid Doyle and our colleagues at the *Sunday Tribune*. A special word of thanks for *Sunday Tribune* picture editor Maureen Gillespie.

Michael Clifford wishes to thank his friends for their help and particularly his family, Pauline Sweeney and Luke and Tom, for the space and patience they afforded him to research and write. He also wants to thank his parents John and Aideen Clifford for their helpful suggestions and support.

Shane Coleman wants to thank his family and friends for their encouragement and support in writing this book, most especially Ev, Cúan, Donagh and Aoibhinn for their ever-present love and understanding.

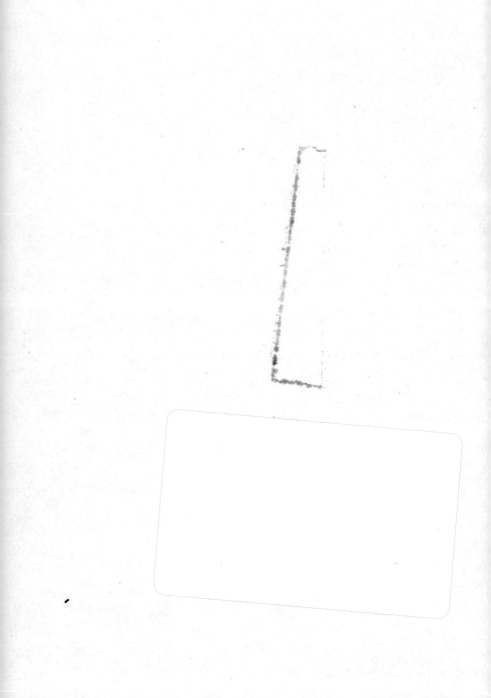